STRATEGIC SURVEY 1980-1981

D1725825

The International Institute for Strategic Studies
23 Tavistock Street London WC2E 7NQ

Published by
The International Institute for Strategic Studies
23 Tavistock Street, London WC2E 7NQ

This publication has been prepared by the Director of the Institute and his Staff, who accept full responsibility for its contents. These do not, and indeed cannot, represent a consensus of views among the world-wide membership of the Institute as a whole

First published Spring 1981

ISBN 0 86079 046 0
ISSN 0459-7230

Printed in Great Britain by Spottiswoode Ballantyne Ltd., Colchester

CONTENTS

PERSPECTIVES

1980 was, above all, a year of reassessment: reassessment of security priorities, of the future of East–West relations as well as third-world security and stability, of the requirements for deterrence and defence, and, for most industrial societies, of the difficulty of reconciling economic constraints with the financial demands of military security. The need for reassessment reflected a deep sense of uncertainty about the future in both East and West, and it occurred at a time when East–West dialogue and co-operation seemed to have reached their lowest for well over a decade.

The uncertainty was particularly marked for the two major powers, the Soviet Union and the United States of America. Both found their ability to control events diminished, and both sought in the experience of the past remedies for the future.

The Soviet Union: Burdens of Empire
For the Soviet leadership, the need for reassessment was increased by the failure of earlier policies, and by the evidence that a constant build-up of military force could solve neither economic problems at home nor political problems abroad. The most serious example of this was provided by the year's events in Poland, the most populous and important of the USSR's affiliates. The Polish economic crisis, which led first to a massive strike movement, then to the toleration of an active trade union not under the control of the Communist Party, not only revealed the deficiencies of earlier Soviet policies towards Eastern Europe but also faced the Soviet leadership with a crisis to which there was no ready answer. It also underlined the security problem for Europe as a whole that is posed by the Soviet inability to develop a relationship with the East European countries which reflects their interests as well as those of the Soviet Union, and which can function without a constantly implied threat of military action.

From the Soviet point of view, the Polish crisis was above all political. Because the Communist Party exercises a monopoly of power in a Communist state, any manifestation of dissent and dissatisfaction is inevitably a political challenge to the Party's authority. But events in Poland went far beyond this: the acceptance of *Solidarity*, a trade union organization independent of the Communist Party, had institutionalized that challenge.

At the beginning of 1981, Poland was governed by a Communist leadership anxious to regain initiative and authority and yet – against a background of serious and seemingly inescapable economic deterioration – dependent upon the co-operation of trade unions which were anxious to consolidate the gains they had made in August. The possible implications are momentous: if the Polish compromise succeeds, it could herald the beginning of political pluralism in the East European part of the Soviet empire – and perhaps eventually in the Soviet Union herself.

To leave Poland to sort out the problem by herself threatened to undermine the authority of the Party not only in Poland but beyond, at least in the worst-case vision of Soviet leaders. On the other hand, to use military force for a direct intervention held out prospects no more promising and potentially highly dangerous. An invasion, if successful, might stop Polish workers from striking, but it would not get them to work more effectively; it would not be able to establish political authority for a Party in internal disarray; and it would offer no remedy for the ills of the economy. And the success of any invasion was far from assured, and the operation would be fraught with dangerous uncertainties. Would the Polish armed forces, who had carefully fashioned a nationalistic image for themselves, resist a Soviet military move? If they did, might not the spectacle of protracted fighting between 'Socialist brothers in arms' lead to challenges to Soviet control elsewhere in Eastern Europe – further West in East Germany or Czechoslovakia, or futher east in the Baltic provinces? If so, the question in Moscow, no less than in the West, must be whether a general challenge to Soviet power in Eastern Europe might not raise the spectre of events getting out of hand and slipping into a conflict between East and West.

Soviet reaction to the Polish events suggested that these dangers were understood in Moscow. The Soviet leadership clearly sought to avoid a situation in which direct military action would become unavoidable (although the necessary preparations for it were completed by December). Instead, the Soviet Union, together with other East European countries, encouraged the Polish Communist leadership to claw back the concessions it had made in August, backing it in this difficult task with economic assistance, diplomatic presence and repeated reminders that, if these measures should fail, the military option would remain available. And it was the very seriousness of the situation which continued to give this option credibility, Polish confidence and international hopes to the contrary not withstanding.

The challenge of Poland, however, while the most serious, was not the only challenge confronting the Soviet empire. Internally, the economic situation failed to improve. The unsettled question of the succession to a leadership well advanced in years and weakened in December by the death of former Prime Minister Kosygin, tended both to sap confidence and to discourage major new initiatives to solve pressing problems. On the periphery, the Soviet force in Afghanistan was still, a year after its invasion, far from effectively controlling the country and providing the puppet regime of President Karmal with a basis of legitimacy. Even increased Soviet military pressure on Pakistan, while perhaps consolidating the Soviet presence, would not make that presence any less controversial and would stop short of securing unchallenged regional dominance for the USSR. In the Gulf, the war between Iraq and revolutionary Iran demonstrated Soviet inability either to control the former, a formal ally, or tangibly to increase her influence with the latter. In the Middle East, even the Israeli-Egyptian deadlock in the Camp David peace process failed to improve the Soviet position, and the signature of the Soviet-Syrian Treaty of Friendship and Co-operation (at the request of Damascus), through the uncertainty prevailing both in the region and in Syria, would tie the USSR more closely to Syrian actions which she could scarcely hope to control. In Asia, China's domestic problems seemed to justify a more relaxed view of dangers of Sino-Soviet rivalry, but a sequence of warnings to Japan in the latter part of the year bore witness to the Soviet Union's continuing inability to establish a relationship of mutual respect and advantage

with Asia's leading economic power. And from the non-aligned and developing world there came – for the first time – widely supported condemnation of the USSR for her military occupation of Afghanistan, expressed in resolutions of the UN General Assembly in January and November.

• More important for future Soviet security than these diplomatic set-backs was the failure of Soviet policies toward the West, and particularly the United States. To the Soviet leaders, so often incapable of seeing their own moves other than as a reaction to those of 'hostile forces', the deterioration of Soviet-American relations was primarily the result not of Soviet but of American behaviour. Yet they could not but be worried by the consequences of that deterioration: the further sharpening of American concern about Soviet military power, leading to growing demands for new military programmes, imbuing American policies with a much stronger sense of the need to contain Soviet action world-wide, and encouraging closer ties between the US and China. Moreover, the traditional option of seeking to intensify detente with America's allies at times of strain in the super-power relationship, while not totally foreclosed, was constrained by the uncertainty over Poland and by the USSR's need to protect her empire from what was seen as the disjunctive impact of detente.

Securing the empire thus became the first priority. If, at the beginning of the year, Soviet policies abroad were shaped by the confidence of power, this confidence has been severely undermined by subsequent events. Time is no longer clearly working in the Soviet Union's favour in the 1980's. The central question for Western policy is how to cope with a Soviet Union that no longer sees time on her side, is incapable of finding solutions to her increasing political problems, yet is in possession of unprecedented military power.

The United States: A New Impatience
In marked contrast, the United States, after years of uncertainty, seemed to view the future with more self-assurance. Well before the 4 November elections which brought Mr Ronald Reagan to the Presidency and ended two decades of Democratic Party control in the US Senate, the United States seemed to have moved towards what many inside and outside

the country had long hoped for: a measure of consensus on America's role in the world. Yet in early 1981 it was still a consensus born more of impatience and frustration than of self-confidence and purpose.

The effect on the American public mood of the protracted crisis involving the 53 US Embassy staff members held hostage in Iran cannot be overstated. The situation was a humiliating one in any case, but President Carter's strategy, for much of the 444 days the hostages were held, of making their plight the central issue of his Administration's policies violated an important principle: since terrorism seeks attention, providing that attention is the worst possible response. Indeed, the Carter strategy may even have prolonged the detention of the hostages beyond the point at which it continued to serve any of the factions in Iran's internal power struggle. Moreover, the crisis bred a nagging sense of humiliation in American public opinion, and this was further aggravated in April by the dismal failure of an attempt to rescue the hostages by a raid on the Embassy-turned-prison in Tehran.

In terms of American public opinion, the political effect of the hostage crisis was to reinforce a general trend toward a narrower and tougher nationalism, profound suspicion of Soviet motives, impatience with allies and a call for stronger military efforts. Mr Carter himself had sensed the force of this trend during the latter half of his term and had sought to follow it, though with reservations. Mr Reagan, on the other hand, clearly reflected the new mood in American public opinion rather than resisting it. All the same, many of the policies that the new Administration was likely to pursue in foreign and security matters did not seem to differ much in substance from those articulated by its predecessor over the previous two years. Both sought increased defence spending. Both were wary of pinning high expectations on negotiations with the Soviet Union, and sceptical about what they saw as illusions about detente among some of their allies. Both agreed on the central strategic significance of the Gulf region and the need to hold military force available to meet contingencies there. And in the Middle East both wanted to maintain the advantages of the Israeli-Egyptian peace treaty (though Mr Reagan seemed less intent on pushing the process toward a degree of Palestinian autonomy).

Even on those issues which had looked like major points of difference during the election campaign, major substantive disagreement seemed unlikley. On human rights, the Carter Administration had long since toned down the more idealistic pronouncements of the earlier part of its term. In relations with the Soviet Union, both camps favoured some dialogue with the other side. On Latin America, the toughening of US responses to the festering civil war in El Salvador predated Mr Reagan's inauguration; and the new Administration took pains to explain away campaign statements suggesting that it would fundamentally readjust US policies towards China.

What was likely to change after January 1981 was therefore not the substance of US policies so much as their spirit. Mr Reagan seemed to have caught the mood of the nation, and his electoral success thus laid the basis for a consensus on US foreign and security policies which had been missing since the mid-1960s. But at the beginning of 1981 it was too early to judge how durable this basis would be. There are both opportunities and risks. The most significant opportunity is that President Reagan and his team may be able to banish the American public's mood of irritation and frustration and replace it with a new sense of self-confidence – the confidence in military strength which is the precondition for arms control and other agreements with the Soviet Union, the confidence in the fundamental support of allies which is essential to tolerate the inevitable differences of interest within alliances, and the confidence in the international role of the United States which will make her policy more generous and less sensitive to unpredictable crises in the Third World.

The major risk, on the other hand, lies in a danger which the Carter Administration had experienced: that events would overtake original intentions and force the Administration to follow the thrust of public opinion rather than lead it. After all, a change of outlook and style will not dissipate the problems that have circumscribed American power and influence in the past decade. Much of the rhetoric of the election campaign smacked of remedies that might have applied in the simpler world of the 1950s but will scarcely suffice in the more complex one of the 1980s. Realities will impose themselves: the realities of strategic nuclear parity with the Soviet Union and of a

Western Alliance whose members are increasingly reluctant to subject their own interests to that of the alliance leader; the reality that military force will take time to build and that it cannot in any case replace political solutions, though it may facilitate them; the reality that much of the turbulence in the Third World escapes effective control by either superpower. The central issue for the future of America's policies lies here: how will the American mood react to these realities? Will disappointment at the complexities of the world of the 1980s spur the search for other, more appropriate, strategies? Or will the United States blame the world instead of her own policies, and thus reinforce the trends, which have been gaining ground in recent years, towards more impatient nationalism and American unilateralism in place of Western collectivity? It will take all the new team's professionalism and all the President's ability as a communicator to avoid the risks and profit from the opportunites the emerging consensus provides.

Priority for Western Defence
The American consensus found most concrete expression in widespread support for a stronger defence. In January 1980 the Carter Administration announced a 5% increase in real terms in defence spending over each of the next five years, and in February 1981 President Reagan called for an additional 2% for 1982. Yet even with defence budgets which would reach nearly of $300 billion by 1984, expenditure priorities will still have to be set, and as 1981 began it was still uncertain which programmes would and should take precedence over others.

Much of the American debate, in particular the views expressed by Mr Reagan's supporters, suggested that priority should go to the nuclear strategic forces. This reflected the now-familiar concern over the theoretical vulnerability of America's land-based missile force to a pre-emptive Soviet attack, and also the sense that technology was now offering a range of new possibilities – for strategic offensive and defensive systems alike. Both considerations were combined in the latest expression of a strategic deterrence doctrine which had been evolving since the early 1970s. Formally outlined by Secretary of Defense Brown in August as Presidential Directive (PD) 59, this represented a nuclear targeting concept which envisaged more limited options for using nuclear strategic weapons against Soviet military targets, endorsed greater flexibility in targeting and emphasized new kinds of political targets in the Soviet Union.

Despite the apparent consensus of the American strategic community, PD 59 raises a number of questions. There are obvious advantages for deterrence in giving the US President more options for a nuclear response than that of all-out nuclear war. But, since PD 59's emphasis on military, economic and new types of political targets is essentially open-ended, how can it answer the old question of 'how much is enough?' other than by leaving it to the size of the defence budget? More important, should targeting doctrines be based on the doubtful possibility that nuclear exchanges can be kept limited and that nuclear war can be controlled once it has broken out? The very technological advances that have made land-based missile silos more vulnerable to attack also threaten the survival of installations like command centres, satellites, radars and communication networks which are essential to implement selective nuclear options and keep a nuclear war limited. And in any case, even if strategic experts may contemplate limited nuclear conflict, political leaders are likely to remain as convinced as they have always been that too many risks and uncertainties attend the first use of a nuclear device for it to be seriously contemplated unless the awesome decision for a general nuclear war has been made. Technology notwithstanding, nuclear weapons are therefore likely to remain what they have been since the Soviet Union acquired a secure second-strike capability – useful for deterring but not for fighting a war.

Conventional – that is to say, usable – forces are thus likely to provide a more appropriate response to the conflicts of the 1980s. As the Western, and in particular the American, security commitment was extended to areas outside the traditional regions of Europe and the Far East, the need to rectify shortcomings in conventional forces became particularly apparent. The presence of two US carrier task forces in the Arabian Sea for more than a year, in connection with the Iranian hostage crisis and the Soviet invasion of Afghanistan, greatly strained American naval resources, especially manpower. Reports also accumulated of deficiencies in the readiness of US ground and air forces caused by lacking trained personnel, munitions and spare parts. The abolition of the draft in 1973, under the impact of the Vietnamese War, and the change to a smaller, more professional voluntary army had produced more problems than it had solved, since the new system generated neither the number of longer-serving, skilled soldiers that was needed nor a pool of reservists which could be drawn upon in the event of a crisis. These shortcomings prompted a gradual reversal of opinion in favour of the draft. In July President Carter called for the registration of young men for the draft, ostensibly as a response to the Soviet invasion of Afghanistan, and though the new Administration did not hide its philosophical scepticism of such an increase in 'government interference', the thrust of the debate suggested that there was growing support in the United States for some form of military conscription.

The realization of the strains affecting conventional forces led the new Reagan team to alter somewhat the priorities that it had developed while in opposition. Though it remained convinced of the need to halt what it saw as the decline in US nuclear strategic capabilities, manpower and readiness took over as the issues most urgently in need of increased attention and spending: the need for usable force overshadowed concern for for the 'non-usable' deterrent forces. Nor is this just an American problem. The next few years are likely to reveal similar difficulties in much of the industrialized world. Even in countries with conscription, stagnating birth-rates since the mid-1960s will reduce the number of those eligible for military service below the level required for existing military structures, while the spiralling cost of modern weapons will soon exceed the funds available. The conservative tendency of Western military planners to retain familiar force structures, in the hope that somehow the problems will turn out to be less severe than feared, will no longer be adequate, and calls to 'do more' in defence have to take account of the fact that the basic structure of the Western military effort needs to be redesigned to meet the new challenges. It will not be easy to maintain affordable and yet credible conventional forces in the 1980s.

These problems are aggravated by the extension of Western security concerns to areas of the Third World, and particularly to the Gulf.

While the necessity of this move was widely accepted, and there is little doubt that some kind of military preparation will be required, both to reassure friendly states and deter hostile ones, doubts continue over how to translate this consensus into appropriate strategies and capabilities.

The problems were highlighted in US planning for a Rapid Deployment Force of some 200,000 men, intended to be available for military crises outside Europe. For contingencies in the Gulf region, the US stationed a total of seven cargo ships in the Indian Ocean in August, with munitions and supplies sufficient for one marine brigade. She completed negotiations for access to facilities in Oman, Somalia and Kenya, and began talks with Egypt on the development of a major US staging post there. The logistic capacity of Diego Garcia, the island base some 4.000 kilometres from the Straits of Hormuz which she leased from Britain, was also to be considerably upgraded.

Yet, assuming that all these preparations would work according to plan, what kinds of military action could be undertaken? To overcome the Soviet military advantages of proximity to the Gulf region would always be a daunting task. Some military presence could help to deter Soviet military action against a local Western ally. But once deterrence had broken down the same level of presence would clearly be insufficient, and massive reinforcements would be needed. These would take weeks, not days, to arrive and even then would depend on logistical support of a magnitude which could scarcely be taken for granted in realistic plans (it has been estimated that for an expeditionary corps of 80,000 men operating in the Gulf region fuel and water supplies alone would demand a lift capacity of 9,600 tons per day). For American planners to emphasize the need for forces and logistics in the region was therefore only sound military logic; and yet that same logic ran clean against the political concern of countries like Saudi Arabia to avoid being too visibly associated with a US military presence on their soil, for the sake of their own internal stability.

The debate on the US Rapid Deployment Force thus tended to underline the contradiction between the need for planning and the possibility that the scenarios on which plans were based would be rendered politically or militarily unrealistic by the unpredictability of third-world crises. Probably the only way of overcoming this basic dilemma lies in accepting the uncertainties involved and seeking not so much a specific military capability to meet a specific military problem as enhanced flexibility to enable existing forces to meet unforeseen contingencies, and in developing the ability to react quickly to minor threats. To give Western, and specifically US, forces enhanced flexibility will, however, be costly and require more attention to be paid to reserve forces – a particular shortcoming of the US voluntary system. In addition, it will mean that US strategic reserves will no longer be wholly available for Europe. Indeed the Defense Department informed NATO in the Spring of 1980 that units stationed in the US and hitherto destined for use as reinforcements in Europe, could in a future crisis be diverted for military contingencies outside the continent.

Finally, more general military flexibility to respond to both the traditional East–West threat in Europe and Asia and the uncertainties of third-world events will imply equipment, training and deployment that is less than ideal for one of these roles. But only a superpower has a military arsenal large enough to provide such flexibility. If the United States is to acquire and employ it, her allies will have to concentrate their military effort in their immediate areas to make up for increased US flexibility. The idea – much discussed during the year – of European contingents assisting the American military presence in the Gulf region had its merits, less in the sense of military efficiency than in demonstrating to the Soviet Union and reassuring the United States that she was not alone. But to dilute Western European military efforts in order to become involved, if only symbolically, in meeting the new security threats outside Europe would risk making them marginally relevant there and inadequate at home where their primary task will continue to lie.

A Future for Detente?
In their relationship with each other, the two super-powers were confronting the need for reassessment of both the objectives and the means of detente. This was most apparent in the United States, where the new Administration seemed to be convinced that old-style detente had not served American interests and

that the basis of US military power would have to be rebuilt before any serious initiatives in East–West relations could be undertaken. The Soviet leadership, on the other hand, conveyed an impression of continuity: it reiterated the need for improved East–West relations and, in President Brezhnev's February 1981 address to the Twenty-sixth Party Congress, called for a Soviet–American summit without preconditions. Nevertheless, other preoccupations and concerns suggested that, for the Soviet Union also, detente would have to be adapted to new circumstances if it was to remain relevant in the 1980s.

It seemed likely, therefore, that neither side would be prepared in the near future to do more than express a readiness to talk; concrete agreements would have to wait for later. To declare a readiness to talk had distinct advantages for both. For the Soviet Union, the ability to exploit differences within the Western Alliance depended on her ability to demonstrate a continued willingness for detente, preferably in such a way as to make the United States appear as the main obstacle to significant progress in East–West relations. For the United States, endorsing the principle of detente was the condition for continued leadership in the Alliance; otherwise West Germany, France and even Japan, in addition to the smaller European countries, might dissociate themselves from her position.

Yet tactical considerations alone cannot create a long-term policy. For the Soviet Union, the substantive objectives for detente policy in the 1980s seemed clear: to prevent the West (in particular the United States) from significantly increasing its military strength and aggravating the Soviet security problems in Eastern Europe, South-west Asia and the Far East; to gain the technological and financial advantages of economic co-operation with the West which the Soviet system needed more than ever after the events in Poland; and where possible to profit from the European interest in detente to put indirect pressure on the US to be more accommodating towards the USSR and more reluctant to counter Soviet efforts to extend influence in the Third World.

Yet in two aspects of detente policy – arms control and restraint in third-world conflict – there were signs that the Soviet Union might be willing to be more co-operative than hitherto. In the 1960s and 1970s, when she was engaged in catching up with and matching US strategic strength, her interest in arms control had been primarily political. But in the 1980s, with her strategic position under challenge from new American efforts, arms control might offer intrinsic attractions as a means of protecting Soviet strength by slowing and restricting US programmes – even if it were to demand substantive Soviet concessions. It would therefore seem wrong to regard the Soviet Union's proposals for new arms control as mere propaganda.

Similarly, the recognition that Soviet interventions in the Third World have undermined support for detente in the United States, plus the growing problems within the empire requiring their attention could well make the Soviet leaders less disposed towards military adventures beyond it, especially where the cost is high, and might even facilitate some tacit agreement with the United States not to interfere actively in areas of primary Western strategic concern. The Reagan Administration's sharp reaction to Soviet involvement in Central America was likely to produce greater Soviet caution and greater reliance on the indigenous forces of change. Similarly, the Soviet Union could not but watch with considerable foreboding American attempts to establish an increased military presence in the Gulf region, along her periphery. It may have been this which prompted both President Brezhnev's repeated assertions that the Soviet Union recognized the importance of the area for Western energy supplies and would not want to interfere with them, and the Soviet proposal for an international conference on guaranteeing access to Gulf oil.

Western reservations to these signals resulted as much from a general distrust of Soviet intentions as from the profound difference in the meaning of the '*status quo*' in the Gulf that each side professed to seek. For the East, the term has an essentially military meaning and implies no increase in Western military presence in adjacent areas; for the West, however, it means primarily regime stability, implying Soviet abstention from attempts to undermine pro-Western Governments in the area. In spite of more encouraging signs from Moscow, the definition of Gulf stability is likely, therefore, to remain contentious.

But if the Soviet Union knows what she wants from detente, can the same be said for the United States? Neither the previous Administration nor the new one seemed to have a clear and agreed concept. Like his predecessor, President Reagan knew what behaviour he did not want from the Soviet Union but found it much more difficult to define what, for the US, would be the positive function of a realistic detente, and it was here, rather than in the assessment of the nature of Soviet power and its dangers that the United States differed from her major European allies. This uncertainty applied to both the objectives and the instruments of detente, and, unless it is reduced there is unlikely to be either a sustainable American policy towards the Soviet Union or an effective co-ordination of East–West relations in the Western Alliance.

Even if the basic objectives are clarified, the instruments will require re-examination. Could arms control encourage more co-operative Soviet behaviour outside Europe? Past experience suggested otherwise. To make agreements on arms limitation dependent on Soviet respect for American interests in other fields – the concept of 'linkage' firmly endorsed by President Reagan – would seem to make little sense if, like SALT II, the agreement is in itself in the US interest. The new Administration seemed, for both military and economic reasons, to tend towards a more positive stance on arms limitations of the SALT type. But even here there was little reason to expect that future negotiations could be quickly concluded.

Can economic incentives foster restraint on the Soviet use of force – in Poland or Afghanistan? Together with shortfalls in the Soviet grain harvest, the partial grain embargo imposed by President Carter in the aftermath of the Soviet invasion of Afghanistan no doubt added to the difficulties affecting Soviet food supplies during 1980 and made the USSR aware of the seriousness of the US concern. But would the earlier threat of such an embargo have prevented the invasion, or could a promise to lift it move the Soviet Union to reduce her involvement in that country? Similarly, would a Western commitment to cancel all financial and economic assistance to the Soviet Union and Eastern Europe make the use of Soviet forces against Poland less likely? Economic relations are probably less suitable as a precise policy lever than as a means of building vested interests in stability. On the other hand, events in Poland suggested that the way in which Western financial and economic assistance to that country had been administered in the past did not promote economic achievement and political stability, but rather the opposite. Should Western credits in future therefore continue to be given without conditions? That economic interdependence works both ways, particularly if, through dealings with the East, West European countries can reduce unemployment or dependence on energy supplies from other sources, was clearly brought out during the year. Yet where should the limits of acceptable dependence be drawn? And which side would be more dependent on the other, particularly in a crisis?

In the Third World, how could Soviet restraint be more readily obtained, and in what regional circumstances: by excluding the Soviet Union, through containment and military deterrence, or by making her acccountable through co-operative arrangements?

At the beginning of 1981 there were no clear answers to these questions, either in the United States or in Europe and Japan. Past experiences were only of limited relevance, future conditions still not fully assessed, and it was unlikely that a comprehensive strategy would emerge in the near future. Detente in the 1980s, even more than in the previous decade, will scarcely be able to solve any of the major outstanding problems between East and West. But perhaps it can reach the modest objective of helping to manage the crises that are bound to occur. Even this will require not less but more dialogue between East and West, particularly between the two major powers.

Third-world Conflicts
The year which reminded the world of the intensity of super-power rivalry also reminded it of the limits of the super-powers' ability to control events. Nowhere was this more evident than in the region which President Carter, in his 1980 State of the Union message, had declared to be an area of 'vital interest': the Gulf. qThe most telling event was the outbreak of war between Iraq and Iran in September 1980, when neither the Soviet Union – with both military weight in the region and a treaty of co-operation with Iraq – nor the United States were able to halt a conflict that neither saw as in her interest. There were other examples. Against the wishes of both the major powers, movement towards nuclear proliferation appeared to continue in Pakistan and Iraq. Libya's attempts to extend her influence into black Africa through control over Chad were largely unchecked, and countermeasures, if any, would depend primarily on the local states' actions. Even in El Salvador, the small strife-ridden Central American state within the US strategic perimeter which the Reagan Administration chose to make the first symbol of its foreign policies, the ability of outside actors to determine events was limited. The United States could increase military and economic aid for the junta and, probably, reduce the flow of arms shipments from Cuba and others to the armed guerillas. But whether the junta would succeed in pacifying the country and gaining legitimacy for itself would be determined primarily by indigenous forces.

This does not imply that outside influence has become negligible, but that rarely can it be decisive. While it might be legitimate to view third-world conflicts in the light of their implications for East–West competition only, this is clearly insufficient to define either their causes or the remedies needed to defuse them. Yet it was precisely the uncertainty of how to identify the causes and apply the remedies which tended to encourage the propensity to assess third-world conflicts by the more familiar yardsticks of East–West competition. There was widespread agreement in the West that instability in the Gulf region affects Western strategic interests, yet there were few certainties about the most effective means of response. Western military reasssurance to Saudi Arabia could be helpful during a crisis – witness the dispatch of four US early-warning aircraft to that country during the Iran–Iraq war – yet before the crisis occurred it could be harmful and might even precipitate it. As events in Iran had demonstrated, over-rapid economic development would strain the traditional structures of authority and political legitimacy, yet so would too slow a development. Economic aid to developing countries, even if considerably greater than that provided by Western countries, could not hope to make up for the huge financial deficits experienced by all but the oil-rich developing nations.

The problems of third-world stability therefore look like necessitating a major reassessment of the concepts of the past three decades. This process will probably suggest two directions for future Western strategy: first, to seek to prevent undue and disturbing outside interference in regional affairs, and to allow the precarious process of domestic development to proceed; second, to encourage regional security arrangements where possible. The Camp David process and the Zimbabwe settlement provide recent examples that, while difficult, this need not always be impossible.

Strains in the Western Alliance

The period of reassessment in East–West relations and third-world conflicts coincided with a similar period in the Western Alliance. For thirty years, the Alliance produced a sense of identity of interests on both sides of the Atlantic. At the beginning of the new decade, this identity has become less self-evident. The general deterioration of detente has brought home to Europeans the obvious fact that, because of geography, they have a higher stake in the absence of friction in Central Europe than the United States has; and to many Europeans, conscious of their greater energy dependence, an American approach to the Middle East which exposes the United States to the wrath of Arab oil producers and whose success is doubtful seems too costly to pursue. In nuclear matters, although nuclear war remains improbable, the growing emphasis on theatre nuclear weapons seems to make European targets more vulnerable than Soviet or American ones – an impression unhappily strenghtened by the often uncritical embrace of nuclear warfighting and limited nuclear war scenarios in the US strategic debate.

Differences of interest are not surprising in an alliance of sovereign states. Yet such differences acquire considerable political weight during the year, for two reasons: subjectively, because of heightened American sensitivity to what many in the US saw as a lack of solidarity by allies in a period of crisis; and objectively, because the Alliance needed to adapt both to new intra-NATO power relations and to new external threats. The most obvious manifestation of this occurred after the Soviet invasion of Afghanistan, when the Alliance could not agree about its impact on East–West detente and on future relations with the Soviet Union. Even if the rift was narrowed as the year went on, particularly when common concern over the Polish crisis united the Western Alliance, the residue of strain remained. On the American side there were additional grievances over the alleged reluctance of Western Europe and Japan to recognize the seriousness of the threat to overall Western security posed by Soviet action in the Gulf, and over the half-heartedness of European support when the protracted hostage crisis in Iran frayed American tempers.

A major effort of reassurance on the part of Western Europe will be required to restore American popular endorsement for the Western Alliance – and the visit of the British Prime Minister, Mrs Thatcher, to Washington in March 1981 indicated that this was recognized by political leaders in Europe. But the underlying problem of the Western coalition ran too deep to be avoided for long by mere assurances of loyalty and solidarity. Transforming an alliance built around the assumption of undisputed American leadership into an alliance of shared responsibility implied tasks for both sides of the Atlantic: for the United States to recognize that differences of view between the allies are inevitable, legitimate and not a sign of European unreliability; for Western Europe to understand that shared responsibility implies shared commitment, and to resist the temptation to plead diversity of interests as an alibi for inaction. In the United States, European political manoeuvring was all too readily interpreted as a sign of creeping neutralization – particularly in the case of West Germany, which is most directly affected by the cooling detente. European difficulties in upholding earlier defence spending commitments were read not as genuine problems in meeting the rising costs of defence at a time of economic strain but as fear of provoking the Soviet Union. And the deal arranged by Belgium, Holland, France and Germany, under which they hoped to obtain major deliveries of natural gas from the USSR, is seen not as a sensible move to diversify supplies and reduce import vulnerability but as symptomatic of a willingness to become more dependent on the Soviet Union. Conversely, many influential Europeans (and not only those on the left of the political spectrum), fearing a new world-wide policy of containment, remain sceptical of America's emphasis on increased military power and her failure to ratify the SALT II Treaty. The past four years of at times inconsistent US leadership in the Alliance have left their mark and, *faute de mieux*, have encouraged greater self-confidence and a greater sense of independence in Europe which will not now be removed merely by manifestations of American displeasure or assertions of leadership.

Nonetheless, the learning process did get under way during the year. European governments came to realize that most of their policies, even when they differed from US policies, still depended on the United States for success. President Giscard's and Chancellor Schmidt's visits to Soviet President Brezhnev in May and July 1980 could not promote East–West detente in the absence of US backing, and the resolution passed by the European Summit in June, suggesting an approach to the Middle East different from that envisaged by the Camp David framework, could not succeed without American agreement. In formulating their own distinct policies, European governments have to be aware of the risk that their efforts might merely be used by others to bring pressure on the United States which she is bound to resent.

Conversely, the Reagan Administration has repeatedly emphasized the importance it attaches to the Alliance and, at least initially, has shown understanding for European concerns. It has seemed prepared to mute its earlier scepticism over arms control in order to accommodate the European governments' desire for progress in this field, and demands for greater spending by European allies have been framed not as ultimata but as appeals for support.

It was, of course, possible that the apparent consensus of 1980 would give way to more profound and public disagreement – with the Middle East, the search for a settlement in Namibia, increased allied defence contributions and East–West relations the most obvious points of discord. All the same, the level of agreement between the two sides of the Atlantic on basic security issues was more impressive than the Alliance was often given credit for: consensus ranged from concern over the Soviet military build-up and the need to counter it to the recognition that Western security is at risk not only in Europe and the Far East but also in the oil-producing region of the Gulf. West European governments accepted that the need to hold US forces available for contingencies there would reduce American reinforcement capabilities in Europe and that they, and not only the United States, would have to use their influence to support stability in the region.

There was even movement, however slow, towards improving the conflict management role of Western institutions: the June 1980 summit of the major member states of the OECD (the Organization for Economic Co-operation and Development) in Venice devoted most of its time to discussing the security challenges to the West, and in December the NATO foreign ministers, learning from the lack of Western coordination over Afghanistan, decided to convene immediately if Soviet troops should march into Poland.

The chief task for the Alliance in the 1980s will be to build on this consensus and these institutions so as to prevent understandable differences in secondary interests from undermining the common primary interest – security. This will be a difficult and sensitive task, since the recognition of differing interests was at times accompanied, on both sides of the Atlantic, by a domestic political mood less generous towards transatlantic differences and more prepared to ascribe them to ulterior motives than to legitimate political disagreement; this was particularly and disturbingly marked in the US–German relationship. And it was likely to be aggravated further if the new Administration in Washington were to equate leadership with mere toughness, thus creating expectations at home and resentment abroad. As the new team took over in Washington, there were signs that this danger was recognized. But more will be needed, on both sides of the Atlantic: a move to define together both the problems and the priorities of Western security in the 1980s – perhaps by means of a new version of the 'Harmel Exercise' of 1969 through which the Alliance members had jointly developed their positions on deterrence, defence and detente.

Security and Economy
Yet such a joint exercise will not depend only on a consensus among political leaders and governments as to the threats and how to meet them. It will also overnments as to the threats and how to meet them. It will also depend on popular support and on the ability to maintain a credible defence at a time when economic stringency is increasingly affecting the whole industrialized world.

The problem of reconciling the growing cost of defence with the other demands of modern society is not new. What is new, though, is that the combination of recession and inflation is forcing governments to face the problem head on, rather than fudging the issue as they have done in the past. Spending one's way out of recession by means of increased defence and other public outlays used to be seen as a means of overcoming economic stagnation and unemployment, albeit at the cost of creating some inflation, but in the economic conditions of the early 1980s this interaction has collapsed, and inflation, stagnant economies and high unemployment all coexist. This puts all governments under pressure to make major cuts in public expenditure, and, as the cost of defence grows, so it becomes less realistic to exempt it from cuts. It is thus no longer certain that both a credible defence effort and the public support it requires can be maintained unless the main economic problems can first be overcome.

Even in the United States this recognition is likely to limit the size of the major new defence spending programmes foreshadowed during Mr Reagan's election campaign. In Britain, the deep concern over the Soviet threat expressed by the Conservative government did not prevent some reneging on earlier pledges to increase defence spending. In other West European countries, the 1977 commitment to real increases in defence expenditure of 3% a year was watered down, often significantly, as it became clear that maintaining the commitment would impose politically costly sacrifices in the domestic sectors of public spending. Even Israel, traditionally prepared to sacrifice economic stability for the sake of strong defence, now sought to reduce the burden; faced with a 1980 inflation rate of over 130%, the Begin government voted to reduce the defence budget by 15% in 1981. Nor was defence spending a matter of concern only to the Western world. In China, recognition that earlier economic forecasts had been too optimistic is likely to add to the difficulties of military modernization. And in the Soviet Union and Eastern Europe pressing economic problems, further aggravated by the Polish crisis, are bound to render increases in defence spending more problematic than they have been during the 1970s.

Economic capabilities will thus circumscribe defence capabilities more directly than at any time in the post-war period. This is not simply a military problem but one with direct domestic political consequences, as the British experience showed. Frustration over the economy was expressed in growing opposition to defence in general and the nuclear effort in particular, and the Campaign for Nuclear Disarmament, reflecting the antipathy to nuclear technology that is present to some extent in most European societies, found its ranks swelled by those directly affected by the economic crisis. In other European countries, the tension between policies for economic recovery and defence, though perhaps less obvious, was no less real. The combination of social resentment at home and the need to strengthen defence against threats from abroad is likely to introduce into defence policies a new and disturbing controversiality and thus to threaten the continuity on which they depend for their credibility.

The process of adjustment to these new realities will be a painful one in all Western societies. It is unlikely that the consensus on foreign and security policies which has been the rule over the past years will emerge unscathed from the experience.

NEW FACTORS IN SECURITY

TRENDS IN STRATEGIC FORCES

The developments in strategic nuclear weapons systems and national strategic policies that were being debated at the outset of the 1980s were entirely different in nature from those taking place ten years earlier. The 1970s began with the Soviet Union achieving parity in the central nuclear balance with the United States; hard-target counterforce capabilities on both sides were relatively limited; and the successful negotiation of the first Strategic Arms Limitation agreement, which limited each super-power's deployment of anti-ballistic missile weapons to 200 interceptors (reduced to 100 each in July 1974) and set quantitative ceilings on strategic ballistic missiles, was commonly regarded as institutionalizing the strategic concept of Mutual Assured Destruction (MAD). During the 1970s, however, the apparent stability of this situation was seriously undermined by the development of increasingly accurate guidance systems for ballistic missile re-entry vehicles, by the deployment of multiple individually-targeted re-entry vehicles (MIRV) on a large proportion of American and Soviet land-based intercontinental ballistic missiles (ICBM) and sea-launched ballistic (SLBM), and by increasingly sophisticated strategic command, control, communication and intelligence (C^3I) systems. These developments allowed strategic nuclear weapons to be targeted against a wide range of military and economic-industrial installations and facilities – including missile silos and command centres hardened to withstand blast pressures of thousands of pounds per square inch (psi) above normal atmospheric pressure – and opened up the possibility of limited and controlled nuclear exchanges.

Mutual Assured Destruction was in fact never accepted as an operational strategic doctrine by either the United States or the Soviet Union. In the Soviet view, deterrence of nuclear attack is best achieved not by the ability to inflict assured destruction but, rather, by the ability to win a nuclear war – the better the Soviet armed forces are equipped and trained to fight a nuclear war, the more effectively they will deter a nuclear attack on the Soviet Union. Should deterrence fail, then those forces would be used purposefully and massively to achieve military victory. Strikes would be undertaken simultaneously against US strategic nuclear forces, theatre nuclear weapons and associated facilities, conventional military forces and installations, command-and-control systems, politico-administrative centres and economic-industrial facilities.

US strategic nuclear policy was formally codified with the signing by President Carter of Presidential Directive 59 on 25 July 1980. Contrary to some claims about the novelty of the concepts embodied in PD 59, it is in fact in direct historical line of descent from a series of studies initiated soon after President Nixon took office in January 1969. These studies led to National Security Decision Memorandum 242, signed by the President in January 1974, via the promulgation of the *Policy Guidance for the Employment of Nuclear Weapons*, signed by Defense Secretary James Schlesinger on 4 April 1974, to the preparation of a new Single Integrated Operational Plan, SIOP-5, which took effect on 1 January 1976. The target base for SIOP-5 includes some 40,000 potential targets divided into four principal groups, each of which contains a wide range of target types. The four principal groups are the Soviet Union's nuclear forces, her general purpose forces, her military and political leadership centres, and her economic and industrial base. SIOP-5 not only allows great scope for choice between the 40,000 targets but actually requires it, since there are less than 10,000 weapons in the SIOP forces. PD 59 directed that US war planning should emphasize improving the effectiveness of attacks against military targets, although retaining the destruction of the Soviet economic and industrial base as a principal objective.

New Technologies

These developments in the United States' strategic nuclear policy reflected not only the technological superiority that she maintained throughout the 1970s, particularly in the area of MIRV and missile guidance techniques and sophisticated command-and-control systems, but also the fact that the Soviet Union made unexpectedly rapid progress in these same areas during the late 1970s.

At the beginning of the decade the US had slightly less than 5,000 deliverable warheads: one on each of her 1,910 ICBM and SLBM, and about 2,800 bombs and *Hound Dog* air-to-surface missiles carried on FB-111 and B-52 bombers. By 1976 the total of deliverable warheads had doubled, to more than 8,000, principally because of the deployment of *Minuteman* III ICBM and the *Poseidon* SLBM (with three and fourteen MIRVs respectively), which together accounted for 6,610 warheads. This greatly increased the number of conventional military targets (airfields, army bases, ports, rail marshalling yards, tank concentrations, etc.) and economic and industrial facilities (petroleum refineries, power stations, factories, etc.) that could be attacked by the SIOP forces, besides enhancing the flexibility of choice available to US planners.

Developments in US missile accuracy were also dramatic. In 1970 the CEP (circular error probable: the radius around a target within which 50% of warheads aimed at it are expected to fall) of the *Minuteman* II ICBM was about 2,000 feet, and that of the *Polaris* SLBM about 3,000 feet. By 1980, the improved NS-20 guidance system on the *Minuteman* III gave a CEP of between 600 and 700 feet, while the *Poseidon* SLBM had achieved 1,200–1,500 feet. These developments greatly increased the hard-target counterforce capability of the *Minuteman* force and also enhanced the capability of *Poseidon* against a wide range of semi-hardened military targets.

With respect to the command and control of the US strategic forces, more than $25 billion was spent on strategic C³I systems during the 1970s. By 1980, the *World-Wide Military Command & Control System* had been rationalized; four of the six E-4 aircraft that will comprise the *Advanced Airborne National Command Post System* were operational; procurement of 18 C-130 TACAMO aircraft to provide survivable communications with the ballistic-missile submarines was virtually completed; and a wide range of satellites had been developed for early warning (*Defense Support Program System*, of three *647* satellites), communications (*Defense Satellite Communications System, Satellite Data System and Air Force Satellite Communications System*), navigation (NAVSTAR *Global Positioning System*) and electronic and photographic surveillance (*Code 467 Big Bird* or *Hexagon* and *Code 1010 Hexagon* and *Code 1010 Keyhole* satellites).

In the case of the Soviet Union, the first MIRV-equipped ICBM (SS-17, SS-18 and SS-19) were deployed in 1975, and the first such SLBM (SS-N-18 Mod 2) in late 1978. As a result, the number of warheads in the Soviet strategic nuclear forces increased markedly in the late 1970s – from 3,000 in 1975 to about 7,000 at the end of 1980. Moreover, the accuracy with which these warheads can be delivered also improved dramatically. When the SS-17, SS-18 and SS-19 were first deployed the US Department of Defense reckoned their CEPs to be about 1,500 to 2,000 feet. By mid-1980, however, refinement of their guidance systems had given them CEPs ranging from 850 feet for the SS-19 Mod.1 to 1,460 feet for the SS-17 Mod.1. Moreover, totally new guidance systems for the SS-18 and SS-19, first flight tested in November 1977, have achieved a CEP of 600 feet; fitting the new systems to existing missiles is currently under way and should approach completion by 1983–4 (i.e. some five years after the US fitted the improved NS-20 to all her *Minuteman* III ICBM).

The Soviet Union has also invested heavily in strategic C³ systems. While many of them lack the technical sophistication of their US counterparts, they provide a much better capability to protect the political and military leadership, and the survivability of many of the Soviet communication systems is greater.

Counter-Military Potential

By the end of 1980, the US technological lead was therefore much narrower than it had been a decade before. The prospect of a 'window of opportunity' favouring the Soviet Union is not merely an issue for legitimate debate, but is accepted as incontrovertible by many analysts and observers, including some senior members of the new Reagan Administration. At the very least, the 1970s is going to look like a period of certitude and stability in comparison to the confusion and uncertainty surrounding the strategic developments of the early 1980s.

The debate in the United States has been plagued by problems of semantics, particularly where different usages of the term 'counter-force' are concerned. In the press and many academic writings, counterforce is identified with operations against hard targets – most especially ICBM installations. On the other hand, both Soviet and US practice has long been to plan counterforce attacks on a wide range of conventional military forces as well as against both strategic and tactical nuclear forces. In 1961–3, when counterforce was avowed US policy, more US strategic nuclear weapons were targeted on Soviet conventional force installations (such as barracks and air fields) than on Soviet nuclear forces – a situation which continued through the 1960s and 1970s and was effectively confirmed for the 1980s by PD 59.

The concept of counter-military potential (CMP), or lethality, provides an index for assessing relative capabilities against a range of military targets, from hardened ICBM silos and underground bunkers to radar antennae and army barracks. The CMP of a weapon is a combined index of its explosive power and expected delivery accuracy expressed in

$$CMP = \frac{Y^x}{CEP^2}$$

where Y is yield in megatons; x is 0.666 for yields of 0.2 megatons and above, and 0.4 for smaller yields. The index does have some major weaknesses. Total lethality is highly dependent on the CEP, which is extremely difficult to measure for a missile. The capability to destroy certain numbers and types of targets is not simply a function of aggregate lethality of the individual bombs and warheads in the offensive force. And it fails to take account of the means of delivery, enemy defences, or the targets (the blast resistance of SS-17, SS-18 and SS-19 silos is rather greater than the 2000 psi of most *Minuteman* silos; the USSR has thousands of hardened political and military command centres, communication systems and associated control facilities; and Soviet industry is generally more protected than US industry). Nonetheless, CMP is a means of assessing counterforce capabilities.

At end of 1980 the total CMP of the US strategic nuclear forces was almost three times greater than that of the Soviet Union. However, its rate of increase will be relatively low until air-launched cruise missiles and MX ICBM become operational in the second

half of the 1980s. In the interim, Soviet strategic nuclear programmes as currently projected will produce a Soviet advantage in CMP. More significantly, the CMP of the Soviet ICBM force surpassed that of the US *Minuteman* and *Titan* II ICBM during 1980, and is expected to exceed it greatly during the period 1983–6.

The imminent preponderance in CMP of the Soviet strategic forces is the basis of concern about the 'window of vulnerability'. In April 1979 the Commander-in-Chief of Strategic Air Command, Gen. R.H. Ellis, wrote to Defense Secretary Harold Brown that the survivability of the US ICBM silos was declining and 'is now under 40 percent' and during 1980 several officials testified that a Soviet attack in the early 1980s could theoretically destroy more than 90% of US ICBM. This prospect, taken in conjunction with a Soviet capability to destroy US non-alert bombers and submarines in port, has generated concern that the USSR might exploit this theoretical vulnerability. Such concern has led, in turn, to the notion of the 'window of opportunity', according to which the Soviet Union could be tempted to launch diplomatic, political and even military offensives around the world in early or middle 1980s. This has commonly been regarded as the most important national security problem facing the US at the outset of the 1980s.

Unfortunately, the debate on this problem has suffered from a tendency to see the part but not the whole. To begin with, the problem affects not only US ICBM but also Soviet ICBM. During the early 1980s the Soviet capability to destroy US ICBM will indeed be greater than the US capability to destroy Soviet ICBM. But this will be a temporary situation, and the US will in any case retain a significant counter-ICBM capability, even though the USSR may enjoy counter-ICBM superiority. Completion of MX ICBM deployment in the late 1980s will return counter-ICBM superiority to the US.

The perspective of the debate has also been restricted by the almost exclusive emphasis on ICBM vulnerability. Since the Soviet Union has chosen to invest relatively heavily in ICBM at the expense of SLBM and bombers, while the United States has chosen to deploy a more balanced 'Triad' consisting of land- and sea-based missiles, plus a major strategic bomber force, it is not surprising that the former now has the advantage in purely ICBM calculations.

(The 1,398 Soviet ICBM carry 75% of the megatonnage and more than 5,000 of the 7,000 warheads in the Soviet arsenal, whereas the 1,054 US ICBM carry 35% of megatonnage and 2,154 of the 9–10,000 warheads in the US arsenal.) But just as these choices have logically resulted in a Soviet ICBM advantage, they have equally logically left the US superior in both SLBM and bombers. The imbalance of vulnerability is particularly marked for the SLBM forces. Of the 31 US ballistic-missile submarines currently operational, about 20 (with about 3,200 warheads) are generally at sea at any given time, and these are regarded as invulnerable to current Soviet anti-submarine warfare (ASW) capabilities. On the other hand, the Soviet Union generally maintains only 7–10 such boats permanently on station, and they are continuously monitored by US ASW forces. Thus the advantage in SLBM which the US derives from her lead in anti-submarine technology tends to balance the Soviet advantage in SLBM.

Finally, the vulnerability of US ICBM is much more a theoretical than an operational concern. To destroy the 1,064 US ICBM silos, the Soviet Union would need to use some 2,000 perfectly co-ordinated warheads – including a second (and perhaps even a third) wave to compensate for failures in flight and on detonation in the first wave – all of them spaced and timed to avoid mutual destruction by the phenomenon known as 'fratricide' which can cause the nuclear explosions of some warheads to affect other warheads before detonation. The command and control requirements of such co-ordination border on the infeasible. Moreover, the United States could avoid the destruction of her ICBM force by recourse to tactical measures such as launch-on-warning (LOW) or launch-under-attack (LUA), which would leave only empty silos for incoming Soviet warheads to destroy. At the very least, the possibility of LOW or LUA tactics could deter the Soviet Union from undertaking a counter-ICBM attack in the first place. Hence, as Secretary Brown reported to Congress in early 1980: 'the hypothetical ability of the Soviets to destroy over 90 percent of our ICBM force cannot be equated with any of the following: a disarming first strike; a Soviet advantage that could be made meaningful in an all-out nuclear exchange; a significant contribution to a damage-limiting objective; or an increased probability of a Soviet surprise attack'.

Therefore, if the Soviet Union were able to make political gains during the period of the 'window of opportunity', this would not be because of any objective strategic balance in her favour, but rather, because the limited perspectives of the American strategic debate had led to an underestimation of the conditions of nuclear deterrence and of US capabilities.

The MX Missile
US defence planners have nevertheless judged the long-term vulnerability of the ICBM element of the strategic forces to be politically and strategically unacceptable, and have sought a remedy by means of less vulnerable basing for the new MX missiles.

In September 1979 the Carter Administration decided to deploy 200 MX ICBM in a system of 4,600 horizontal multiple protective shelters. As originally configured, each missile was to be carried on a transporter-erector-launcher (TEL) vehicle within a closed loop, or 'racetrack', consisiting of 23 shelters about 7,000 feet apart on spurs running off a road some 10-15 miles long. The number of loops per complex were to range from three to seven or eight, depending on the surrounding terrain, and there were to be about 40 complexes, all located in a single field in southern Utah and Nevada. In addition to the MX missile, the TEL was to carry a 140,000-lb 'modesty shield', designed to prevent satellite observation of the missile and its deployment to any particular shelter. With a speed of 15-20 mph, the TEL was expected to be able to move from one shelter to another in the time available between receipt of warning of a Soviet missile launch and the arrival of the warheads, giving the system some residual survivability even if the Soviet Union had identified the locations of the MX missiles within the shelter complexes.

This plan was very much a compromise and was immediately subject to severe and wide ranging criticisms. Whereas the USAF estimate of the cost of the system was $33.2 billion in 1980 dollars – including ten-year operation and maintenance costs but excluding some $2 billion for the 2,000 MX warheads – the General Accounting Office of the US Congress reported the likely cost as 'at least $56 billion', and some unofficial estimates went as high as $100 billion. The programme's environmental impact also came under fire, since the construction project was to be the largest in history and was to be carried out in an area where the balance of nature is extremely delicate. Questions were raised, too, about the counterforce potential of the MX missile, about the programme's sensitivity to assumptions about the character of the Soviet threat to the system and about the problems of maintaining Soviet uncertainty as to which particular shelters actually contain missiles.

In May 1980, in response to the Congressional and public criticism, the Pentagon abandoned the 'racetrack' system in favour of the 'loading dock' basing mode. This entailed a number of changes to the plans. The 'closed loop' configuration of shelter deployment was replaced by a linear version, which reduced the construction involved, and hence the cost, and diminished the environmental aspect by requiring less land. The transporter-erector-launcher vehicle was replaced by a separate transporter and mobile launcher. This reduced the size and cost of each shelter (or loading dock), because only the erector launcher had to fit into it, and rendered the separate 'modesty shield' unnecessary, since the transporter itself could shield the launcher from observation while being placed in the shelter. Also, shortening the average distance between shelters from 7,000 feet to 6,000 feet further reduced the amount of land the system required. This resulted in an estimated saving of $3 billion but implied a reduction in the speed with which the missiles could be moved between shelters after receipt of warning of a Soviet attack. By the end of 1980 the Air Force, in response to Congressional pressure, was also giving serious consideration to 'split basing' of the MX – deploying some in the southern high plains region of western Texas and eastern New Mexico as well as in Utah-Nevada – so as to lessen the environmental impact on any one region. However, these modifications did little to soothe the critics of the programme, and it was clear by the end of the year that a further complete review would have to be undertaken by the new Administration.

Ballistic Missile Defence
One consideration in any review of the MX programme will be the possibility of defending the missile complexes against Soviet ballistic missile attack. The technologies of ballistic missile defence have progressed rapidly since (and despite) the Anti-Ballistic Missile (ABM) Treaty of May 1972, particularly with respect to the defence of hard point targets such as ICBM silos. The concept most frequently advanced in the United States, and favoured by several high-level officials in the Reagan Administration, involves a two-layer system of interceptors outside the atmosphere using non-nuclear warheads, plus a lower layer of hypersonic interceptor missiles inside the atmosphere, armed with nuclear warheads. (More exotic concepts, using space-based high-energy lasers and particle-beam weapons, are also under development. But though lasers might be deployed by the mid-1980s for anti-satellite use, it is most unlikely that either could be deployed in an ABM mode before the 1990s.) The lower layer, known as the Low Altitude Defense System (LOADS) has been developed to the point where 100 interceptor missiles and the necessary number of small phased-array radars permitted under the existing ABM treaty could be deployed by 1983–4. LOADS has been specifically designed by the US Army for deployment, in the first instance, with the 150 *Minuteman* III ICBM at Grand Forks, but it could later be used with the MX complexes. It would seek to engage specific incoming warheads (not missiles) aimed at specific missile shelters and would operate up to about 30,000 ft. This would simplify the system's task, since atmospheric filtering would separate out the warhead from most of the missile debris and decoys that posed such overwhelming difficulties for previous ABM concepts. LOADS interceptors could be sited at set locations within the MX complexes or, for greater effectiveness, could employ the same random movement and deception techniques as the ICBM themselves, and the deployment of 100 of them would increase by 50% the number of warheads the Soviet Union would need to destroy the 200-missile MX system. Further deployment of ABM missiles and radars would be in breach of the ABM Treaty, but strong pressures have already developed in the US for the amendment or even abrogation of the Treaty. These pressures could well prove irresistable if the concern about ICBM vulnerability is not put in its proper perspective. A review conference on the Anti-Ballistic Missile Treaty is scheduled for 1982.

Technology and Stability

The current developments in counter-military potential and ballistic missile defence indicate an extremely complex relationship between military technology, strategic policy and perceptions of the strategic balance. It is clear that developments in military technology are neither autonomous nor uncontrollable. Some of the particular developments were a direct response to the demands of the avowed strategic doctrine – this was especially true of developments in C³, since this was identified in the Nuclear Targeting Policy Review of 1977–9 and in PD 59 of July 1980 as inadequate to support any policy involving extended nuclear war. Conversely, some technologies were consciously not pursued. More accurate guidance systems could have

been developed for the *Poseidon* SLBM during the 1970s so as to enhance the counter-military potential of the US SLBM force; ABM deployment, too, has been eschewed for nearly a decade. However, in an era when the certitudes of the 1960s and 1970s have been replaced by great uncertainties, when relatively stable doctrines such as Mutual Assured Destruction have given way to more open-ended notions of possible protracted nuclear war, and when vulnerabilities are commonly perceived as being unacceptable, the promise of the new technologies is difficult to resist. The irony is that, without strong and discriminating resistance, the instabilities and uncertainties that dominate the strategic debate at the outset of the 1980s will only be exacerbated by the end of the decade.

PROJECTING POWER

The sequence of events in South-west Asia from the fall of the Shah and the taking of American hostages to the invasion of Afghanistan and the Iran–Iraq war have highlighted the range of conflict in the Third World and suggested the continuing relevance of outside military power. For the Western countries, in particular, it made it clear that possible military contingencies beyond Europe could not be treated as the lesser included case of European defence. Yet if the events before and during 1980 indicated the range of ways in which developments in the Third World could affect critical Western interests, and suggested the need for a capability to respond with military force if necessary, they did not make clear exactly how military forces might be used, and under which conditions they might be effective.

For the Soviet Union, events in 1980, nowhere more than in Afghanistan, indicated a different perspective on power projection. Soviet capabilities to project military force over long distances, while growing, remained distinctly inferior to those of the United States. Yet the most obvious places where events might threaten important stakes of America or the Soviet Union and tempt one or the other to intervene – namely South-west Asia and the Persian Gulf – are far from the United States and relatively close to the Soviet Union. The

USSR's preoccupation with nations on her periphery was clear, a geographic advantage for the Soviet Union which the United States could scarcely overcome. This suggested less need for far-flung bases as a means of moving men and equipment and more emphasis on naval forces as a symbol of political presence, and as a means of shadowing Western fleets and interdicting Western projections of power.

US Plans for Rapid Deployment

The United States has not lacked power projection forces, or even the capacity to deploy ground forces far from her borders. In fact, the basic forces available have remained, and will remain, relatively constant. They consist of: the 82nd Airborne Division (15,200 men), the 101st Airmobile Division (17,900) – both in the United States – one or two light divisions (10–15,000), one or two Marine divisions (19,800 each, plus own aircraft), 600 to 1,000 combat aircraft, somewhere around 700 cargo aircraft (70 C-5As, 234 C-141s, plus several hundred KC-134 tankers), and two to four aircraft carriers which might be available with their supporting ships.

What has changed is America's assessment of how many forces she might need to move and with what equipment. The previous emphasis was on moving small numbers (several thousand at the most) of lightly-armed troops quickly. Moving larger forces took time. For instance, moving the combat elements of the 82nd to the Persian Gulf would take around 700 C-141 sorties or equivalents, a matter of fifteen days; moving the closest Marine division, that on Okinawa, to the Gulf would take 12 to 14 days by sea. Against the worst conceivable case – a massive Soviet move into Iran – even an American force of several divisions could serve as little more than a 'trip wire' – a demonstration of force which implies the readiness to escalate if it is not heeded by the adversary.

American planning for 'quick strike' forces can be traced back at least to Secretary McNamara's interest in mobility in the late 1960s. In the Carter Administration, Defense Secretary Harold Brown articulated the need for a rapid deployment force as early as 1977, and planning was accelerated in the wake of events in Iran. In March 1980 the Rapid Deployment Joint Task Force (RDJTF, or simply RDF) was established, and the full programme emerged in the Fiscal Year 1981 budget:

– No new forces were created, but a new headquarters was established. Some 200,000 troops were identified for the RDF, including the 82nd and elements of the 101st; one Marine Amphibious Force (a division plus associated air wing and support); the 24th Mechanized Division, which had been designated for a European contingency; and a minimum of the two carrier battle groups (6–8 ships with 7–8,000 men) that had been on station in the Indian Ocean since late November 1979. Tactical air force units were included but no specific units identified. The establishment of the RDF did result in plans for a Strategic Air Command Strategic Projection Force of B-52Hs, some of which already had begun reconnaissance missions in the Indian Ocean, and accompanying tanker aircraft.

– Initial funding was provided for a new long-range medium-sized cargo aircraft, the CX, to be able to operate from short, relatively primitive airfields. The CX programme was necessary in order to increase the US capacity to lift heavy cargo over long distances, particularly since the 24th Mechanized Division had been included in the RDF. However, it would be the late 1980s before the CX could be deployed in large numbers; decisions on numbers and type of plane were yet to be taken,

but the CX would be the most expensive item in the RDF planning.

–The plan also included a new class of roll-on/roll-off cargo ships intended as a partial substitute for forward bases. They were to hold the equipment for a Marine Amphibious Brigade (MAB) with more armour than a Marine division. Based at Diego Garcia, they would meet Marines flown in by civilian aircraft. Since this programme, like the CX, could not be completed before the late 1980s, the US pre-stocked equipment for the MAB by August, aboard seven chartered cargo ships which were deployed in the Indian Ocean.

The American plans were dependent on access to facilities in the region where forces might be used. Upgrading Diego Garcia, the base leased from Britain, was the centre of such planning, but even it is 3,400 kilometres from the Straits of Hormuz. After considerable negotiation, the United States reached agreement for American access to facilities in Oman, Somalia and Kenya (but not for the setting up of bases), although the agreement with Somalia was held up due to American concern that the United States might be dragged into Somalia's conflict with Ethiopia over the Ogaden, and it was not until early 1981 that the American administration accepted Somali assurances that no US weapons would be transferred to rebels in the Ogaden. Finally, the Reagan Administration reportedly planned a major development of facilities in Egypt at Ras Banas on the Red Sea. Overall, the US was to spend $2 billion over five years to improve facilities in the region. In the emerging US–Egyptian military relationship, American AWACs early warning aircraft began operations from Egypt in June; American F-4 *Phantom* were deployed there in August and September; and 1,400 troops from the 101st conducted a joint exercise there in November, the first American operation in the Middle East in over twenty years.

The new Reagan Administration embraced the RDF, and added $2 billion funding for it to the FY 1982 budget, an increase of 85% over the Carter Administration request. The Administration also sought to solve a number of issues in the implementation of RDF planning. One was the tangled command structure of the RDF, with the Marine lieutenant-general in command reporting to both the Joint Chiefs of Staff and the Commander of US Readiness command, an army general. This issue took on much greater significance after it became clear that the lack of a clear chain of command within the RDF had been a principal cause of the debacle of the US attempt to rescue the hostages from Iran in April. The Reagan Administration examined a number of alternatives, the main one being to assign the RDF to the US Commander-in-Chief, Europe. That appeared to make sense once the focus of the RDF had been narrowed to south-west Asia, given the involvement of European-based forces and facilities in supporting any major deployment in the Persian Gulf. However, it would still leave the RDF Commander some 4,000 kilometres away from the Persian Gulf.

A second major issue was the role of the Navy. At the beginning of 1980, over 30 American ships were operating in the Indian Ocean, including not only the two carrier task forces – one each from the Sixth (Mediterranean) and Seventh (Pacific) Fleets – but also the Bahrain-based Middle East Force (MEF), which had been expanded from three to five war ships. Given these commitments, it became clear that the former deployment pattern of the carrier task forces, with two each in the Mediterranean and the Western Pacific, was unlikely to be re-established; one of the Marine Corps' 1,800-man amphibious units would be more or less permanently shifted from the Pacific to the Indian Ocean. New aircraft carriers would take time to build, even if there were money to construct them and personnel to man them; as an interim solution, the Administration sought to return one or two mothballed carriers and one battleship to the active fleet, but it would be two and a half years before even those could be made ready.

A third specific issue was how to arm and support the RDF. It was all too clear that heavy tanks designed for the war in Central Europe did not make sense for rapid projection forces, and that moving those tanks was a serious problem, since only the giant C-5 air transport and the proposed CX would be able to carry an M-1 battle tank, and even then only one tank each. By contrast, even the much smaller C-130, of which the United States has over 450, could carry two light armoured vehicles of the type the Pentagon moved to develop in 1980.

Beyond these specific issues, the new Administration would continue to confront the questions of how much force was enough, and for what. It highlighted the role of the RDF in preventing a Soviet move against the oil-producing regions, and sought to ensure that the RDF need not be merely a 'trip wire'. As Deputy Secretary of Defense Frank Carlucci said in March 1981: 'It is over 2,500 kilometres from the Transcaucasus to the Straits of Hormuz – over mountainous terrain with few roads and many bridges. Our airpower could be used for interdiction and our RDF land forces could confront such a Soviet attack ... The RDF would assure that the time involved in such a campaign would be protracted. The Soviets, hence, must calculate the course and the consequences of a long war.' Yet it would not be easy to balance military requirements with the political realities of the region. Sea-lift and air-lift requirements could be vastly diminished if American soldiers were stationed in considerable numbers within the region – in Egypt (perhaps in the former Israeli bases), in Saudi Arabia herself or elsewhere in the Gulf, or even in Israel. Yet, even if one of the States in the region were willing to host a major US deployment – and none came forward in 1980 – the strain on regional politics caused by such a deployment could outweigh the military benefit derived from deterring Soviet threats.

America's Allies
The major allies of the United States had some capability to project power outside Europe, especially into South-west Asia, and all took steps during 1980 to increase those capabilities. British Prime Minister Thatcher's visit to Washington in March 1981 suggested that Western co-operation might actually result in some form of allied deployment force. Yet there remained a number of questions. Some of America's allies clearly were reluctant to become too deeply involved in multilateral arrangements. More important, the potential contributions of the allies would remain small, but would the marginal military benefit of increased effort by the allies beyond Europe, plus possible political advantages – in reassuring the United States and perhaps regional actors as well – outweigh the danger of weakening the defence in Europe?

France's activities were the most important. Her naval presence in the Indian Ocean, based in Djibouti and Reunion Island, increased from 14 to 20 ships, and during the war between Iran and Iraq, deployed a 5-ship minesweeping force in the Arabian Sea. The 3,500 French Marines and Legionnaires based at Djibouti constitute the largest Western intervention force close to the Persian Gulf, and in addition France maintains several other units earmarked for intervention. However, France's air-lift is limited, as was demonstrated by her request during the Shaba operation in May 1978 for American transport assistance, but she has ordered 25 additional Transall C-160 aircraft (to add to the 56 already in the fleet), and the first of those will be delivered in September 1981. French increases in defence spending in 1981 included plans for two 32,000-ton nuclear-powered aircraft carriers, the first of which is to join the fleet about 1990, when one of the two existing carriers will have to be retired. At the same time, much of the French effort has been focused on former French colonies and only loosely co-ordinated with American activities. In January 1980 France deployed a five-ship task force to Tunisia to demonstrate support for that country after the Libyan-inspired raid on the town of Gafsa, and in early 1981 she increased her modest deployments in the Central African Republic in an effort to contain the Libyan intervention in Chad. She has insisted on only bilateral and *ad hoc* operations with the United States, announcing for instance, that her mine-sweeping force would not operate in any integrated fashion with other Western powers, while she has continued to grant the United States only limited access to her facilities in Djibouti.

Anglo-American co-operation in planning for security contingencies outside Europe has been more direct – the British defence White Paper of April 1980 argued that the task should 'not be left to the United States alone' – but Britain's forces are modest. The Royal Marine Commandos and Army units, especially the Eighth Field Force, were joined in a pool with one parachute battalion (about 600 men) available for operations at seven days notice. British air-lift also remains limited, although two-thirds of Britain's 45 C-130 cargo aircraft were to have their fuselages stretched to increase lift capacity by 1983. During the year, Britain organized a 'Gulf patrol' in the Gulf of Aden outside the Straits of Hormuz, which by late November consisted of two major comba-tants plus a tanker and support ship. She also

continued to deploy forces in the Far East, with the result that for some time during the war between Iran and Iraq she had at least six ships operating in or near the Indian Ocean.

Few of America's other allies have been prepared, or able to take steps paralleling those of Britain and France. There has been some support within NATO for creating a Standing Naval Force Mediterranean, to offset, in part, the redeployment of one American carrier group from the Sixth Fleet to the Indian Ocean. During 1980, the Federal Republic of Germany agreed to take on a more broader naval role within NATO's boundaries and the Nether-lands, which deploys forces into the Indian ocean on occasion, announced in October a small increase in her planned rate of ship-building. Australia's activities in the Gulf region increased, but she, too, was reluctant to co-ordinate her actions too closely with those of the United States. She deployed two ships to the Arabian Sea and four more to the Indian Ocean in the wake of the Iran–Iraq war. The Fraser Government also announced a major new naval expansion programme, including construction of new amphibious ships and vertical/short take off and landing (V/STOL) aircraft carriers, and offered the United States home-porting rights for one aircraft carrier at Cockburn Sound, Western Australia.

Soviet Capabilities

Afghanistan was the prime example of Soviet power projection during 1980, and it indicated the extent to which those capabilities have improved; in the 1950s the Soviet Union would have been hard-pressed to mount such an operation even into an adjacent state, much less to have done so quickly. Soviet actions in Afghanistan during the course of the year showed the change in Soviet military practices, reminiscent of the American experience in Vietnam: Soviet forces moved from a highly centralized command structure to the creation of seven military sectors in the country; from occasional forays into the countryside to more persistent search and destroy tactics; from the deployment of heavy tanks, air defence and surface-to-surface missiles, such as the *FROG*, to heavy reliance on Mi-24 helicopter gun ships, ground attack aircraft, mostly MiG-21s, and air mobile and motorized rifle infantry, the latter generally operating from light armoured BMPs.

Soviet capabilities for projecting power over longer distances also steadily increased during 1980, enabling the Soviet Union to demonstrate presence, to support regional allies and to prevent or complicate Western countermoves. This development in capability was most obvious in the Navy, which between 1964 and 1976 had expanded its operations beyond Soviet waters by a factor of almost 14, from less than 4,000 ship-days annually to nearly 48,000. This latter figure meant that over 130 Soviet naval ships operated out of Soviet waters every day. In 1980 the Soviet Union operated two *Kiev*-class vertical take-off and landing (VTOL) aircraft carriers; a third was completed and a fourth was under construction, and there were indications that the building of the first Soviet large-deck aircraft carrier was planned. The most striking new Soviet warship, the 32,000-ton battle cruiser *Kirov* – about the same size as a World War II battleship – underwent sea trials in 1980, and a second 13,000-ton *Ivan Rogov*-class amphibious ship was also built. In the wake of the Iran–Iraq war, the Soviet Indian Ocean squadron, present since the early 1970s, grew to roughly 30 vessels, including about a dozen combat ships and 500 Naval Infantry.

The closest Soviet equivalent to the proposed American RDF is the airborne force – seven line divisions, each composed of about 7,300 men. By contrast, Soviet marines, the Naval Infantry, are few by comparison to their American counterparts, comprising 5 regiments each with about 2–2,500 men. The airborne forces are not just another element of the ground forces, but are directly subordinate to the Ministry of Defence, emphasizing their special role; airborne forces were the first to be sent into Czechoslovakia in 1968, and were at the forefront of the campaign in Afghanistan. The Soviet air-lift fleet remained smaller than the American; in 1980 it comprised 100 of the newer Il-76s, somewhat comparable to the US C-141s, 50 An-22s (the only Soviet aircraft capable of carrying tanks and tracked missile launchers) plus 550 of the older An-12s (in addition the Soviet civil airline, *Aeroflot* had 25 Il-76s, 36 An-22s and 150 An-12s). Limitations on air-lift would be a serious obstacle to any Soviet effort to move large forces and equipment over long distances in a short period of time. However, the Soviet air transport force had been effective a number of times in air-lifting military hardware to Soviet associates – in the Middle East in 1973, in Angola in 1975–6, in Ethiopia in 1977–8 and in Afghanistan during the past two years.

The Soviet Union has also made moves to overcome her lack of distant facilities, which have constrained operations far from her borders. She appeared to have deployed several nuclear submarines near the Straits of Malacca and had sent a supporting submarine tender to Cam Ranh Bay, Vietnam, although there were reports that Vietnam continued to place restrictions on Soviet use of her facilities. During 1980 she constructed a new facility in Cambodia at Kampong Son, on the Gulf of Siam, which, in conjunction with Cam Ranh Bay, would make it easier to support a large fleet operating either in the South-west Pacific or in the Indian Ocean. There was also evidence that the Soviet Union was developing a base at her anchorage at the Dahlak Islands, off Aden; she was already operating aircraft from Aden, as from Cam Ranh Bay, and had another anchorage at Socotra, in the Red Sea.

In Afghanistan, the Soviet Union extended the runways at major airfields, and the two air bases in southern Afghanistan, in particular, not only placed much of the Persian Gulf region within range of Soviet tactical aircraft but shortened the air route to more distant Soviet clients, such as South Yemen or Ethiopia. In a crisis, they would also give the USSR a route to the Arabian Sea which would only involve over-flying the poorly defended Baluchistan area of Pakistan.

For America and her allies, projecting power into South-west Asia will continue to pose a number of problems: new capabilities will take time to create, and it is not clear that the effort can be accomplished without weakening NATO forces in Europe. Even if the Soviet Union is judged unlikely to attack the oil-producing regions of the Persian Gulf, she will continue to enjoy the advantages of relative proximity to that region. That proximity also means that she is likely to regard Western efforts in the region less as efforts to insure oil supplies than as measures which increase the military weight of the West in a region near to the Soviet Union.

FOCUS ON CENTRAL AMERICA

The first major initiative of the Reagan Administration towards its European allies, in February 1981, dealt with a country which had not hitherto been a focus of either Atlantic or East–West relations: El Salvador. Developments in Central America clearly aroused concern in the United States, and it was by the deliberate choice of the new Administration that they became a strategic issue not only in the context of intra-American but also in that of US–European and East–West relations. Of these, the last two were the most important: the Reagan Administration deliberately declared El Salvador – traditionally an area of predominant US influence – a test case for its future foreign policy, expecting the Soviet Union to respect and West Europeans to support US interests there. Yet doubts remained as to whether this particular test case was the one best suited for those purposes. Beyond that, it remained a question to what extent the turmoil in Central America and the Caribbean posed a strategic concern, even to the United States.

El Salvador

During 1980 the conflict in El Salvador took 9,000 lives and brought the country closer to full-scale civil war than at any time since the 1930s. As in many other countries of Central America and the Caribbean, the potential for conflict had been clear. El Salvador was a country of 4.5 million people affected by extreme poverty and income inequalities worse than any in the region, with a near-feudal oligarchy of a few thousand people owning 60% of the arable land and receiving over half the national income. Economic growth in the 1960s had increased the urban population and had raised expectations which could not be met in the aftermath of the costly 1969 war with Honduras and in the international economic conditions of the 1970s.

After the overthrow of strong man Gen. Carlos Humberto Romero in October 1979, a five-man civilian-military Junta took power. On 4 January 1980 this split when two of its three civilian members resigned in protest at alleged police violations of human rights and failure to implement promised land reform. The same day leftist guerrillas seized six radio stations, and, as the civilians who had resigned from the Junta were replaced exclusively by Christian Democrat politicians, violence from both Left and Right intensified. On 11 January leftists seized the Panamanian Embassy and took hostages, whom they released three days later after the Government had agreed to release seven leftists from jail. On 22 January sniper fire turned a left-wing demonstration of 100,000 people into a riot in which 22 were killed and 135 wounded. Mass kidnappings reached epidemic levels, with over 400 hostages taken between 18 and 20 February alone.

On 18 February, after 10 demonstrators had been killed during a seizure of the Education Ministry, the Archibishop of San Salvador, Oscar Romero, wrote to President Carter asking that no more military aid be sent to the Junta. The United States had promised $50 million in economic aid and over $5 million in military assistance, contingent upon land reform. On both 23 and 24 February, the United States warned rightist elements in the Salvadorian military not to stage a coup, and on 6–7 March the Junta, under American pressure, announced a nationalization of the banking system and a land redistribution programme ultimately affecting all farms over 250 acres. Those moves, coupled with declaration of a state of siege, drew limited support from groups of the Centre and Right, but violence escalated. Archbishop Romero was murdered on 25 March, and the United States charged that a right-wing Cuban exile may have been the assassin. The American Ambassador publicly expressed doubt about the utility of military aid and charged elements of the Salvadorian military with 'excesses' of violence.

As the Junta moved rightwards, rifts became apparent between the 'progressives', led by Col. Adolfo Majano, and the conservatives under Colonel Jaime Abdul Gutiérrez. However, on 16 October the Junta announced that a referendum on a new constitution would be held in 1982, to be followed by elections for civilian government in 1983. This move was coupled with the offer of an amnesty to those who laid down their arms and with efforts to contain the excesses of the Right.

On 28 November six leaders of the opposition Democratic Revolutionary Front (a coalition ranging from Marxist guerrillas to Social Democrats and dissident Christian Democrats) were abducted and killed, and on 4 December

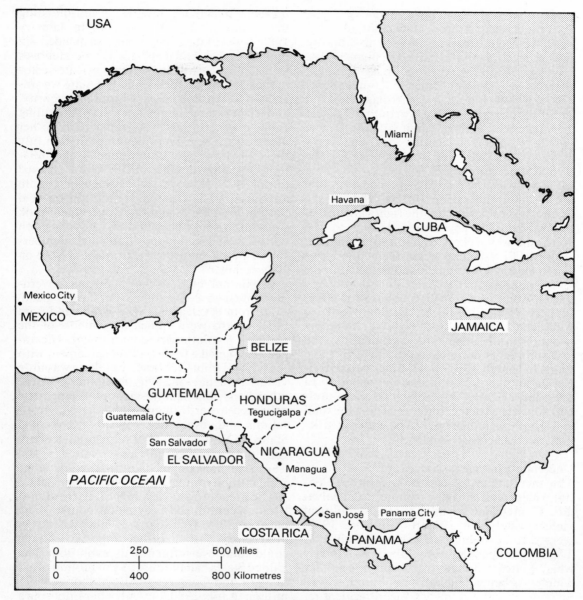

Central America and the Caribbean

the bodies of four murdered US missionaries were found. In both cases, the Right was suspected, and the United States suspended new aid pending a clarification of the Army's role. On 8 December, another shake-up of the Junta ousted Col. Majano, who had alleged that rightist militants had been responsible for most of the deaths, and Christian Democrat José Napoleon Duarte became President, with Colonel Gutiérrez as Vice-President. The US State Department announced that it would resume economic aid to the re-organized Junta.

On 9–10 January 1981 the opposition groups began a major guerrilla offensive in northern El Salvador. When this was repulsed by Government forces, and when workers failed to heed calls for a general strike, left-of-centre groups in Latin America and Europe which had supported the opposition began to rethink their position. Even the Sandinista

Government of Nicaragua, under pressure from the Reagan Administration for allegedly allowing its territory to be used to tranship arms from Cuba to the Salvadorian guerrillas, expressed support for a political solution. Nicaraguan Interior Minister Tomás Borge said of El Salvador: 'The guerrillas could not defeat the army and the army could not defeat the guerrillas. Things cannot continue like this. It is convenient neither for the Government nor for the guerrillas, neither for the United States nor for us'.

For her part, the United States had been able to forestall military coups during 1980, but she had not been able to arrest the rightward drift of the Salvadorian government. More to the point, she was seeking to build-up a political centre in El Salvador which seemed less and less to exist. Citing Cuban and Soviet support for the opposition in El Salvador, the outgoing Carter Administration had reversed itself in January 1981, freeing $5 million worth of American equipment for the Junta, including two transport helicopters and small arms – the first shipments of 'lethal' equipment in three years. In March, the new Administration decided on another $25 million in arms aid to El Salvador, and was to despatch 20 more military advisers to that country (bringing the total to 54), although they were to be under instructions not to engage in combat.

Uncertainty in Central America
The uncertain prospects for the future of Central America were hardly confined to El Salvador. Guatemala, where Left–Right political violence had been a fact of life since 1954, seemed to be sliding the way of El Salvador. Thirty-nine people were killed in January when police stormed the Spanish Embassy which was being held by peasant groups. And in September the country's Vice-President resigned in disillusionment at the government's human-rights record – thus further discrediting the regime of President Romeo Lucás García.

In Nicaragua, the ultimate direction of the Nicaraguan revolution remained in question eighteen months after Sandinista revolutionaries brought down the Somoza regime. Internal tension remained high in 1980, but an uneasy balance was maintained between the Sandinista-dominated Government and non-marxist elements in commerce, the church, labour unions and the press. The regime did,

however, make some progress in consolidating the country's internal situation. In January 1980 it reinstated civil rights, suspended six months earlier, and it also made several moves to reassure the private sector – private-sector representation on the Council of State was increased in April from one-third to a majority, and when two moderate members of the ruling Junta resigned, they were replaced by other moderates. The Government indicated in July that it had met agricultural targets, and inflation, running at 60% in 1979, was halved during 1980. However, on 23 August the Junta announced that elections would not be held until at least 1985, and the Government took steps to curtail the activities of opposition parties. As a result, opposition party members staged a walk-out from the Council of State on 12 November.

In external relations the Sandinista Government pursued a dual course. On the one hand, visits from PLO leader Yasser Arafat and from Fidel Castro were valued as symbols of the regime's revolutionary commitment. Nicaragua also signed a trade and aid agreement with the Soviet Union in March, but there was little visible evidence of Soviet assistance. On the other hand, the Sandinistas took a pragmatic approach towards international lending institutions and, especially, towards the United States. In September, after nine months of negotiation, a consortium of private US and European banks agreed to re-schedule some $600 million of outstanding Nicaraguan debt.

The predominant view in the Carter Administration continued to be that the course of the Nicaraguan revolution was not yet determined, and that a forthcoming US attitude could therefore influence its evolution. The United States had promised $156 million of aid in 1979 and Congress finally authorized $75 million in July 1980, but only after imposing a stipulation that no aid could be provided if Nicaragua were found to be supporting terrorism in Central America. When the Reagan Administration took power it did not move immediately to cut off aid, as campaign rhetoric had suggested it might, but aid did remain suspended pending resolution of Nicaragua's role in aiding the Salvadorian opposition.

The Caribbean
On the surface, the string of victories by conservative parties in free elections in the Carib-

bean during 1980 contrasted with the turbulence of Central America. Yet beneath the surface many of the same sources of instability were present: extreme poverty and severe inequalities in income, often compounded by racial and ethnic cleavages; young populations with rising expectations; dependence on imported energy and single-product exports; and frequently anachronistic political systems.

In marked contrast to the leftist coup in tiny Grenada, which had shocked American policy-makers in March 1979, the electoral trend in the Caribbean in 1980 was conservative. This was demonstrated most dramatically in Jamaica, but conservative governments were also returned in Dominica, where Mary Eugenia Charles' Freedom Party took power in July, in St Kitts/Nevis in February, in Antigua in April and in Bermuda in December. Jamaica had suffered a severe economic decline before the October elections, and a sharp increase in political violence. In March, negotiations between the Manley Government and the International Monetary Fund over a $231-million aid package had broken down. In April, five members of the opposition Labour Party were shot and killed, and in June Manley announced that 20 members of the Defence Force were being detained on charges of plotting to overthow the Government. Political violence continued in Jamaica right up to the election.

The elections, on 30 October, brought a landslide victory for Edward Seaga's Jamaican Labour Party, which won 52 of 60 Parliamentary seats. Seaga's first move was to expel the Cuban Ambassador in Jamaica for alleged interference in the election, and he also sought to stimulate private enterprise and rebuild the economy. Seaga was among the first heads of state to visit the new US President, in January 1981 when he secured agreement to a timetable for rescheduling Jamaica's debt to the United States and received IMF loans totalling about $550 million. While Jamaica would remain a member of the non-aligned movement, clearly she was building a relationship with the US that was very different from that implied by Manley's 'Democratic Socialism'. However, whether the Seaga Government would succeed in restoring the economy, let alone whether its election would set a pattern in the Caribbean, would become clear only with the passage of time.

The Role of Cuba

Cuba faced a number of challenges in 1980, both external and internal, which raised questions about her future role in the region. Her effort to take the lead in the non-aligned movement was tarnished by her support for the Soviet invasion of Afghanistan. After a long silence on the issue, Cuba voted against the UN resolution condemning the invasion; subsequently, in November, she lost her bid for the Latin American seat on the Security Council. Disease struck hard at Cuba's vital sugar and tobacco crops during 1980, unemployment and shortages were evident, and the faltering economy underlined her dependence on the Soviet Union, requesting aid of about $3 billion per year. She signed a five-year, $35-billion economic exchange agreement with the USSR in October, and the Soviet military presence in Cuba continued to increase, as Soviet pilots used Cuban facilities to stage surveillance missions off the American coast and to monitor NATO naval exercises.

Anti-Castro slogans and pamphlets appeared for the first time in January, and the extent of discontent was underlined by the exodus of over 125,000 Cubans (1% of the population) to the United States between April and September. This began on 6 April, when over 10,000 Cubans crowded the Peruvian Embassy in Havana after the government withdrew its police from the gates and announced that safe passage would be granted to all those wishing to leave the country. After rejecting offers from the UN and the Organization of American States (OAS) to arrange an orderly emigration, Castro announced on 21 April that the Cubans in the Peruvian Embassy and others with Cuban-American relatives could leave on the private boats which, acting on rumours of the forthcoming exodus, had put into Mariel.

The most contentious issue, however, was Cuban and Soviet assistance to the opposition in El Salvador. Following efforts to spread revolution in Latin America in the 1960s, Cuba had changed course as a result of clear Soviet pressure and the fear of alienating nervous neighbouring regimes. She had provided help, perhaps even including arms to the Sandinistas and to the radical regime in Grenada, but this had been given only once the regime was in power or visibly on the way there. In the case of El Salvador, however, the United States charged that Cuba and the Soviet Union had arranged for some 600 tons of arms to be delivered from Ethiopia, Vietnam and Eastern European countries to the Salvadorian opposition – and that they had done so in late 1980 and early 1981, when the outcome of the conflict in El Salvador was very much in doubt. Such assistance hinted at a more venturesome Soviet approach, perhaps reflecting a judgment that revolution was more likely in Central America, or that the United States was less able to resist it, than the Soviet Union had previously believed.

Dilemmas for Policy
The first indications of the Reagan Administration's policy towards Central America and the Caribbean suggested some continuity with the Carter Administration approach. It was clear, however, that the new team would see regional turmoil in the context of East–West rivalry, and not merely as a regional matter. While many of the practical consequences of this shift remained unclear, further increases in military assistance to the Junta in El Salvador seemed likely. The United States might be able to persuade her allies that this course was justified by Soviet and Cuban assistance to anti-Junta forces, but it was a course fraught with danger: political polarization in El Salvador had decimated just those moderate elements which the US sought to support, and even if the Junta proved more successful than anyone in Washington expected, the violence was still likely to persist for several years.

More important, there was little evidence the United States' friends in the region were prepared to underwrite policies that emphasized military instruments, let alone military intervention; US efforts to arrange an OAS force to facilitate the transition in Nicaragua in 1979 had been rejected by most OAS members. And while the region's major states, Venezuela and Mexico, shared American concern about instability, they both emphasized the need for political and economic measures (in 1980 they agreed to recycle up to 75% of their oil revenues from Latin America as low-interest loans to the region). Mexico also had generally good relations with Cuba, and Mexican President López Portillo, visiting Havana in August, repeated earlier calls for an end to the US economic blockade of Cuba.

These issues were related to the larger questions of American – and Western – strategic interests in the region. The Soviet military presence in Cuba remained a specific but limited problem. On the other hand, the economic and human links between the United States and the region would grow larger (as much as one-fifth of the Mexican population was to some extent dependent on income remitted by family members working in the US). And, while internal turmoil in the region would continue to be tragic for the people concerned, would it in fact endanger vital American interests? The Soviet Union clearly was unwilling and probably unable to finance another client in the region, a fact not lost on Nicaragua's Sandinistas. Good relations with Mexico, the United States' third largest trading partner and an increasingly important source of oil, represented a more concrete stake, and the narrow Mexican political structure – the legacy of a revolution grown old – could be vulnerable over the longer term. Yet US policies designed to contain the Left in Central America, by force if necessary, would increase rather than diminish the risk of internal strain in Mexico.

AMERICAN MILITARY MANPOWER

As American military commitments expanded, US forces were stretched thinner during 1980, and in the United States and among her allies, there was growing concern about her military manpower. The problems of her all-volunteer force (AVF) were real and sure to worsen. Most immediately troubling was the difficulty of retaining soldiers with critical skills; beyond that, both the number and quality of new recruits and the state of US reserve forces gave cause for concern. The overextension of US forces was highlighted in 1980 when one aircraft carrier in the Indian Ocean spent 300 days at sea and only five in port.

The United States' problems were not unique among Western armed forces, and her problems with the AVF (which had been recommended by the Gates Commission in 1970, amidst the turmoil of the Vietnam war, and implemented fully in 1973) bore some resemblance to those Britain had faced when she abandoned conscription in the early 1960s.

Table 1: US Active-duty Military Manpower

	Strength 30/9/80 (000)	% of author- ized	Recruitment as % of target (fiscal years) 77	78	79	80
Army	777	100	99	97	92	100
Navy	527	99+	96	94	93	100
Marine Corps	188	102	95	101	97	99
Air Force	558	100	100	100	97	100
Total	2,050	100	98	97	92	100

SOURCES: Office of Assistant Secretary of Defense (MRA&L) (MPP), 17 October 1979, 31 October 1980; US Department of Defense. *Manpower Information Book* (1977), p.B-40.

But even those Western military establishments which had retained conscription were confronted, by the end of the decade, with the need to take increasing fractions of diminishing populations of draft-age men. However, America's problems were worse and bigger, not only absolutely but also relatively (Britain's armed forces, for instance, were about 0.6% of her population in 1980, compared with about 1% for the United States).

The AVF: Successes and Limitations

The record of the AVF as a whole has been by no means totally bleak. Indeed, most of its critics even conceded that it had come a long way from the ravaged forces that shambled out of Vietnam in the early 1970s and attempted simultaneously to adjust to an all-volunteer recruiting environment. As Table 1 shows, the active-duty forces of over 2 million were being maintained at authorized levels, and recruiting of enlisted personnel in Fiscal Year (FY) 1980 – 1 October 1979 to 30 September 1980 – was markedly better than it had been in FY 1979. Those forces were buttressed by a Selective Reserve (including the National Guard) of over

800,000 and an Individual Ready Reserve (IRR) numbering more than 400,000, making a 'Total Force' of 3.2 million military personnel – a considerable establishment by any standard. Clear progress had also been made in reducing institutional 'turbulence' due to absenteeism, desertion and rapid attrition of recruits. As Tables 2 and 3 show, only the Navy had been plagued by deteriorating discipline, and all the services seemed to have achieved greater institutional stability than in the AVF's early years, with additional progress anticipated. Finally, manpower-related costs seemed to have been brought under control, after rising during the first years of the AVF. Those costs peaked in FY 1976, when they accounted for approximately 61% of all defence outlays, but it was estimated that they would account for no more than 54% of the defence budget in FY 1981.

Nonetheless, the apparent success was misleading. In the first place, although the Active and Selected Reserve components were maintained at or near their authorized levels, these levels were below what was considered necessary for full peacetime manning of the forces and barely four-fifths of the number required for mobilization. Four of the Army's sixteen Active divisions had only two brigades apiece, their third brigades (along with at least eleven battalions required by other divisions) existing only in the Selected Reserve (National Guard). Some Army line companies had only two platoons instead of the three required, and nearly one-sixth of the rifle companies in the Marine Corps existed only on paper.

What was true of the active force was even more true of the reserves, and this raised questions about how far and how quickly the United States could mobilize in a major war. The Selected Reserve itself was woefully short-handed, and the Individual Ready Reserve (IRR) – veterans who do not train but are liable

Table 2: Absenteeism FY 1971-80 (rates per 1,000)

	1971	1972	1973	1974	1975*	1976*	1977*	1978*	1979	1980
Army	176.9	166.4	159.2	129.9	95.4	70.3	47.0	40.4	38.0	41.6
Navy	19.0	18.3	21.7	53.8	73.0	77.5	76.9	78.3	83.4	82.0
Marine Corps	166.6	170.0	234.3	287.5	300.9	201.8	103.5	97.5	86.7	83.6
Air Force	9.4	17.2	16.1	17.3	13.0	7.8	3.8	4.6	5.9	6.7

*Reporting procedures for the different services changed at different points between FY 1975 and FY 1978, and abrupt year-to-year changes in this period should be read with caution.

to call-up in time of emergency – had been decimated during the 1970s. While the draft was in force the reserves had little trouble maintaining their authorized strengths, since those joining the National Guard were exempt from draft, and the ranks of the IRR were filled with the turnover of conscripts after their two years of service. Despite improvements in 1979–80, the IRR still had less than half the 900,000 authorized strength presumed necessary for effective total mobilization. Even after the re-introduction of draft registration (as oppposed to the draft itself) announced by President Carter in July, it would still take about 115 days to induct and train new conscripts and move them to the battlefield if the draft were begun during a war.

Furthermore, each of the active services had significant shortfalls in various areas. The Army and the Navy were each short of approximately 20,000 non-commissioned officers, and with the hardships imposed by overstretched forces, especially in the Navy, it was hard to foresee any improvement. Career re-enlistment rates in all services (though better in FY 1980 than in FY 1979) were still well below the levels maintained in the early years of the AVF, as Table 3 shows, and this was expected to continue, even allowing for further improvements. Both the Navy and the Air Force were short of pilots (the Air Force being 3,000 short), and the Marine Corps lacked more than 3,000 skilled technicians. Finally, while the actual and projected decline in turbulence did reflect some increase in institutional stability (the Navy, as indicated earlier, being an exception), all the services had far to go.

The Question of Quality

If the statistics raised questions, a far more serious concern was what had been done to acquire those numbers. Except for the Marine Corps, which chose to accept reductions in authorized levels, the tendency has been to let quality slip in order to acquire a sufficient quantity of volunteers. To be sure, the FY 1980 precentage of recruits with high-school diplomas (usually seen as an indicator of individual reliability rather than technical competence) was 68%. Although this was below the FY 1979 figure of 73%, it was still equal to the figure for the pre-Vietnam era. The problems, however, lay in the mental capacity of the recruits. For years the AVF's supporters had argued that, based on the tests, the quality of the new volunteers was as high as that of their pre-Vietnam predecessors. In FY 1979, for instance, only 5% of recruits were presumed to be in the lowest mental category eligible for enlistment, as opposed to 15% in the FY 1964 force. In the summer of 1980, however, the Defense Department was compelled to concede that the mental aptitude tests used to classify recruits had been incorrectly assessed, and that in fact 30% of all FY 1979 recruits were in the lowest category, while for Army recruits the figure was 46% instead of the 9% previously claimed. Even more disturbing was the fact that, even with the lowering of standards to these levels, a shortfall in total recruits of as high as 35–45% was projected by FY 1982 – a potentially crippling blow to the all-volunteer Army. This would not only affect the total size of the forces but also their ability to make use of the sophisticated equipment that had been introduced in

Table 3: First-Term Attrition
(percentage not completing minimum three-year obligation)

	Fiscal Year Entering Service									
	1971	1972	1973	1974	1975	1976	1977	1978*	1979*	1980†
Army	26	28	31	38	37	37	34	31	32	34
Navy	28	32	34	38	35	31	29	26	27	27
Marine Corps	31	24	32	37	38	35	29	30	29	28
Air Force	21	26	30	31	29	26	26	29	27	27
Total	26	28	32	37	35	34	31	29	29	30

*Estimated   †Projected

SOURCES (tables 2 and 3): Office of Assistant Secretary of Defense (MRA&L) (MPP) 31 October 1980, February 1981; R.W. Hunter and G. Nelson, 'The All-Volunteer Force: Has It Worked? Will It Work?', paper presented to Hoover Institution Conference on Military Manpower and the All-Volunteer Force, Stanford, California, December 1979, p.37.

the past years so as to compensate for lower manpower by means of increased firepower.

There were two other consequences of the AVF's quest for enough soldiers, one deliberate and the other unintended. The deliberate one was a significant increase in the number of women serving in the armed forces, coupled with a corresponding expansion of their role in the military. In FY 1964, women had comprised less than 1% of the active force. By FY 1974, with the AVF fully under way, that percentage had risen to 2.5%; by FY 1980, the enlisted force included 150,000 women on active duty (some 7.5%) and the figure was projected to rise to 254,000 (12.5% of the active force) by FY 1985. Women were most prominent in the Army and the Air Force, and least apparent in the Marine Corps. The first women were admitted to the service academies in 1976 and commissioned in 1980.

The second, unexpected, consequence was a striking increase in racial minorities, especially blacks, in the armed forces. Black enlistment rates declined from 26% of enlistments in FY 1979 to 22% in FY 1980, but the trend was nonetheless striking. In FY 1964, blacks had constituted only 11% of all initial accessions, with the Army having the largest share (14%), but during the 1970s the proportion more than doubled for the defence establishment overall. For fiscal 1978–80 inclusive about a third of the Army's recruits and a quarter of the Marine Corps' were black, whereas the national population was less than 13% black. Compounding this was the sharp disparity between black representation in the officer corps and the enlisted force, despite 'affirmative action' efforts by the Defense Department. Once again, the Army stood out: 32% of its enlisted force was black in 1980 as against only 7% of its officer corps.

While historically there has been no clear relationship between the representativeness of a military institution and its effectiveness in the field, the racial character of the US military was worrisome on three grounds. One was moral concern that a society was being defended by those who had profited least from it. The second was concern over the military danger of a heavily black Army in the light of the continuing possibility of renewed racial turbulence in America. The third was the related worry at the prospect of combat producing black casualty rates disproportionate to the black population of the country as a whole, and of operational liabilities being induced by the resulting domestic outrage.

Cost

Finally, there was a question of cost. Military manpower outlays having declined as a proportion of the defence budget in recent years, the AVF could not be held accountable for all the increases in manpower-related costs. The largest single increases in military pay and benefits occurred in 1969–71, well before the AVF had come into being, and the growth in military retirement pay as World War II and Cold War career personnel finished their service was also substantial (retired pay and benefits, accounting for barely 5% of all manpower costs in FY 1964, were projected to triple in FY 1981 to nearly 18%). All the same, US military manpower costs were high in an absolute sense, and were well above the 47% of the defence budget which they had absorbed in FY 1964. There was also a supplemental cost associated with the AVF, estimated at upwards of $20 billion, due to the increased recruiting costs and bonuses paid to entice volunteers to enter and remain in the military. Whether or not all these costs could be laid at the AVF's door, they had the effect of reducing the funds available for all other military functions (training, maintenance, procurement) and pushing defence budgets higher.

Priorities for the Future

There could be little doubt about the combined effect of manpower considerations on the operational readiness of the armed services. Nonetheless, it is important not to overstate the problem or the extent to which it could properly be attributed to the AVF alone. Aggregate US striking power, especially in the essential strategic forces, remained impressive, and the pre-Vietnam mixed force of conscripts and volunteers was by no means the elite force some later came to believe.

All the same, the manpower problems in 1980 were serious, and likely to worsen. Demographically, the proportion of eligible males in the prime 18–21-year age group would continue to decline by up to 24% into the mid-1990s. Economically, while relatively high unemployment rates do make the military more attractive to young people, this is especially true for those with the fewest skills – so

Table 4: Percentage of eligibles re-enlisting in the AVF, FY 1973–80

	73	75	78	79	80	change 73–80
First-term Personnel						
Army	38	39	36	43	51	+13%
Navy	23	40	40	38	37	+14%
Marine Corps	13	20	29	20	23	+10%
Air Force	20	40	41	38	36	+16%
Total	24	37	37	37	39	+15%
Career Personnel						
Army	63	75	69	66	69	+6%
Navy	92	80	64	62	67	–25%
Marine Corps	82	73	69	52	50	–32%
Air Force	93	90	82	82	82	–11%
Total	83	82	72	68	71	–12%

SOURCES: Hunter and Nelson, *op. cit.* in Tables 2 and 3; Office of Assistant Secretary of Defense (MRA&L) (MPP), 31 October 1980.

that it was far from clear that the military would be able to attract enough of the right kind of volunteers. Inflation would both create pressures for increases in military pay and benefits and push up defence outlays (or else compel further reductions in readiness if such increases were not forthcoming). And, while public opinion was plainly disposed to endorse a larger American defence effort, and perhaps to contemplate a return to the draft, conscription did not have many staunch advocates, and few were anxious to risk a repetition of the anti-draft riots of the Vietnam-war era. Even a return to the draft would not solve all the manpower problems, however, and it would raise new issues of its own. It would have little immediate effect on the most pressing problem – that of retaining skilled personnel – and it would be expensive, perhaps prohibitively so. It was difficult to imagine public support for selective conscription, even based on some sort of lottery. Some form of compulsory national service would be fairer (although there were doubts whether it was constitutional) but, because there would then be more manpower available than the services could handle, it would raise the problem of how to employ some 3.5 million young Americans in non-military government service programmes. Such a service could cost upwards of $25 billion per year, and it would not entirely solve the dilemma of how to select those who would serve in the military.

The United States faced a choice between three principal courses of action. One was to accept the continued desirability of the AVF and reduce manpower levels to lessen the pressure on it. A second was to abandon the AVF and turn to some form of conscription. The third was to sustain both the AVF and existing manpower levels, and to continue to search for remedies.

Neither President Carter nor President Reagan was ready to adopt the first alternative. In 1980 Mr Carter seemed to have begun to move in the direction of the second option. His reinstatement of registration – widely seen as the first step in that direction, despite White House denials – would probably have been followed by classification and, finally, by induction through a selective service or a national service scheme if conditions in the AVF continued to worsen.

Mr Reagan, in contrast, seemed likely to try to make the AVF work, at least for a time. He was philosophically opposed to conscription, and many of his advisers and supporters also saw the end of conscription as a positive legacy of the last (Nixon-Ford) Republican era. Yet most of the remedies had been tried. Lowering enlistment standards would mean reduced proficiency and greater 'turbulence', even though it would reduce recruiting problems. There were legal, financial and practical limits to how far civilians and women could be substituted for men in the areas of greatest shortfall – the ground combat arms and naval combat units. Increasing the size of the career force by extending terms of service would work to the advantage of the Active Force but would exacerbate the problems of the Reserves, which had depended on recruiting larger numbers of prior-service personnel to offset their own recruiting shortfalls. Technology could not be readily substituted for manpower, both because of its cost and because the technology already in use by the forces appeared to exceed the average skill levels of the people required to man and maintain it. Finally, more use of bonuses and other economic incentives would push manpower costs up still further and increase the pressure on the defence budget, without any guarantee that more money would buy enough soldiers, better soldiers and longer-serving soldiers – in short, the kind of armed forces the United States required to meet her commitments in the 1980s.

ANTI-SUBMARINE WARFARE

Since their inception, nuclear-powered ballistic-missiles submarines (SSBN) have been regarded as the strategic force least vulnerable to pre-emptive strike by the enemy. Hence, at a time when land-based intercontinental bombers and missiles are becoming increasingly exposed to the high accuracies of modern delivery vehicles, the sea-based deterrent remains the most reliable 'secure second-strike force', and the one on which Western (and perhaps Soviet) nuclear doctrine is based. Yet the development of strategic anti-submarine warfare technologies in which both major powers have invested considerable effort in recent years may, over time, render even these forces more vulnerable to attack.

As traditionally conceived, anti-submarine warfare (ASW) involves three steps: detecting a submarine; pinpointing its position (and ascertaining that it belongs to a specific group or class of enemy submarine); and firing weapons to destroy or incapacitate it. These tasks are carried out in the context of three types of operation which are analytically distinguishable but blend together in practice – open-area, barrier and trail operations. In open-area operations, sensors survey thousands of square miles, either instantaneously or (as in the case of a satellite) within a very short period of time. If targets can be localized and classified, then an immediate attack can be considered if the appropriate weapons can be delivered quickly to the target. If the location is too imprecise or appropriate weapons are not available, then the large-area sensor can direct mobile sensor/attack platforms (such as aircraft) to a position from which they can pinpoint and destroy the target. Barrier operations can be conducted at geographic choke points, along enemy transit routes, and off enemy ports. Large-area sensors may provide the initial information to the ships, submarines or aircraft manning the barrier, but if such sensors are not available, or their coverage leaves gaps, the barrier forces divide the uncovered area and attempt to locate and attack enemy submarines on their own. Trail operations are the best way to main-

tain assured contact with an enemy submarine, with the trailer picking up its quarry as the latter leaves port or passes a choke point on the way to the open sea. The most effective trailing is covert – with the trailer (another submarine) relying on passive sensors to establish the position of its target. But overt trailing of one surface ship by another is a regular naval practice in peacetime, and the technique could conceivably be extended to submarines as well. An SSBN would find it difficult to lose a faster submarine which used active sensors to maintain contact, though the trailer would itself be vulnerable.

This description makes clear that effective ASW depends on a complex combination of operations and requires co-ordination, communication and patience. This difficult task could be made easier by major technological breakthroughs – for instance by using satellite surveillance of large areas to detect anomalies on the ocean surface produced by submerged submarines. But the future balance of ASW capabilities is likely to be the result not so much of a specific breakthrough by one side or the other as the steady development of trends and techniques already evident.

American Advantages
In the balance of ASW strength between the United States and the Soviet Union, the former will continue to hold a number of advantages, as well as suffering several important vulnerabilities. A crucial advantage has been the undisputed US lead in hydro-acoustic sensing and processing technologies. Water is a good conductor of sound, and low-frequency signals, for instance, often travel thousands of miles. Active acoustic sensors transmit pulses into the water and listen for the characteristic echo as the pulse is reflected off a submarine's hull. Passive sensors receive the sounds generated by a submarine – from the flow of water over its hull, the rotation of its propellor, or the continuous operation of the pumps which are a necessary feature of nuclear reactor systems. The echoes or sounds produced by a specific

type of submarine constitute an acoustic 'signature' which allows it to be identified.

American acoustic systems include fixed undersea listening arrays cable-connected to the shore, powerful surface-ship and submarine sonars, and dipping sonars suspended in the water from helicopters or from expendable buoys (sonobuoys) which are usually dropped from and monitored by aircraft. They also provide guidance for torpedoes and triggering mechanisms for mines. American acoustic systems have a sophisticated computer-based capability for identifying the signals they are seeking, distinguishing them from the ocean's background or ambient noise and filtering out and amplifying the true submarine signals. The United States has also benefited from the tendency of Soviet nuclear submarines to be 'noisy'. While the USSR is making incremental improvements to lessen the noise, according to the US Navy's Director of Research and Engineering, they 'show no major trends towards quieting. Major strides in quieting would entail sizeable and costly new approaches to submarine construction. There are no indications the Soviets are moving in that direction.'

The second American strength is geography. The coasts of the United States and her allies front ocean basins, transit routes and choke points traversed or patrolled by enemy SSBN; most notably, Soviet submarines from the Northern fleet in Murmansk must travel through the so-called Greenland-Iceland-United Kingdom gap to reach open ocean, while submarines from the Pacific Fleet in Vladivostok must transit the Kunashir Channel. American and allied facilities and forces along those coasts facilitate large-area search and barrier operations.

A third and very significant strength is the US large-area system, SOSUS (Sound Surveillance System). Deployed off both American coasts and in areas where Soviet submarines sometimes transit or patrol, its passive listening hydrophones are anchored or moored so as to receive sounds from passing submarines; underwater cables transmit the signals from the hydrophones to shore-based processing facilities. It has been claimed that, under proper conditions the sytem may be able to place a target within a 50-nautical-mile circle. SOSUS is thus critical to the efficient use of American mobile ASW systems, especially aircraft and

submarines, since, by prompting them where to look, it allows them to intercept hostile submarines.

Further improvements were made to SOSUS to enable it to find quiet submarines and overcome recent increases in ocean ambient noise levels resulting from increased merchant ship traffic, offshore oil drilling, etc. The US Defense Advance Research Projects Agency (DARPA) listed as the first among its FY 1980 accomplishments the 'continuous tracking of [a] simulated quiet submarine' in the deep ocean. DARPA also reported some success with experiments aimed at 'development' of (long-range, low-frequency) active surveillance techologies' at sea, which, being active, would not be dependent upon hearing the noise generated by a submarine.

The US Navy's land-based ASW aircraft and submarines constitute a fourth strength. While the US surface vessels are well-equipped for tactical ASW, their commitment to convoy and carrier battle group duties means that they would probably have little direct involvement in strategic ASW. That would be the responsibility principally of P-3 *Orion* aircraft and various classes of nuclear attack submarines. The P-3 is well suited to ASW, with a combat radius of 2,400 nautical miles and an endurance aloft of 17 hours. It can quickly respond to SOSUS cueing and can patrol large areas in short time periods. Its primary search and localization sensors are a magnetic anomaly detector and sonobuoys. The former, which searches for disturbances in the earth's magnetic field caused by a passing submarine, has a fairly restricted area coverage. The latter, however, are capable of much wider coverage when laid in patterns across a submarine's expected path and operating either passively or actively. Their signals are processed by sophisticated on-board computers which can direct an attack with the P-3's depth charges or torpedoes. In 1980 the Navy had approximately 350 P-3s distributed around a world-wide basing network that allowed them to be within flying range of likely SSBN deployment areas.

The United States' most effective single ASW units, however, are her nuclear attack submarines (SSN). These have been much quieter than their Soviet counterparts and have superior acoustic sensing and processing capabilities which allow them to detect a Soviet SSBN long before it is aware of the American boat's presence. The United States had 74 SSN in 1980, and construction of the *Los Angeles* class would increase the number to 90 by the end of the decade.

Limitations on American ASW

A principal limitation to set against the strengths of American ASW has been the Soviet Union's effort in protecting her strategic submarine force. One element of this is the sheer size of that force. In 1980 the Soviet Union had 62 first-line operational SSBN, and she was expected to maintain that total (the limit originally set down in the SALT I Treaty). By contrast, the United States never has had more than 41 SSBN, and that number could drop to 32 by the end of 1981 before rising again to about 40 by the end of the decade. Given the monumental expense of SSBN (the new US *Ohio*-class boats cost $1–2 billion each), the Soviet effort to build 62 of them suggests a strong desire for security in numbers. In addition, older Soviet submarines – which, because of the limited range of their missiles, had to hazard transits to mid-Atlantic and Pacific waters to be within range of North America – are being phased out, and the newer *Delta* III boats, carrying SS-N-18 missiles with a range sufficient to hit the US from defended sanctuaries near the Soviet homeland, are replacing them. In 1980 there were 33 *Delta* I, II and III boats carrying SS-N-8 or SS-N-18 missiles, with a range of 8,000 km. The improved range of submarine-launched missiles will thus permit the Soviet Union to keep the bulk of her submarines behind a maritime defence perimeter around the immediate homeland. (For SSBN operating out of the Northern Fleet bases, this perimeter might extend to the central Norwegian Sea or beyond; for the Pacific Fleet, it would include the Seas of Japan and Okhostk and waters extending hundreds of miles east of the Kamchatka Peninsula.) Soviet writings and exercises attach high priority to securing this perimeter against enemy ASW operations, probably using a high proportion of Soviet naval forces as well as significant percentages of Long-Range Aviation, National Air Defense, and Strategic Rocket Forces. The US air and surface ASW units would thus find it difficult to survive within the perimeter, much less locate and kill Soviet SSBN, and her SSN would face a daunting task if they were to challenge SSBN in such sanctuaries.

Another limitation on American ASW is the inherent vulnerability of large-area acoustic search and command, control and communication (C^3) systems. Since the Soviet Union may well know where SOSUS arrays are located and where their data transmission cables came ashore, those cables could be cut or the shore-based processing facilities destroyed. In 1980 the United States was developing two mobile systems which could either replace SOSUS if it were neutralized or simply supplement it where its coverage was poor or non-existent. One, SURTASS (Surveillance Towed Array Sensor System), consists of long hydrophone cables towed by civilian-manned dedicated surface ships which would collect acoustic data and relay it to shore facilities for processing, display and analysis. The other, RDSS (Rapidly Deployable Surveillance System), consists of large sonar buoys laid in 'fields' by aircraft or submarines; these moor themselves to the ocean floor and for up to month or so serve as a detection and tracking system whose signals are either transmitted directly to aircraft or relayed via satellites to other processing facilities.

Both these back-up systems are themselves vulnerable, however, although less so than SOSUS. Enemy submarines could use signals from SURTASS ships transmitting their data to shore processing facilities to locate the ships and destroy them. Even if SOSUS, SURTASS and RDSS survived, the effectiveness of these acoustic systems could be greatly impaired if enemy submarines stayed out of those ocean layers which best conducted the sounds they make. Their ability to operate at critical frequencies could also be swamped or crippled by the effects of great volumes of noise in the water – for example, nuclear explosions. The United States will remain dependent on acoustic systems for some time to come since she did not initiate a programme to develop non-acoustic wide-area search systems until 1979.

C^3 systems in general are notoriously fragile, and, even if they seem generally adequate, those supporting ASW are no exception. They are susceptible to jamming, and the strong Soviet emphasis on 'radio-electronic combat' makes this a likely countermeasure. In addition, missiles, aircraft or sabotage could render many communications ground sites useless. Whether communications satellites would be damaged is uncertain – it depends on the scenario assumed, the progress of the Soviet anti-satellite weapons programme begun in 1976, and the prospects for restraints on such weapons being agreed between the two super-powers – but recent improvements in American C³ have made the United States more dependent on satellites for transmitting data among ASW forces.

A further limitation on US ASW is the lack of adequate numbers of reliable weapons systems. For example, the *Los Angeles*-class SSN now being built are so expensive (approximately $500 – 600 million each) that only one or two a year can be purchased, which is inadequate to sustain the projected force level of 90 SSN by the end of the decade. Another example is the Navy's phasing out of its long-range rocket-assisted ASW weapon SUBROC before a replacement becomes available (programmed for the end of this decade). This could seriously limit the present advantage of US SSN, since they would need to approach within torpedo range to strike at Soviet submarines which carried their own long-range ASW weapons. A third example is the US Navy's mine development effort. American officials have acknowledged that mines have a key role in ASW, but programmes to enhance the Navy's mining capability have been plagued with recurring technological problems. The CAPTOR deepwater mine, for instance, originally hailed for its great ASW potential, has been in development for twenty years and its problems were so great that Defense Secretary Brown at one point ordered the termination of the programme. Only the lack of an alternative deepwater mine persuaded him to rescind the order, and as a result in 1980 CAPTOR was still being produced at a trickle, as attempts were made to correct its deficiencies.

The Soviet Potential
The Soviet Union initially concentrated her strategic naval efforts on systems for tracking and destroying the aircraft carriers which she viewed as the primary naval threat. However, the development of American *Polaris* SSBN in the 1950s and 1960s led to a broad and well-funded ASW programme involving intensive research into both acoustic and non-acoustic systems. That effort notwithstanding, the Soviet ASW potential in the near future seems to be the converse of America's: few strengths and severe limitations.

The strength of Soviet ASW has been in local operations. If the location of a submarine is known and lies in an area where her forces are free to operate, the Soviet Union has a good capability to mount effective barrier or local search-and-destroy operations by massing air, surface, and sub-surface forces. While Soviet systems may not be as sophisticated as their American counterparts, their numbers may make up for any lack of quality. The quality of acoustic sensors and weapons on Soviet naval units is believed to be adequate for such operations, as is the C³ system – to which the Soviet Union always has assigned high priority. In addition, the Soviet mine inventory reportedly numbers in the tens of thousands. Submarines and even merchant and fishing ships could covertly mine suspected enemy SSBN transit routes, and in wartime aircraft and surface combatants could also lay them – the USSR might accept the loss of many aircraft if she thought that US SSBN would be bottled up in their ports as a result.

The new Soviet *Alfa*-class SSN is another important ASW improvement. Soviet submarines have attempted to trail American SSBN in the past, but, since it seems clear from repeated US official claims that American SSBN on patrol remain secure, the trailing must have been unsuccessful. The *Alfa* attack submarine could make a critical difference. It is reputed to be the world's fastest and deepest-diving submarine, and if it engaged in overt trailing by using its active sonar it might be difficult for an American SSBN to escape without the use of decoys or the support of other forces. There were two *Alfa* boats in the Soviet inventory in 1980, and their production was continuing at a slow rate.

Despite these advantages, however, the factors degrading the Soviet ASW potential remain far more significant than those enhancing it. One such factor is C³, which, for the USSR as for the US, is both critical to the efficiency of ASW operations and vulnerable to disruption (although the Soviet emphasis on avoiding dependence on one system alone may have rendered Soviet C³ somewhat less vulnerable than American). A second factor is geography. Except in the Pacific, the Soviet homeland does not offer direct access to the waters where US SSBN operate, thus restricting Soviet deployment of wide-area acoustic systems and complicating the operation of ASW forces from

Soviet bases. The USSR has apparently been unable to secure access to foreign ports or facilities in the Atlantic or Pacific, either to deploy ASW forces regularly or establish ASW ground sites.

American efforts to counter Soviet ASW capabilities have been an important third factor. For example, underlying the deployment of the new *Trident* SSBN was a determination to stay well ahead of any Soviet ASW developments. With its 7,400-km missile, *Trident*'s patrol area can be ten times the size of that available to its *Polaris* and *Poseidon* predecessors carrying 4,600-km missiles; it is also quieter than its predecessors, and was specially configured to incorporate existing and developing ASW countermeasures. By 1980 two *Trident* boats had been built but were not yet operational, and construction was to continue at a rate of one a year until 1984.

A fourth factor degrading its potential against Western SSBN is the Soviet Navy's primary role in maintaining a defence perimeter around the homeland. This task will place such heavy demands on the Soviet Navy in wartime that it is difficult to see how it could seriously challenge American SSBN outside that perimeter. The Soviet Navy had only 40 long-range ASW aircraft in 1980 – a remarkably small number – and, while its inventory of 271 major surface combatants and 189 attack submarines seems impressive in the abstract, these units are distributed among four fleets (Northern, Baltic, Black Sea and Pacific) and two squadrons (Mediterranean and Indian Ocean). The small number of aircraft, the distribution of the remaining forces, and the tendency towards unit-intensive operations simply would not leave enough capabilities to pose a decisive challenge to US SSBN, especially since these would not need to enter the Soviet defensive perimeter in order to strike targets deep in the Soviet Union.

Finally, the Soviet Union still has no large-area sensor. She has assigned high priority to developing one, and her focus on non-acoustic research is eliciting considerable concern in the West. Soviet writings have exhibited interest in a wide variety of non-acoustic phenomena produced by a passing submarine: changes in water level; magnetic, electromagnetic, and gravity anomalies; increases in radioactivity because of neutrons leaking from a submarine's reactor; and ocean surface reflectivity

and thermal effects resulting from the wakes and waves a submarine generates. Radars, infra-red sensors, magnetic anomaly and nuclear detectors, gravitometers, superconductors and lasers all have the potential to detect at least one of the phenomena, and lasers have the additional potential for finding a submarine directly by bouncing a beam off its hull. Converting the potential of any of these systems into a reliable and practical capability for submarine detection over a wide area would be a breakthrough of great significance.

The US Navy's Research Director, David Mann, said in censored testimony in 1979 that the 'Soviets are expected to have ... improved acoustic sensors, and probably towed-array sonars ... These improvements will give better technical capabilities to deter, track and attack submarines operating near the USSR, ... in confined waters, or ... transiting choke points'. His Defense Department counterpart, William Perry, stated in 1980 that the USSR was 'in the early development phase of new submarine detection systems which by the early nineties could have some level of effectiveness against our current nuclear submarines' – that is, submarines other than *Trident*. But Perry added that American deployment of the long-range *Trident* I missile and the very quiet *Trident* submarine would offset 'the potential new ASW system'. Both Mann's and Perry's statements imply that the systems referred to may, for technical and operational reasons be restricted to covering the *Polaris/Poseidon* patrol areas, and thus may be of doubtful effectiveness against newer US systems.

Implications

Neither the Soviet Union nor the United States seems likely in the foreseeable future to be able to destroy the other's nuclear missile-carrying submarine force in an extended war. The factors limiting Soviet ASW potential remain overwhelming by comparison to the factors enhancing it, and the clearly greater American potential suggests that the United States would be able to locate and destroy at least some of the Soviet submarines operating outside the sanctuary of waters adjacent to the Soviet Union. Yet within these sanctuaries Soviet submarines were likely to survive because of Soviet ASW countermeasures and because of the fragility of US systems – C^3 and large-area search systems in particular.

Perhaps a more critical question is the vulnerability of SSBN to a surprise pre-emptive attack. In the near term the lack of an effective large-area sensor would prevent the Soviet Union from launching such an attack. The United States would seem to have a greater potential to do so, given that only some 15% of Soviet SSBN (or 10 boats) are kept on patrol at any given time, leaving the remaining 85% in port where they would be vulnerable to a ballistic missile attack. Yet it is far from obvious that the US would be able to attack even those 10 boats simultaneously without the necessary preparations being detected, causing the USSR to send more boats to sea, triggering countermeasures and creating a risk of pre-emption.

Even without any major (and unlikely) technological breakthrough, however, individual SSBN are becoming more vulnerable to detection and attack. The oceans will become less opaque, and will offer modern submarines much less protective cover than they have enjoyed for the two decades since the advent of strategic SSBN. This will be partly offset by the introduction of longer-range submarine-launched missiles, which will enable both major powers' SSBN forces either to roam much larger areas of open sea or to stay close to their home shores in defendable sanctuaries. The 'creeping vulnerability' of ballistic missile submarines will therefore be a slow process and not a rapid one.

THE SUPER-POWERS

NO SIGN OF A NEW BEGINNING

In 1980 relations between the United States and the Soviet Union reached the lowest point in over a decade. Lines of communication between the two were more strained than at any time since the death of Stalin in 1953. The assumptions and expectations that underlay the American conception of the mutual relationship in the 1970s had been shattered by the Soviet invasion of Afghanistan, the tone was embittered by continuing turmoil in Iran and the Persian Gulf, and the process complicated by the American presidential election. Almost every aspect of super-power detente – from arms control to bilateral trade and diplomatic interchange – was deadlocked, and super-power relations seemed to be flawed by a fundamental and unresolved difference between the two over what should be, in the 1980s, the rules of the game. By 1980 both sides seemed to have recognized, albeit from very different premises, that there was little left for them in the detente process. Far from ordering international relations, super-power relations had themselves become a victim of international disorder.

Nor did the events of 1980 offer signs of a new beginning. The incoming Reagan Administration pledged its readiness to continue talking to the Soviet Union – for example, over strategic arms limitation – but there was little evidence that fundamental differences in perspective would become less marked. Even over the war between Iran and Iraq, where the interests of both seemed to favour an early end to the conflict, there was no explicit coordination and considerable mutual suspicion. The mood in the United States remained frustrated and truculent, and Americans seemed to hope that improving the military balance vis-à-vis the Soviet Union somehow would make the world an easier place. For her part the Soviet Union continued along familiar lines: the economy stagnated, military strength increased and the long-awaited rejuvenation of the leadership was still delayed. The trace of arrogance and the feeling that the 1980s would be a Soviet decade, which seemed to underlie many Soviet comments at the beginning of the year, was gone by the year's end, being replaced by a mixture of apprehension, confidence and irritation, with events in Poland and Afghanistan and the election result in the United States the major causes for the change.

Future Tests: Poland and Third-world Conflict
If one thing was clear, it was that new international crises would tend to render the Soviet-American relationship even more difficult. The most threatening of these was Poland. If the Soviet forces should be sent into the country to try to re-establish control, that would have profound repercussions on East-West relations in general and Soviet–American relations in particular. In the worst case, a Soviet military invasion of Poland might lead to resistance not only there but also in other parts of the Soviet empire in Eastern Europe and raise the spectre of a drift to war in the centre of Europe – a prospect even more disturbing, given the bad state of relations between the super-powers and hence of their ability to manage a crisis. But even if a Soviet invasion succeeded in suppressing the Polish trade union movement, the effect on the prospects for detente would be serious indeed, and the reaction in the West very different to that in 1968, when East–West contacts and negotiations were only marginally delayed as a result of the Soviet invasion of Czechoslovakia. The reason would be twofold: first a Soviet march into Poland in 1981 would violate the major international document of East–West relations, the Helsinki Final Act, to which the Soviet Union had pledged herself (the march into Prague in 1968 had violated only Western hopes). Second, and more important, an invasion of Poland would jeopardize the very basis of the Western understanding of detente: that it would gradually increase respect for human dignity in Communist regimes. The invasion of Czechoslovakia had been directed against a government which had disclaimed the Soviet doctrine of power, but an invasion of Poland would be directed against people who had obtained precisely what detente, in the Western view, was intended to provide. There

would be an outcry all over the Western world, and in the United States no political leader would be willing to maintain or enter any negotiations with the Soviet Union.

If Poland was the most threatening issue for future Soviet–American relations, during most of 1980 the primary issues were outside Europe and in areas beyond the clear control of either nation – a continuation of the pattern that had persisted since the Angolan conflict in 1975. Older conflicts continued: unchanged Soviet hostility to the Camp David peace process in the Middle East was reflected in support for the confrontation states, Syria and Libya in particular; activity by the USSR and her allies in the Horn of Africa continued, as did Soviet backing for Vietnam; and the Soviet invasion of Afghanistan in December 1979 marked the definitive end of the hopes of a decade of super-power detente.

The invasion of Afghanistan and the American reaction to it dominated 1980, both reflecting, and contributing to, the deteriorating super-power relationship. Soviet actions in the preceding years already had helped to generate an emerging American consensus about the need to respond to Soviet power, a trend which the invasion of Afghanistan could not but strengthen. At the same time, it also suggested how hard the task would be, and how little progress the super-powers had made since the 'Code of Conduct' signed by President Nixon and Secretary-General Brezhnev in 1972.

It seemed clear that the immediate motivation for the Soviet invasion of Afghanistan derived from the deterioration of Soviet control within the country. Yet, as the Soviet leaders weighed the possible damage to detente, they may have regarded it as already damaged beyond repair. The demise of the SALT Treaty in the US Senate, the NATO decisions to increase defence budgets and deploy new medium-range missiles in Europe, and the broad American support for doing more in defence – all suggested that intervention would be relatively free of risk to Soviet-American relations, since there was little left to lose. Moreover, the USSR, already frustrated with what she saw as the unpredictability of the Carter Administration, must have calculated that little of benefit could be expected from that Administration, especially once it was into an election campaign in which hostility to Soviet policy was a matter of course.

The initial American reaction to the invasion was sharp. President Carter called the Soviet action a 'threat to world peace' which had 'made a more dramatic change in [his] opinion of what the Soviets' goals ultimately are than anything they have done'. On 4 January the United States announced a series of diplomatic and economic sanctions: a cut in grain sales from 17 million tons to the 8 million pledged by earlier treaty agreements, suspension of Senate consideration of the SALT II Treaty, a virtual embargo on high-technology exports, curtailment of Soviet fishing rights, and the threat of an Olympic boycott. In addition, the US indicated that she would speed up the establishment of military bases in the Persian Gulf and south-west Asia, offered $400 million in economic and military aid to Pakistan (later rejected by Pakistan as insufficient) and moved to improve her links with China. In his State of the Union Address on 23 January, President Carter reinforced these moves, articulating a firm, if vague, new policy of containment in the Persian Gulf: 'An attempt by any outside force to gain control of the Persian Gulf will be regarded as an assault on the vital interests of the United States'. In sum, the American moves either suspended or cancelled virtually every surviving process of super-power detente. And many of the moves hurt the United States no less than the Soviet Union, which suggested that their purpose was as much to deter future Soviet actions by indicating their costs as it was to induce a Soviet withdrawal from Afghanistan.

The Soviet Union reacted to the Western moves with indignation and hostility. She vetoed two Security Council resolutions – one calling for sanctions against Iran, the other condemning the Soviet invasion – increased her military presence in Afghanistan, and sent the leading dissident Andrei Sakharov into internal exile. Soviet officials accused the Carter Administration of 'shameless lies and falsehoods designed to poison the atmosphere of detente', suggesting that the US had become an 'absolutely unreliable negotiating partner capable of violating international obligations and cancelling treaties and agreements' and seeking to blame her for the breakdown of detente. The USSR offered a variety of crude justifications for her invasion, but by December 1980 Leonid Zamyatin, President Brezhnev's chief spokesman, was offering publicly a more straightforward rationale: 'We were against the appearance on our southern border of a state that might be hostile to us and endanger our security; not 1,000 miles away but right on our doorstep. This is the crux of the matter.'

The positions of both super-powers remained frozen throughout the year. President Carter had little freedom for manoeuvre during the election campaign in any case, and the United States saw the Soviet Union's vague proposals for negotiations over Afghanistan as little more than reflections of a desire to legitimize the Soviet presence there. Even if Soviet leaders were surprised by the extent of the reaction to the invasion, once they were committed the difficulties encountered on the ground suggested that any serious Soviet interest in withdrawal was unlikely. Instead, Soviet officials branded American policy variously as hegemonistic, militaristic and hysterical; they saw Afghanistan as merely a pretext for a new American expansionism and a return to the Cold War. The American and Soviet prerequisites for discussions on Afghanistan remained far apart: for the United States, a Soviet troop withdrawal was the precondition, while Moscow emphasized the need for regional discussions which would have the effect of recognizing the government in Kabul and implicitly justifying the Soviet invasion by calling for an end to interference by others in Afghanistan.

Turmoil in the Persian Gulf, and in particular the 14-month captivity of the American hostages, provided an additional source of tension between the United States and the Soviet Union. The USSR remained ambivalent towards developments in Iran, sensing the dangers of continued chaos and Muslim extremism on her borders; nevertheless, and despite anti-Soviet statements by Iranian leaders after the invasion of Afghanistan, she continued to exploit anti-American sentiment within Iran. She did offer a mild, formal condemnation of the hostage-taking, but at the same time vetoed the Security Council resolution calling for sanctions against Iran, in partial retaliation for Western condemnation of the invasion of Afghanistan. She also labelled the attempt to rescue the hostages in April a 'reckless gamble'. In the same vein, during the delicate negotiations over the hostage affair in December 1980 and January 1981 Soviet media made repeated charges that the US, using the hostage issue as a pretext, was preparing to invade Iran. Such a desperate effort to prevent release of the hostages hinted at deep concern that the end of the hostage affair might mean the beginning of some rapprochement between Iran and the United States. Whatever its motivation, the Soviet stance could only aggravate the mood of suspicion in the United States.

Arms Control and Deterrence

If there had been any doubt, 1980 made clear that SALT no longer could serve as the centrepiece of Soviet–American relations. By deferring Senate consideration of SALT II as a reaction to the Soviet invasion of Afghanistan, President Carter tied the SALT prospects to a Soviet withdrawal from that country. Moreover, neither the climate within Congress nor that in the nation as a whole would have permitted serious consideration of ratification before the beginning of the next administration. The Reagan Administration's insistence that SALT II was inequitable and 'fundamentally flawed' suggested that progress in new SALT discussions would be slow at best. In addition, President Reagan explicitly stated at his first press conference in January 1981 that 'you can't sit down at a table and just negotiate that [SALT] unless you take into account ... at that table all the other things that are going on. In other words, I believe in linkage.'

The year saw the beginning of preliminary Soviet–American discussions on medium-range nuclear systems in Europe. But the future of these discussions remained uncertain as 1981 began, and in the absence of a more certain future for SALT the possibilities for progress were slim. All the same, there were considerable political pressures to get the talks under way. NATO governments, in agreeing on the introduction of new American long-range theatre nuclear weapons, had coupled this with an invitation to the USSR to negotiate mutual ceilings on medium-range missile systems. The Soviet Union had at first insisted that negotiations could not be started unless NATO governments first cancelled or delayed their modernization plan, but she abandoned this after Chancellor Schmidt's visit to Moscow in July. The Soviet leadership may have changed its position for a variety of reasons, calculating that talks were more likely to induce disunity within NATO over the modernization decision than Soviet intransigence; that they offered some promise of sustaining momentum in the detente process, at least with Western Europe, while maintaining pressure on the US to ratify SALT II; and that they might restrict the expansion of Western theatre nuclear forces.

The American decision to enter the preliminary talks reflected a recognition that the United States could hardly refuse negotiations which (through NATO) she had demanded. Secretary of State Muskie and Soviet Foreign Minister Gromyko met in New York on 25 September to lay the basis for talks. Preliminary technical discussions opened in Geneva on 16 October, adjourning on 17 November with little evidence that the two sides had moved further beyond vague agreement that the talks should be bilateral, should focus on other than strategic nuclear systems and should somehow be related to SALT.

The temper of the strategic relationship, as well as the difficulty of discussing nuclear issues between the two sides, was suggested also by the formal change in American strategic doctrine announced on 20 August and embodied in Presidential Directive 59 (for greater detail see pp. 12, 44). It was emphasized that the new Directive was only the latest stage in a decade-long evolution, and that it arose from the need to sustain the credibility of deterrence at a time of increasing official worry about the vulnerability of the American land-based *Minuteman* missile force. Yet the Directive – coupled with the increased US defence budget, the strong attention given to strategic nuclear forces, and the NATO nuclear modernization plan – provided new ammunition for Soviet arguments that the United States was seeking military superiority. Tass observed that the Directive signalled the abandonment of detente and the principle of parity, and President Brezhnev labelled it 'extremely dangerous'. Much of this reaction was motivated by the desire to paint the United States as an enemy of detente, but some of it seemed to reflect underlying Soviet concerns, both political and strategic, as to how the new Directive would affect future Soviet strategic problems and the future of Soviet–American relations.

The New American Administration
Soviet statements during the American Presidential election suggested that Soviet leaders were frankly unable to decide which candidate they preferred. While some specific Carter positions – for instance, the commitment to bring back SALT II for ratification – might hold some promise, the sense of frustration with the Carter Administration ran deep, and with memories of the Nixon Administration, Soviet leaders may have looked hopefully towards the election of another Republican President, despite the anti-Soviet rhetoric of Mr Reagan and many of his closest advisers. Moreover, both candidates clearly seemed to be caught up in the conservative tide sweeping the United States. Following Mr Reagan's election, Soviet statements adopted a wait-and-see attitude, calling for 'realism' on the part of the new President, and in November President Brezhnev said that 'any constructive steps by the United States Administration in the sphere of Soviet–American relations and pressing world problems will meet with a positive reaction on our part'. In his report to the Party Congress in February 1981, Brezhnev suggested an early summit between himself and Reagan, and he also made a number of proposals in arms control, including the possibility of extending military confidence-building measures under the Helsinki Final Act to all of European Russia in return for some unspecified extension on the Western side.

Poland was the issue immediately at hand. As the Polish crisis neared the boil in December, the Carter Administration issued several warnings of an 'unprecedented build-up of Soviet troops along the Polish border' – clearly trying to avoid repeating its over-mild reaction to Soviet military movements before the invasion of Afghanistan. For their part, Soviet leaders appeared to have decided in December to give the Polish Communist Party more time to set its house in order. In early 1981, however, statements accusing the Polish union *Solidarity* of working to undermine socialism in Poland became sharper, and there were accusations of subversive assistance from Western trade unions and governments. More fundamentally, there was little sign that the USSR was willing to accept a fundamental change in the structure of Polish society.

A second set of issues was super-power arms control. With regard to SALT, little was clear beyond the fact that a Reagan Administration would take months to decide what it wanted from the SALT process, and that SALT would be less prominent on the agenda than it had been in the past. Whether the Reagan Administration's commitment to sustaining the SALT process would be substantiated by actual proposals was less clear. The prospects were equally uncertain for the talks on nuclear missiles in Europe. The new Administration faced requests from its allies in Western Europe that the talks should continue in some form, and its willingness to begin NATO consultations again on the subject in March 1981 suggested it was persuaded. Yet the obstacles to progress were awesome: the Administration's own insistence that restoring the military balance was the necessary prelude to any serious negotiations, the technical difficulties of the talks themselves, and the uncertain fate of the SALT process, to which both American and Soviet leaders wanted the European talks to be linked.

A third imponderable in the future of super-power relations was China. The evolution of Sino-American relations was given new meaning and impetus by the Soviet invasion of Afghanistan. Congress approved the granting to China of Most-Favoured-Nation trading status in January, and in the absence of a similar agreement with the Soviet Union, that spelled the end of even-handed diplomacy. Defense Secretary Brown's visit to Peking in the same month underscored the parallel American and Chinese approaches, and increased the military aspect of their co-operation. The sale of a *Landsat* satellite ground station (with possible military utility), announced during Brown's visit, was followed later in the year by agreements to sell transport aircraft, computers, radar and communications technology, all of which indicated virtual blanket approval of defence-related sales apart from so-called lethal weaponry.

Sino-American co-operation was reflected in a series of meetings during the year. In March there were joint talks on Afghanistan, which included Japan, in May Deputy Premier Geng Biao visited the United States, and in July President Carter, meeting Chairman Hua Guofeng in Tokyo, observed that close links with China were necessary to 'minimize the threat of the Soviet build-up'. Statements of support for Taiwan by Mr Reagan and his advisers raised questions about the future of Sino-American relations, but as the new team took office those statements gave way to a recognition of the practical necessity and strategic advantages to be obtained from building on past American policy. The overriding interest of the new Administration in countering Soviet power seemed unlikely to break the pattern of Sino-American links so far, and might go well beyond this to the provision of offensive military equipment to China – further raising Soviet concerns.

Finally, there was the question of super-power relations in potential areas of turmoil outside Europe. Mr Reagan and his senior advisers seemed certain to push that question to the top of the super-power agenda. The new President had clearly stated his belief in linkage, yet recent history suggested that linkage – making improvements in direct super-power relations conditional on Soviet behaviour as a whole – would not always affect Soviet behaviour and thus would risk undermining further American support for arms control and other co-operative ventures in the process. Even if the United States and the Soviet Union were to agree to make understanding on extra-European issues a central focus of their relationship, their mutual suspicions over Iran, let alone over Afghanistan, suggested how far apart the two sides' conceptions remained.

THE UNITED STATES: FRUSTRATION AND ASSERTIVENESS

Two issues dominated the American approach to the world in 1980: the presidential elections and the continuing crisis of the hostages in Iran. The Soviet invasion of Afghanistan during the hostage crisis intensified the American mood of combined frustration and assertiveness, almost truculence. In January 1980 President Carter devoted his State of the Union address almost entirely to foreign policy and defence. The economy was dealt with more in passing, despite the fact that the 'misery index' (the rates of unemployment plus inflation) stood at about 19%. In the public mood which brought Ronald Reagan to the presidency there were undertones of nostalgia and of unilateralism. The former was a yearning for simpler times in a simpler world which, in retrospect at least, American military power had seemed able to control, while the latter was not a return to isolationism, but a sense that the United States could not ultimately count on friends and allies and had to be prepared to act alone if need be.

The Hostage Crisis

The immediate object of American frustration was the continued captivity of 53 US hostages in Iran. It was ironic that the hostage episode, which did much to lift President Carter from the depths of unpopularity in the autumn of 1979, should have played such an important role in his presidential defeat a year later. Although the US response to the hostage-taking was restrained, the anger went deep, and the issue never left the front pages of American newspapers. Its dominance was so clear that US foreign policy itself at times seemed to have become a hostage of the hostages.

The United States explored various policy responses. She halted imports of oil from Iran and froze Iranian assets in the US. A UN Security Council resolution calling for sanctions against Iran was vetoed by the Soviet Union in January, and although resort to the International Court of Justice produced a decision against Iran in May, this had little practical effect. On 20 April, under great pressure, America's European allies agreed to reduce diplomatic staffs in Iran and to impose economic sanctions on Iran if there were no progress by 17 May. It came as a surprise when the White House announced in the early hours of 25 April that a US military force had aborted a secret mission designed to rescue the hostages. Three of the 8 helicopters used in the mission had failed, and in the ensuing confusion 8 American servicemen perished when a transport aircraft collided with one of the helicopters preparing to leave the area. Secretary of State Cyrus Vance said he had been unable to support the raid attempt and resigned in protest, to be succeded by Senator Edmund Muskie.

In the United States the immediate public reaction to the raid was less indignation at its failure than profound shock and disbelief. Not since the Bay of Pigs debacle in 1961 had the pride of the nation been so humiliated by a

single operation. The President defended his decision as 'better to have tried than not to have tried', and the public evidently agreed with him – 71% of those interviewed in a Gallup poll felt he had been right to try the rescue. In a curious way, however, the failure dissipated the mounting public pressure for military action. There was concern, particularly in Europe, that this humiliation might precipitate a more reckless act, especially in an election year, but in the event the raid seemed to pave the way for a return to negotiations, which started in earnest in September.

Months of meticulous negotiation finally culminated in the release of the hostages on 20 January 1981, after 444 days in captivity. The jubilant welcome the hostages received reflected the relief Americans felt that the painful episode was over, and the relief overshadowed the high cost in national pride that the United States had paid. Yet it was clear that the end of the hostage affair marked no great change in American foreign policy, and that the wounds it had inflicted would take a long time to heal.

Increased Defence Budget

The public mood of support for more defence spending to counter what Defense Secretary Brown called 'the sustained expansion of the Soviet defense effort that has been going on for twenty years' gathered additional momentum in 1980. In January 46% of those polled by Gallup thought too little was being spent on defence, 23% felt present expenditure was about right and only 14% thought too much was being spent (the first time since the question had been asked that the first percentage exceeded the second). In such circumstances it was hardly surprising that the Carter Administration's defence budget for the Fiscal Year (FY) 1981, presented to Congress in January 1980, was assailed as too little. It called for outlays of $142.6 billion, an increase in real terms of 3.3% over FY 1980, and Mr Carter promised future increases of 5% in real terms. Nonetheless, to many inside and outside Congress, there seemed to be a wide gap between the declared objectives of the United States in dealing with the Soviet Union and the military forces available to support those objectives. Some of the specific criticisms of the budget were that it reduced or slowed the procurement of tactical aircraft for both the Navy and the Air Force, and that it did not do enough to increase America's power projection forces, especially in the Navy. Congress ultimately passed, and in mid-December President Carter signed an FY 1981 defence budget authorizing outlays of some $157.6 billion. The President's original budget had been increased in a number of areas – most notably ship-building, where $1.3 billion was added. The largest percentage increases over the previous year's budget were in weapons procurement (a 17.2% real increase) and in research and development (9.1%).

The focus of the defence discussion was how to project American military power into southwest Asia, but apart from funding a new transport aircraft, the CX, the FY 1981 budget was unaffected by the crisis in the Gulf region. However, planning for the Rapid Deployment Force (RDF) – involving mobile forces reorganized for deployment over long distances and backed up by improved transport and logistic support – continued, and its headquarters was formally established on 1 March. The United States deployed a squadron of F-4s to Egypt in July, and in November there was the RDF's first overseas exercise involving some 1,400 of the infantry troops assigned to it. (For detailed discussion of the RDF, see pp. 17–19.) There were a number of criticisms of the force, and particularly of its command structure: former Defense Secretary James Schlesinger wrote that 'just as the Holy Roman Empire was neither holy nor Roman nor an Empire, the RDF cannot live up to its name'. There were clearly problems to be solved – about the command arrangements, about the forces available for the RDF, and about the extent of facilities required in the region to support its deployment. All the same, the RDF did reflect American concern over military contingencies in the Third World, particularly the Gulf region, and it would therefore continue in one form or another.

The defence budget which President Carter bequeathed to his successor in early January 1981 requested outlays of $180.0 billion for FY 1982 (4.4% above FY 1981 in real terms). It contained no striking new initiatives but built on the increases Congress had introduced into the FY 1981 budget, rather than trying to reverse them. Research and development was up 14.1% in real terms over FY 1981, and, with a continuing focus on power projection, the budget funded 14 new and 2 converted ships. It

also provided for full-scale production of the ground-launched cruise missile for deployment in Europe. With the delivery of the *Carl Vinson* in FY 1982, US aircraft carrier strength would rise from 12 to 13, at least for several years until one of the older boats was retired.

The Reagan Administration moved quickly to implement its promise to increase the defence budget still further, proposing supplemental funding of over $6 billion for FY 1981, and adding $25.8 billion to Carter's request for FY 1982. If the Administration were to decide on real increases of 7% a year, it would have nearly doubled the FY 1982 Carter budget by 1986. Yet there were questions about whether even the neglected American defence industrial base could usefully absorb such increases without merely raising prices and creating backlogs of committed but unexpended funds. More important, increases in defence spending of the scale Mr Reagan's advisers had discussed cut directly against the Administration's declared intention to reduce federal spending in order to remedy the country's deteriorating economic situation. Indeed, economic considerations were likely to impose some constraints on the more ambitious defence plans.

Strategic Forces and Doctrine

There was a continuing modernization of American strategic forces during 1980, even as the debate about them continued. The FY 1981 defence budget contained $1.5 billion for the largest and most controversial programme in this modernization – the MX mobile ICBM. The Carter Administration remained committed to the MX, notwithstanding strong opposition from environmentalists and arms-control advocates to the horizontal basing mode agreed in 1979, and continuing doubts about its technical effectiveness, especially in the absence of the constraints on the number of Soviet strategic warheads that SALT II would have imposed. Mr Carter's FY 1982 budget contained $2.9 billion for the MX. Meanwhile, the programme to fit new and more accurate Mk 12A warheads to 300 *Minuteman* III missiles continued throughout the year and was due to be completed by the end of 1981.

Concern about the theoretical vulnerability of American land-based missiles and the specific concern about MX led to renewed interest in ballistic missile defence (BMD). In

July the Republican Party platform called for 'vigorous research and development of an effective anti-ballistic missile system', and in the January 1981 budget spending on BMD research was increased from $268 million to $346 million. The most prominent system under consideration would combine a long-range system, meant to attack incoming Soviet warheads in space, with a Low Altitude Defence System (LOADS), designed to strike remaining warheads within the atmosphere. But any decision to move forward with these plans would confront the Reagan Administration with hard choices, since any deployment of sufficient size to protect MX (and even some testing of components) would require the abrogation or renegotiation of the 1972 Anti-Ballistic Missile Treaty.

The *Trident* programme, involving a new missile and a new submarine, was plagued by production delays and staggering cost rises (from $157 million per submarine in 1974 to $1.24 billion in 1980). The *Ohio*-class boat was due to become operational in December 1981, two and a half years behind schedule. Two *Polaris* boats were dismantled during the year, because their nuclear fuel was exhausted and because the US would have come up against SALT I ceilings had sea trials of *Trident* not been delayed, and the other three remaining began conversion to attack submarines.

The debate over American strategic forces and doctrine was fed by Presidential Directive 59, signed by President Carter on 25 July. PD 59 emphasized more selective, limited nuclear options and suggested a wider range of military, political and economic targets. Together with accompanying Directives (PD 53 on the need to improve communications in a nuclear war environment, 57 and 58 on measures to sustain continuity of political leadership in the event of a nuclear war) PD 59 sought to respond to what were seen as adverse trends in the strategic balance, on the assumption that more limited options would add to the credibility of America's nuclear deterrence. The plans the new Directive called for thus included more options for intermediate, less than all-out, strikes against Soviet targets; for targeting political 'nodes' in the USSR so as to threaten the effective functioning of the Soviet system; for considerable emphasis on the endurance of US strategic forces as well as of command and control installations, in case a

nuclear war had to be sustained; and for improved 'look-shoot-look' capabilities to assess nuclear strikes made on enemy targets.

Whether these objectives made sense, given the fact that the vulnerability of command and control and of national command authorities far exceeded that of nuclear delivery systems, would remain in doubt. There were questions about the wisdom of building limited options that probably could not, in the final analysis, be implemented. American officials were at pains to stress that PD 59 was only the latest phase in a long evolution of American strategy, running back at least to the Nixon Administration, and emphasized that the purpose remained to deter the Soviet Union in the face of adverse trends in the strategic balance. In discussing the Directive, Secretary Brown emphasized that 'PD 59 is not a new strategic doctrine; it is not a radical departure from US strategic policy over the past decade or so'.

However, both the doctrine and the manner of its presentation evoked criticism. Secretary of State Muskie admitted to being unaware of PD 59 before it was announced, and to many critics the Directive seemed an ominous sign that selective nuclear options necessarily implied a greater likelihood of their being used, despite repeated official expressions of doubt over the feasibility of limited nuclear war. Moreover, the way the Directive was presented appeared to have been influenced by electoral politics, to outflank Republicans in an election year and demonstrate the Carter Administration's support for a tough nuclear stance. In fact, the Republican party platform, approved a month earlier in Detroit, had endorsed 'a clear capability to destroy military targets'.

The Reagan campaign had emphasized concern over the vulnerability of America's land-based missiles, and the new Administration seemed to be committed to accelerating American strategic programmes. There were suggestions of strategic 'quick fixes' – such as deploying the existing *Minuteman* III force in a more survivable basing scheme, accelerating air-launched cruise missile deployment, and converting the eight *Polaris* submarines still available to cruise missile carriers – in order to reduce US vulnerabilities in the period before full deployment of the MX and *Trident* systems. There were also calls during 1980 for the production of a new manned bomber, either some variant of the B-1 or a stretched version of the FB-111. In August the Carter Administration announced a technological breakthrough known as *Stealth*: a new bomber, still on the drawing-board, which would use a variety of techniques to greatly diminish its visibility to radar.

The Conservative Trend

Mr Ronald Reagan became President on 4 November, with 51% of the vote (52% of the electorate voted). However, since he carried 44 states, his electoral victory was one of the most decisive of this century. A number of factors contributed to the landslide: public frustration with the hostage affair, vented on the incumbent President; the stridency which crept into the Carter campaign; and Mr Reagan's reassuring performance during the television debate between the two candidates, which demolished the image of him as a dangerous war-monger. And much of the vote was less an endorsement of Ronald Reagan than a rejection of Jimmy Carter (in previous elections no incumbent presiding over similar inflation and unemployment statistics had ever stood any chance of winning).Yet underlying all the more specific explanations seemed to be the simple fact that the country had continued the trend towards conservatism that had been apparent over recent years. This trend was even more strongly reflected in the congressional election than in the presidential one. The Republican Party gained control of the Senate for the first time in 26 years, and a number of noted liberal Democrats, such as Frank Church, George McGovern, Birch Bayh and John Culver, were swept away by the conservative tide and replaced by men and women of staunchly conservative views.

The election outcome provided a basis of strength for the new President, and even the Democratic leaders of Congress pledged to give him a 6-month political 'honeymoon'. Surely, too, the electoral mandate extended to defence, for there were few signs that the public mood would oppose further increases in defence spending. However, the conflict between Mr Reagan's defence aides and his economic advisers – the latter determined to carry out his campaign promises to cut federal spending and diminish the size of the government – promised to be a major and continuing battle.

The implications of the election outcome for America's approach to foreign policy were less clear. American allies – and even her adversaries – who had hoped for a more consistent American policy yet feared the ideological simplicities in many campaign pronouncements, were reassured by Mr Reagan's major appointments, especially that of General Alexander Haig as Secretary of State. On a broad range of early actions, a pragmatic approach was apparent. The Reagan team indicated early on that it was prepared to continue the SALT negotiations in some form, and by February 1981 the new President said that 'any time they [the Soviet Union] want to sit down and discuss a legitimate reduction of nuclear weapons, I want to go to such negotiations'. The European allies, finding defence resources more and more constrained by economic factors, took some comfort when Secretaries Haig and Weinberger indicated at their confirmation hearings in January that the 1977 NATO commitment to defence budget increases of 3% yearly would no longer be the yardstick of the new Administration. At the same time, it was clear that the Administration would make new demands on European governments for increased defence spending, and would do so sooner rather than later. Even in those areas where its ideological overtones seemed strongest, Mr Reagan's team avoided precipitous action: for instance, it did not immediately suspend economic assistance to the Sandinista regime in Nicaragua.

Despite its display of pragmatism, however, the Reagan team, like every new Administration, would have to establish its authority and learn to implement policy, and not merely formulate it. That would take time, and international crises might not wait. At the same time, there was clearly a new tone emerging in American policy: more assertive, more nationalistic, more impatient – in short, tougher towards allies and adversaries alike. With it went a new emphasis on, if not an uncritical belief in, military power, a tendency to view conflicts in the world essentially as the product of East–West detente. These convictions would overlay and shape the pragmatism. But what if the policies failed? Would the American reaction then be to blame the policies and seek to change them? Or would it be to blame the world and strengthen instead the incipient isolationist tendency that lay not far below the surface of public attitudes?

THE SOVIET UNION: CONCERN OVER VULNERABILITY?

If the public mood of the United States in 1980 was worried about the country's near-term weaknesses, Soviet leaders had reason for concern over the USSR's long-term vulnerabilities. Signs of these were obvious, most notably in the unrest in Eastern Europe but also in growing Soviet economic difficulties. Soviet leaders also saw themselves confronted with a deteriorating international climate and with what they must fear most: an America aroused, bent on re-arming, with her allies – in Europe and the Far East – sharing the concern if not always the willingness to increase defence effort. Relations with China remained tense, and the threat of isolation was driven home to the Soviet Union by the fact that, for the first time, she faced overwhelming condemnation by third-world nations when the UN General Assembly criticized her invasion of Afghanistan by majorities of 104–18 in January and 111–22 in November.

It was, however, far from obvious that Soviet leaders accepted such a gloomy view of their situation. They were, after all, men long accustomed to economic 'muddling through'. Also, they could look to their formidable military power as a considerable protection, for if the Soviet Union lacked other attributes of a super-power, she certainly had the military one. Soviet military modernization, estimated to consume more than 13% of a gross national product only 65% as large as that of the United States, continued apace in 1980. Even so, the margin of comfort provided by military might could be precarious over the longer-term, given the emerging momentum of US re-armament. That was most obvious in the strategic nuclear realm. For most of the 1980s, the American land-based ICBM force would be theoretically vulnerable to a superbly timed Soviet pre-emptive attack. However, the MX missile, if deployed by 1989 as currently planned, would give the United States a similar capability against Soviet land-based ICBM – and these constituted more than 70% of the warheads of the Soviet strategic force, whereas US ICBM were only some 30% of the American total. The Soviet Union would not find it easy to respond to the MX threat and remain within the limits of SALT or, more important, the capacities of the Soviet economy. Some assessments predicted that the USSR would simply increase her ICBM warheads from, say, the 8,600 anticipated under SALT II rules by late 1985 to 14,000 or even more by 1990. But such assessments had to be reconciled with the other strategic tasks facing Soviet planners during the same period: an air-defence system against American air-launched cruise missiles, a modernized submarine-launched ballistic missile force, the continued modernization of theatre nuclear strike systems, and perhaps an up-dated ballistic missile defence.

Worsening Economic Problems

The Soviet Union's economic plight worsened during 1980. Impressive growth in GNP during the 1960s and early 1970s (6–7.4%) dwindled in 1979–80 to a mere 2%. The grain harvest, at 189.2 million tons, was only slightly more than 1979's 179 million and fell well short of the planned 215 million tons. The Soviet Union was therefore obliged to purchase 30 million tons of grain on the world market, which was a costly undertaking, given the American grain embargo and bad harvests in many producing nations. Agriculture remained inefficient, employing about a third of the labour force and absorbing about a quarter of total investment but producing only a fifth of the Soviet GNP. The successive crop failures also shattered hopes of increasing the Soviet standard of living – meat consumption for example, remained well below the 'recommended' Soviet standard.

The full dimensions of the economic problem became evident in December 1980 and January 1981 with publication of the results of the Tenth Five-Year Plan and the targets for the Eleventh (1981–5). New land was scarce, new energy resources increasingly difficult to tap, and a labour shortage an ever more acute possibility, so that growth had to come from improved productivity. Yet it was precisely here that the USSR had failed most clearly in the tenth plan: production goals were missed by an average of around 10%, but labour productivity fell short by almost 15%. As a result of these short falls targets for 1985 in the eleventh plan were lowered considerably and set at, or only slightly above, the tenth plan's 1980 goals (see Table). Even those more modest planned targets would be difficult to reach, however. The forecast productivity

Soviet Industrial Production: Goals and Achievements

Selected Industrial Products	1980 (plan)	1980 (actual)	1985 (plan)
Electricity (billion KW–hrs)	1340–1380	1290	1550–1600
Oil (million tons)	620–640	600	620–645
Natural Gas (billion m²)	400–435	425	600–640
Coal (million tons)	790–810	715	770–800
Steel (million tons)	160–170	150	–
Fertilizers (million tons)	143	105	150–155
Chemical Fibres (thousand tons)	1450–1500	1170	1600
Cement (million tons)	143–146	125	140–142

increase of 4.2–5.5% per annum called for in the eleventh plan lay well above the 2.3% achieved in the tenth. Grain production goals set for the eleventh plan (238–242 million tons) seemed unrealistic and would in any case necessitate, as in the past, large new shifts of investment towards the agricultural sector – shifts which would inevitably add further strains to an already overstretched economy.

Next to agriculture, energy production was the paramount problem. Despite the Soviet Union's substantial oil reserves, growth rates in oil production dwindled from over 10% in the early 1960s to 2.4% in 1980, and the dilemma was clear: even if production were stabilized at 1980's 600 million tons, or even continued to increase slightly, there would be less and less oil to export. That would mean a choice between further curtailing exports to Eastern European allies (thereby aggravating their balance-of-payment problems) or reducing supplies to the West (thus producing less hard currency to pay for grain and technology imports). Coal production also virtually stagnated, and nuclear energy production advanced much more slowly than forecast. Only natural gas met its target, and meeting the ambitious goals for further expansion in that sector would depend crucially on the availability of Western credits and technology. A $25-billion barter deal with West Germany,

France and Italy (natural gas against steel pipes, technology and credits), proposed at the year-end, pointed in that direction.

These constraints would make it harder to sustain increases in military expenditure of some 4–5% per year while the economy grew only by 2–3%. The trade-offs between growth in military strength and improvements in the standard of living of both the Soviet population and those in Eastern Europe would become sharper. The events in Poland underscored the delicacy of the choices bearing on Eastern Europe, and even the Soviet Union was not entirely immune from internal turmoil, as was suggested by the strikes at the Togliatti plant in the summer of 1980 and the unrest in Estonia in the autumn. Despite these difficulties, however, the USSR was unlikely to sacrifice defence to sounder economics or to internal political considerations. On the contrary, her view of international trends and the traditional Soviet desire for over-insurance would tend to underline, not weaken, the military priority.

The Price of Imperium
The year underlined the high price of the Soviet quest for global influence. The Soviet Union had been a useful partner for the Third World during the struggle for decolonization, but, as that period drew to an end, she found it harder and harder to compete with the West in providing economic assistance and technology. Soviet influence became more and more dependent on the provision of military assistance. Between 1955 and 1979 total Soviet economic assistance agreements amounted to only $18.2 billion and actual disbursements to barely $8.2 billion, while Soviet arms agreements totalled $47.3 billion during the same period and deliveries reached $35.3 billion. In 1980 alone Western economic assistance surpassed total Soviet non-military assistance for the 25 years to 1979. Moreover, Soviet economic assistance was concentrated on countries in which the Soviet political and strategic stake was clear, with 57% going to Turkey, India, Morocco, Egypt and Afghanistan, and another 24% to Iran, Pakistan, Syria, Algeria and Iraq.

Where the USSR had met with success, however, the price had often been high. Cuba, with her faltering economy, cost the Soviet Union over $8 million a day in 1980; Vietnam between $2 million and $4 million, depending on the season; and Ethiopia about the same. Nor were the costs only economic. Vietnam proved an uncomfortable ally, and her expansionist policies in south-east Asia caused risks to broader Soviet interests, while her reluctance to grant the Soviet Union un-encumbered access to military facilities was frustrating. Iraq's invasion of Iran taught Soviet leaders a lesson the US had learned earlier – that recipients of arms supplies use those arms for their own purposes, and not for those of the supplier state. And the invasion of Afghanistan, whatever else might be said about it, had shown that acting to prevent the loss of a stake could be tantamount to increasing the already threatened stake, perhaps dramatically. While there was little evidence that the Islamic revival would seriously affect Muslims in the Soviet Union in the near-term, the longer term prospects, together with unrest on the USSR's southern borders, were hardly comforting. While the total Soviet population increased by 26% between 1959 and 1979, the Russian population grew by only 21% whereas the population of the largely Muslim Repub-lics jumped by 73%.

The long-awaited rejuvenation of the Soviet leadership again failed to occur during 1980. President Brezhnev, his health apparently improved, held on to the reins of power, and the rest of the Politburo remained largely unchanged. The one exception was the rapid promotion of Mikhail Gorbachev, a Brezhnev protegé and an expert on agricultural issues, who had become a candidate member of the Politburo in the autumn of 1979 and was raised to full member in October 1980. His age of 49 was a good deal less than the Politburo's average age of 69. Other opportunities for renovating the leadership were by-passed, however. In October, Pyotr Masherov, the 62-year old party head from Byelorussia and candidate member of the Politburo, died in a car crash, but he was replaced by Tikhon Kiselev, a former premier of Byelorussia, who was 63. The Politburo was severly weakened when poor health forced Prime Minister Alexei Kosygin to resign only a few weeks later (his death in December and the grand state funeral he received largely dissipated rumours that political reasons might have lain behind his resignation). The nomination of his deputy, Nikolai Tikhonov, 75, as his successor indicated that any real change in the Soviet leader-ship was yet to come and cast little light on the direction of that change. This impression was confirmed by the XXVI Party Congress in February and March which, for the first time in many congresses, left the Politburo un-changed.

THE MIDDLE EAST AND THE GULF

The war between Iran and Iraq and the continuing hostage crisis in Iran during 1980 underscored the general shift of regional conflict from the Near East towards the Persian Gulf. The tensions which had led to the war continued with fluctuating intensity through the last third of the year and into 1981, and promised to be a persistent feature in the region. For both Iran and Iraq, there were important implications also for internal political order, strengthening the role of the military in the short run but carrying the risk of a domestic collapse as the war dragged on.

Regionally, the conflict accentuated the polarization of the Arab world; internationally, it raised afresh, together with other events during the year, the question of appropriate roles for outside powers. For the West, the region had become the 'third strategic zone' after Europe and North-east Asia, but there remained uncertainty about how to deter the Soviet Union without provoking her and, more important, how to maintain the stability of states in the region without creating an obtrusive military presence which would further strain internal stability and regional politics.

WAR BETWEEN IRAN AND IRAQ

The immediate initiator of the war was Iraq, but the conflict had its roots more generally in the Iranian revolution and its international militance, and in the aspirations to regional leadership of President Saddam Hussein of Iraq. Iraq seemed clearly to have miscalculated badly, and the conflict developed into a low-level war of attrition. Both the United States and the Soviet Union had an interest in terminating the conflict, but neither was able to wield much influence over the parties, despite their role as major arms suppliers. It remained difficult to see a negotiated solution before the struggle for power in Iran between the various contending groups had been decided.

The War on the Ground

Armed clashes along the border between Iran and Iraq, which had occurred intermittently since May 1979 with casualties on both sides, intensified throughout 1980. In response to Iranian calls to Iraqis to overthrow Hussein, the Iraqi regime hastily expelled some 30,000 Iraqis of Iranian origin from the country between April and July. On 17 September President Hussein cancelled the 1975 Treaty negotiated with Iran under the Shah, which had redefined their common border. Iran rejected the Iraqi move, and on 20 September Iranian President Abolhassan Bani-Sadr called up Iran's reserves. Two days later Iraqi aircraft

attacked some ten Iranian airfields as well as Tehran, and the next morning Iraqi troops crossed the frontier into Iran.

Iraq's immediate aims ostensibly were limited: a return to Iraqi sovereignty over those portions of the Shatt al-Arab waterway and other territory ceded to Iran in 1975 and an end to Iranian interference in Iraq's internal affairs. Her government denied any intention to occupy the Iranian oil province of Khuzestan or to take the islands of Abu Musa and Greater and Lesser Tumb at the lower end of the Gulf, which had been seized by Iran in November 1971. Yet the Iraqi regime seemed clearly to hope that a quick, decisive victory would undermine the Iranian regime of Ayatollah Khomeini.

Iraqi forces advanced in three main areas along a front that was more than 700 kilometres long: Qasr-e-Shirin in the north, Mehran in the centre, and the main thrust towards Susangerd and Khorramshahr in the south. None of these attacks, nor the defences against them were co-ordinated with close air support. Despite frequent Iraqi claims of success, the advance was slow, as long-range artillery fire prepared Iraqi moves forward. During the first week of the war small air raids by each side penetrated to strike the oil installations of the other, and Iraq's nuclear installation was also hit, apparently by Iranian F-4s. Oil shipments stopped, although some tankers continued to load at Iranian terminals at Kharq, Bushehr and Bandar Khomeini (Shahpur), and Iraq was able to export some oil via the pipeline through Turkey. By early 1981, however, the oil production of both Iraq and Iran was down to about 600,000 barrels per day each, compared to pre-war totals of 3.5 and 1.4 million barrels per day, respectively.

The Iraqi force moving against Khorram-shahr, comprising one division and perhaps elements of another, was in position by 5 October. Despite an apparent lack of co-ordination, reflecting the chaos in the Iranian armed forces that the revolution had imposed, Iran's defenders – a mix of Revolutionary Guards, some regular troops, naval cadets, militia and volunteers – resisted strongly, and the city did not fall to the Iraqi forces until 13 October. The Iraqi advance on the critical refinery city of Abadan was blocked as a crucial bridge to it, in the southern suburbs of Khorramshahr, remained in Iranian hands. On 11 October Iraq put a pontoon bridge across the Karun River about 10 miles north of Khorramshahr, enabling her troops to move down the east bank of the Bahmanshir River which forms the eastern boundary of Abadan island. By the end of October the only Iranian access to Abadan island was by boat or helicopter from the south, but still the city managed to hold on.

By the beginning of 1981 the southern front ran along the Kharkheh river west of Dezful to the Karun and the east bank of the Bahmanshir Rivers. Iraq remained in control of the roads in western Khuzestan, and had begun to build additional routes into that region which would ease, but not entirely solve, the problem of logistical support for troops in their advance positions. In the central and northern sectors the Iraqi penetration was less deep, extending only to the first line of hills above the plains and to the roads into Iraqi territory from the east, apparently a deliberate tactic intended to deny Iran observation posts and good defence points. Towards the end of December, Iraq opened a new front in the mountainous Kurdish area east of Panjwin in Sulaymaniyah province, which had been a frequent target of Iranian air strikes. More generally, however, the winter rains, the low cloud cover and the consequent flooding of the plains kept military operations to a low level after the middle of November.

Minor counter-attacks by Iranian forces regained little territory in the north and centre during the autumn, but they foiled an Iraqi attempt to take Susangerd, bypassed in the initial advance. However, a major Iranian counter-attack south of Susangerd, begun on 11 January, was a definite failure, with heavy casualties on both sides. Iraq lost some 50 T-62 tanks, while Iranian forces, trapped on soft ground, lost perhaps twice as many of their *Chieftain* and M-60 tanks. This ill-timed counter-attack seemed to be a result less of military necessity than of pressure on Bani-Sadr by the clerical factions in Iran to demonstrate the success of his personal command of Iranian forces.

Throughout 1980 it was difficult to assess the size of the forces involved. Of Iraq's 12 divisions (4 each of armoured, mechanized and mountain infantry), about two-thirds were actively involved. The assaults in the north and centre seemed to have been mounted by a mechanized and a mountain infantry division, respectively. One armoured division was believed to have been deployed in the centre, while Khorramshahr reportedly was taken by an armoured division, later relieved by a mechanized division which was then sent against Abadan. The remaining two armoured divisions were deployed against Dezful and Ahvaz, with a mechanized division in support, and the latest front in the Kurdish area was probably the responsibility of a mountain infantry division. That would have left Iraq with one armoured, one mechanized and two mountain infantry divisions in reserve. Iran's border deployments appeared to comprise two armoured divisions (one at Ahvaz responsible for Abadan, and one at Kermanshah) plus two infantry divisions at Sanandaj and Urumiyeh. An armoured division and an 'airborne division' were later dispatched to reinforce the western border area.

Given the lack of independent reporting, losses can only be very loosely estimated. Iraq admitted losing some 300 tanks; her original inventory comprised nearly 3,000, primarily Soviet T-54, T-55 and T-62s, with 50 T-72s, and she retained the advantage of controlling the battlefields, enabling her to salvage and presumably to repair her own and captured equipment. Iran began the war with some 1,500 tanks, half of those British *Chieftain*, the other half American M-47, M-48 and M-60s,

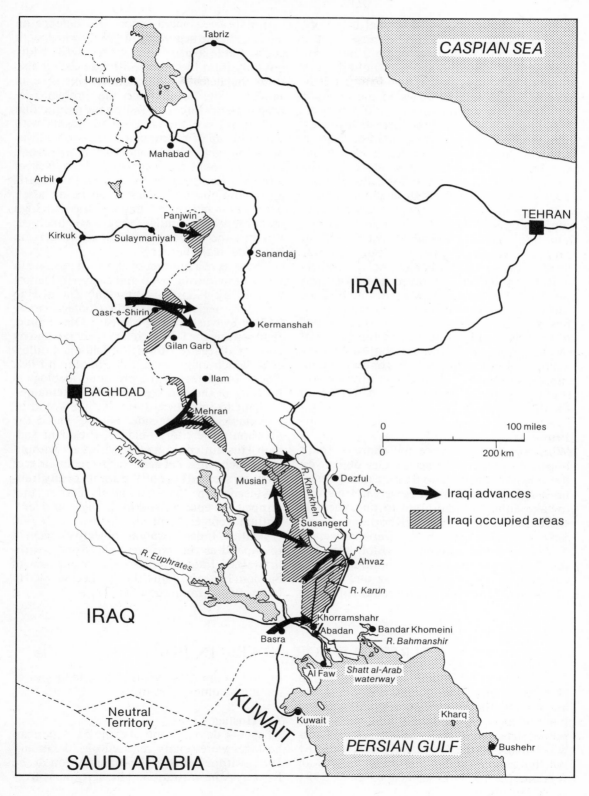

CASPIAN SEA

Tabriz

Urumiyeh

Mahabad

Arbil

Panjwin

Kirkuk

Sulaymaniyah

Sanandaj

IRAN

TEHRAN

Qasr-e-Shirin

Kermanshah

Gilan Garb

Ilam

BAGHDAD

Mehran

R. Tigris

0   100 miles

0   200 km

Musian

R. Kharkheh

Dezful

Iraqi advances

Iraqi occupied areas

Susangerd

R. Euphrates

Ahvaz

R. Karun

Khorramshahr

Abadan   Bandar Khomeini

Basra

R. Bahmanshir

IRAQ

Al Faw   Shatt al-Arab
              waterway

Neutral
Territory

KUWAIT

Kuwait

Kharq

PERSIAN GULF

Bushehr

SAUDI ARABIA

although what portion of the total inventory was serviceable even at the beginning of the war was open to question. Aircraft losses for Iraq were estimated at about 100 of all types (Soviet MiG-21s and -23s, Su-7s and Su-20s). Iranian losses were probably in the range of 150, from an inventory of some 350 American F-4s and F-5s. Most of the aircraft losses on both sides occurred on the ground or through accident. And there was no clear evidence that the Iranian air force was able to put its sophisticated American F-14s into the air. There were many reports throughout the year that one side or the other was receiving more supplies of arms, spare parts or ammunition, and Iraq's Deputy Prime Minister went to Moscow twice during the war, but there was little evidence that either of the two super-powers was directly involved in major ship-ments, although some Western intelligence sources suggested that 100 or more Soviet T-54 or -55 tanks from Eastern Europe were shipped to Iraq via Saudi Arabia during the course of the war. France did, however, confirm that she would go ahead with her 1979 commitment to supply Iraq with 36 *Mirage* F-1 aircraft, and the first four of those were delivered in February 1981.

Prospects

While the Iraqi advance fell short of Iraq's hopes, it did secure some military objectives: the heights in the north and centre and the river lines in the south. Its failures were the inability to take either Abadan, due to unexpectedly stubborn Iranian defence at Khorramshahr, or Susangerd, bypassed in the initial advance. The latter would represent a possible base for a future Iranian thrust against the Iraqi lines of communication towards Ahvaz and Dezful. Tactically, however, Iraq could probably maintain a reasonably successful defence on her lines at the beginning of 1981, though with considerable logistic cost. Iran suffered badly not only from the initial withdrawals but also from the defeat of her counter-offensive in January. She would face the problems of preparing her forces for war on the ground that is more or less of the aggressor's choosing, with the handicap of a command structure that was being built only slowly, shortages of spares and a divided political leadership. In a war of attrition, Iraq's relatively greater spare parts and ammunition reserves could be an asset. The risks of failure in a major battle with high casualties were similar: they were likely to threaten the authority of political leaders on both sides of the border.

There were a number of efforts to mediate in the conflict during 1980 and early 1981, most notably by Pakistani President Zia ul-Haq under the aegis of the Islamic Conference, by former Swedish Prime Minister Olaf Palme, representing the UN Secretary General, and by another delegation from the Islamic Confer-ence, which sought a cease-fire in March 1981. These foundered on the profound ideological hostility of the two regimes, and it remained difficult to imagine a formula that would be acceptable to either side. Having based the invasion on territorial claims, President Sad-dam Hussein could hardly withdraw without some such gain. Yet acquiescing in any loss of territory seemed beyond the ability of any Iran-ian leader in the nationalist fervour that gripped the country and in the light of over 1 million refugees and the estimated 50,000 casualties. Indeed, Iranian objectives seemed to expand as the war went on, from a with-drawal of Iraqi forces to the overthrow of Saddam Hussein. Thus, the prospect seemed to be one of continuing conflict.

STRUGGLE FOR POWER IN IRAN

The crisis over the American hostages in Iran and the Iran–Iraq war so focused international attention on Iran that they obscured the under-lying reality of a continuing and often fierce power struggle between the various elements which made up the revolution there. Aided by the Iraqi attack, the theocratic regime of Ayatollah Khomeini seemed to enter 1981 firmly in command, yet the struggle for power around Khomeini continued.

The Hostage Crisis
After 444 days of captivity, the 52 American hostages were finally released on 20 January 1981, within hours of the inauguration of the Reagan Administration. The agreement free-

ing them – the culmination of negotiations which had begun in September – reflected primarily a recognition by Iran that the hostages had served their purpose. For the United States, there was little alternative to negotiations after the failed attempt to rescue the hostages in April, but the dilemma was particularly painful: to negotiate signalled weakness, yet sanctions threatened to push Iran towards the Soviet Union. For Iran, the hostage crisis was becoming a liability even within the domestic power struggle, and the war with Iraq also drove home the need to seek a formula that would salvage some of the Iranian financial assets frozen in America for the previous 12 months. The actual terms of the agreement represented a failure for Iran by comparison to her original demands: the wealth of the Shah was not 'returned', no apology was made by the United States for past actions, and the death of the Shah in Cairo on 27 July deprived the revolution of symbolic revenge. The American concessions were modest: the United States agreed to free Iran's frozen assets, to forgo any claims for damages against the Iranian government, to assist in identifying the Shah's assets in the US, and to pledge non-interference in Iran's affairs.

Faced with the terrorist take-over of her embassy in Tehran, the United States had tried to balance her outrage with her broader interests in the region. The Carter Administration first exhausted every peaceful avenue: in November 1979 all Iranian assets in US banks were frozen; in January there followed efforts to secure UN resolutions condemning Iran, a UN Commission of Inquiry in February and March, and a condemnation by the International Court of Justice on 24 May. In April the United States turned to tougher measures: on 7 April diplomatic relations were severed, exports banned and future visas for Iranians invalidated. On 17 April imports were stopped and US citizens' travel to Iran curtailed. On 22 April, under the pressure of American hints about military action, the foreign ministers of the European Community unanimously backed economic sanctions against Iran. Fears of America's European allies that precipitous US action would only drive Iran towards the Soviet Union seemed to be substantiated with the announcement of new trade agreements between Iran and the Soviet Union, East Germany and Romania. In practical terms the

Western sanctions made little difference to Iran, since most goods continued to enter via the Gulf States, especially Dubai, though at an additional premium of 15-20%.

Finally, on 24 April the United States attempted a military 'rescue mission' consisting of 90 men and 8 helicopters. Launched from carriers in the Gulf of Oman the helicopters were to reach Tehran from a desert landing area some 400 kilometres away in Tabas, eastern Iran. Because of mechanical failure in 3 helicopters the mission was aborted, but in the ensuing confusion 8 Americans died and 5 were injured in a plane crash. Beyond the specific issues – mechanical failure, inadequate training procedures and lines of command, lack of specific equipment, and poor tactical intelligence – lay the paramount strategic result: a shattered image of US military power and technological efficiency.

After the failure at Tabas, the United States returned to a more patient approach, awaiting the accumulation of pressures within Iran. The first indication that the hostage crisis had become a wasted asset even within the domestic power struggle came on 12 September, when Khomeini set out four conditions for the release of the hostages but omitted any requirement for an apology. The start of the Iran–Iraq war later that month delayed matters, but these four conditions were essentially the basis for the agreements concluded in January 1981.

The Soviet Union's approach towards Iran continued along two lines throughout 1980: tolerance and restraint even when specific areas of difference emerged; and an attempt to portray herself as the 'protector of the revolution' and to support militant opponents of a settlement to the hostage crisis. The Soviet Union continued to benefit from the focusing of the revolutionary rage on the United States. She showed little reaction to the rapid denunciation of her invasion of Afghanistan by Iran's President Bani-Sadr and the tardier one by Khomeini on 4 February. She took both Iran's diplomatic support for the Afghan resistance in the Islamic Conferences of January and May and her refusal to participate in the Olympic Games in her stride. In January the Soviet Union vetoed the UN Security Council measures hostile to Iran, and up to the very end of the hostage affair Soviet broadcasts and commentaries opposed a settlement. On 17 January 1981, three days before the release, *Pravda* charged that the United States was preparing to invade Iran under the pretext of the hostage crisis.

Still, Soviet policy was relatively successful. The revolution's energies throughout remained channelled in anti-Western directions, and the Soviet Union retained links with the political forces in Iran which offered promise of influencing the country's unpredictable future course. However, conflicts between the Soviet Union and the Islamic Republic over specific issues persisted. One was the impasse over the price of Iranian national gas exports to the southern Soviet Union. Though those exports were diminishing in quantity, Iran demanded a five-fold price increase backdated to January 1979, which Moscow rejected. A second issue was the Soviet supply of arms to Iraq, which was criticized by Tehran. After the war broke out between the two Gulf states, the USSR opted for neutrality, though this already implied that she was distancing herself from Iraq, a country with which she is linked in a Treaty of Friendship and Co-operation. A further indication of this was the report, leaked on 5 October by the Iranian Prime Minister, that the Soviet Union had offered arms to Iran and had been refused. A third issue was Afghanistan. If Iran's rhetorical opposition was not matched by any serious commitments to the Afghan resistance, it was clear that the invasion had raised profound suspicion about Soviet intentions. Iran refused throughout the year to enter into any form of dialogue with the 'illegal' regime of Babrak Karmal, rejecting the Afghan peace proposal of 14 May in favour of a Soviet withdrawal based on US-Pakistani-Iranian guarantees to prevent infiltration and the arming of the rebels. A large-scale popular protest against Soviet policies took place in front of the Soviet Embassy in Tehran on 27 December.

Internal Consolidation and Uncertainty

In formal terms Iran completed her constitutional transition in September, with the appointment of a Prime Minister and Cabinet, and the setting-up of a clerical 'Council of Guardians' to oversee all legislation. Only then did the shadowy Revolutionary Council which had run the country since its creation by Khomeini in January 1979 announce its dissolution. Despite growing discontent and his advanced age, Khomeini's control remained firm. Yet around him the power struggle was waged more and more openly, raising uncertainties over the survival of the theocratic regime once Khomeini died.

One obvious source of discontent was the economic chaos, caused by the neglect of the economy during the revolution, the departure of a large part of the managerial and technical class, an ongoing programme of nationalization, interference in the bazaar's traditional trade, disorder in the countryside, and the drying up of foreign credit. Most important, even before the Gulf war Iran had badly misjudged the world oil market; by trying to push crude oil prices up at a time of an impending glut in the world markets, she simply allowed her major customers to go elsewhere, and Iranian oil exports were drastically reduced. In the third quarter of 1980 total oil production was down to 1.4 million barrels a day, less than a quarter of its 1977 peak, and exports of crude amounted only to a few thousand barrels per day. This drop coincided with increasing demands on the state treasury caused by nationalization, unemployment and mounting food imports.

A serious challenge to the unity of Iran came from the growing unrest among the ethnic minorities which make up about half of her 36 million population. The most serious outbreak of violence occurred in January 1980 in and around Tabriz, the capital of the ethnically Turkish region of Azerbaijan, where hundreds were killed in pitched battles between the followers of the leading moderate clergyman in Iran, Ayatollah Kazem Shariat-Madari, and the Government's militia. The conflict brought together two strands of opposition – the demand for a plural society and for regional autonomy – but its bloody repression silenced Shariat-Madari, at least for the time being. By contrast, the Kurds – most of whom are Sunni Muslims, as opposed to the majority Shi'ia sect in Iran, and who straddle the critical border with Iraq – continued to put up effective resistance to the government in Tehran. Tension was high along the hundred-mile strip from Rezaiyeh in the north to Sanandaj in the south and reached a climax in a month-long battle for the city of Sanandaj in April and May, in which over 1,000 people were reported killed. Mahabad, the seat of Kurdish resistance, changed hands several times during the year as the contest swung back and forth.

But in spite of these tensions, there was no realistic alternative to the Khomeini regime in sight. The regime shed its old coalition partners on the Left and among the secular nationalists, and promoted its own ideological vision without serious challenge. The regime had up to 30,000 highly committed Revolutionary Guards at its disposal, retained a grip on its supporters at the grass roots, and controlled the administration of the state. Though economic difficulties mounted, with food shortages, high unemployment and rapid inflation, by early 1981 export earnings from oil were still nearly sufficient to finance vital imports. The disparate exile groups continued to be unable to unite under a single banner with nationalist appeal.

Throughout 1980 the principals in the power struggle were President Bani-Sadr and his associates, the Government of Prime Minister Mohammad Ali Rajai – with links with the dominant Islamic Republican Party (IRP) led by the President of the Supreme Court, Ayatollah Mohammad Beheshti – and the fractious 270-seat parliament, the Majlis. In contrast to the Presidential election in late January, when Bani-Sadr had swept to power with over 70% of the vote and had humiliated his clerical rivals, two rounds of voting for the Majlis in March and May produced a body dominated by traditional clerics from the provinces and other Islamic fundamentalists.

During the war with Iraq, the armed forces began to recover some of their credibility as a coherent military force which previously had been undermined for fear of their potential in the power struggle. In July the more serious of a number of half-hearted coup attempts was exposed and crushed, with over 300 officers arrested, including several post-revolutionary generals, and 92 were later executed. The Revolutionary Guards and the mobs mobilized by the fundamentalists were now a decisive element whenever conflict spilled over into the streets.

The intensity of the internal fight for power was suggested by Bani-Sadr's changing fortunes. Within several months of his stunning victory as President, he was confronted with a Majlis dominated by the IRP, who were bent on reversing the clearly-stated intention of the new Iranian constitution by promoting the legislature over the Presidency as the supreme political institution. The President attempted to restore his influence through his right to nominate the Prime Minister and approve his Cabinet. For three months during the summer of 1980 he held out against the fundamentalists, but in mid-August he was forced to name Mr Rajai, a staunch advocate of the IRP, as Prime Minister. Criticized but not abandoned by Khomeini, he survived largely because of support from Khomeini's son, from the radical wing of the Islamic movement, represented by the Mujaheddin-e-Khalq, from pro-revolution nationalists and the growing number of those who resented the rule of the clerical fundamentalists. The war with Iraq offered him much-needed breathing space as he took personal command of the troops in his role as Commander-in-Chief. This gave him several temporary advantages at least – sparing him identification with the controversial hostage settlement and making an ally of the army – but it also meant that he abandoned day-to-day government to his rivals. Moreover, it meant that he would be judged on the outcome of the war.

IRAQ AND THE DIVIDED ARAB WORLD

The attack on Iran demonstrated both Iraq's bid for leadership of the Arab world and the fragile bases of that bid, within the region and within Iraq herself. Together with other events – most notably the threat of conflict between Syria and Jordan in November – it suggested that the Arab world was more divided than it had been at any time since the war against Israel and the oil crisis of 1973.

Iraq's Bid for Leadership
Iraq had remained isolated in the Arab world until 1978–9. The quadrupling of oil prices in 1973, however, provided the means to break out of this isolation, as it made Iraq the third largest oil exporter after Saudi Arabia and Iran. The agreement with the Shah's Iran signed in Algiers in 1975 terminated Iranian support to the Kurdish rebellion led by Mullah Mustafa

Barzani and his Kurdish Democratic Party (KDP), thus increasing Iraq's internal stability. Equally important were the conclusion of the Camp David accords and the subsequent peace treaty between Egypt and Israel in 1979, which convinced Saudi Arabia that she could not continue her overt support for Egypt, and the collapse of the Shah's rule in Iran in 1978. These events, coupled with doubts about American policy and with the threat of growing Soviet penetration in the region, left the conservative states, Saudi Arabia in particular, uneasy. On the one hand, the interests of a more pragmatic, less doctrinaire Iraq and the conservative states increasingly converged, making possible a stronger Iraqi role. On the other hand, the temporary reconciliation with the rival Ba'athist regime in Syria during 1978 at least reduced differences between Iraq and the radical states of the so-called Steadfastness Front, and the resolution of the Baghdad Summit in November 1978 became a symbol of Arab rejection of the Camp David accords.

The bid for regional leadership formed part of a larger Iraqi conception of a third bloc in world politics between East and West. Iraq's desire to diversify her military supply away from the Soviet Union led to major contracts with France (including extensive co-operation in the nuclear field) and lesser ones with Italy and Brazil. Growing differences with her treaty ally, the Soviet Union, culminated in outright Iraqi condemnation of Soviet intervention in the Horn of Africa and in Afghanistan. In a 'Pan-Arab Declaration' of 8 February 1980, President Hussein called on the super-powers to disengage from the Arab world and declare it a neutral zone whose security is the collective responsibility of the Arab states themselves. Another part of the Declaration pointed to Iraq's role within the Non-aligned Movement, whose 1982 Heads of State Conference would be hosted by Iraq.

If the war between Iraq and Iran underscored the new prominence of Iraq, it also drew attention to the fragile basis of her position. In the face of regional uncertainties and Islamic resurgence, the conservative Arab states of the Gulf – and particularly Saudi Arabia – increasingly saw advantages in a strong and stable Iraq. They had not been as willing to confront Iran because of the possible consequences for their own countries – for example for the substantial Shi'a minority in Eastern Saudi Arabia. Yet most of the conservative Arab states continued to fear that a dominant Iraq would also pose a direct threat to their existence. Iraq had not abandoned her Ba'athist ideological orientation and would, if victorious, emerge as the main regional power with little patience for traditional dynastic rulers which she regarded as anachronisms. Nor did the Gulf States regard the neutralization of the area as an acceptable substitute for American support. Iraq's claim to be the dominant Arab power remained dependent on Egypt's isolation and on the continuation of a rough Arab consensus on the future of the Palestinian question. The conservative states of the Arabian peninsula were in many ways more attuned to the moderate politics of Egypt than to the militant radicalism of Iraq. They had rejected the Camp David formula but were not fundamentally averse to a peaceful settlement with Israel, as was Iraq. The alliance between the conservative Gulf states and Iraq was likely, therefore, to remain an uneasy one.

The Iraqi failure to obtain an early victory in the war with Iran also raised doubt about the internal stability of President Saddam Hussein's Ba'athist regime. Since his assumption of power in July 1979, President Hussein had successfully consolidated his control over the government, the party and the armed forces. He had striven to neutralize opposition by elimination and co-operation, through the offer of nominal participation in the process of government under the umbrella of the National Front of Progressive and Patriotic Parties and through the provision of a National Assembly, directly elected in June 1980, the first of its kind since the overthrow of the monarchy in 1958. Political groups and organizations which refused to co-operate had been suppressed or liquidated: for example, Barzani's KDP and Communist cells in the armed forces. President Hussein had promoted trusted aides and relatives to sensitive positions, had purged or transferred dissident officers, and had maintained tight control and surveillance on political opponents.

Yet President Hussein, a Sunni Moslem, ruled a country in which the Shi'a and Kurdish communities comprise more than 75% of the population. A revolutionary Iran had made efforts to incite the underprivileged Shi'ite community, and Iraq had responded in kind, mounting a campaign for autonomy for the Arabic-speaking Iranian community of Khuzestan. The success of the Ayatollah Khomeini in Iran had inspired a number of religious teachers in Iraq to begin a militant religious organization known as the 'Cause' or *al-Da'wa* whose leader, Ayatollah Bakr al-Sadr, was put to death in prison in April.

Kurdish opposition was also far from stifled, although the war with Iran put Iraqi Kurds – like their Iranian counterparts – in a difficult position, for they could be branded as tools of the enemy. After the 1975 Algiers Agreement between Iran and Iraq the KDP had disintegrated into several factions. One of them, under the leadership of Jalal Talabani, known as the Popular Union of Kurdistan, continued its operations against the Baghdad Government with the assistance of Syria. Another, Barzani's group, maintained a semblance of the KDP organization and rallied to the Khomeini call for the overthrow of the Shah, only to become an instrument of Iranian policy against Iraq. As in the past, the Communists, who supported the Shi'ites, joined the Kurds in their opposition to the rule of President Hussein. When relations between Iraq and the Soviet Union deteriorated, the regime began to crack down on its former ally, the Communist Party, which had provided it with support since 1972, and which now joined a Syrian-backed front of opposition parties. These internal difficulties would not necessarily pose a major challenge to the regime, but what gave them greater weight was that they could combine with failure in the war against Iran to weaken the authority of President Hussein's leadership. Short of an outright victory, which was more and more improbable, Iraq seemed unlikely, as 1981 began, to obtain the predominant position in the region to which her leaders had aspired and which she had come close to achieving as a result of the demise of a powerful Iran.

Polarization in the Arab World

The Gulf War and the threat of hostilities between Syria and Jordan in the latter part of the year confirmed that the Arab–Israeli conflict, though profoundly affecting relations throughout the region, was not the sole, and possibly not the most immediate obstacle, to Arab unity. Clashing interests of member states prevented the Arab summit in November from coming up with any real alternative to the Camp David process which they all officially rejected.

Two rival camps emerged, represented by Iraq and Syria, whose long-standing animosity was exacerbated by opposing aspirations and priorities. Iraqi President Hussein sought to portray the war against Iran as a struggle for Arabism and thus to justify his bid for leadership of the Arab world. For Syria, on the other hand, Iraq's national ambitions in the Gulf were a dangerous diversion of Arab energies from the principal battle against Israel. Yet Syria herself was entangled in Lebanon, exposed to Israeli military might, and confronted by internal unrest fomented by the Muslim Brotherhood which challenged the minority 'Alawite regime of President Hafez al-Assad. Though in control of the higher echelons of the army, Assad's grasp over the Sunni strongholds in Aleppo and Homs looked less certain. Jordan, which had been close to Syria since 1975, moved towards Syria's rival and strongly supported Iraq in the war against Iran. The rising power of Iraq and the centrality of the Gulf in inter-Arab politics increasingly isolated Syria, denying her the status and even some of the financial support from conservative Arab states to which her role as the principal 'confrontation' state had previously entitled her. A fruitless 'union' with Libya, proclaimed in September, changed nothing and only demonstrated Syria's growing weakness and limited options.

In an effort to counter Iraq and to redirect Arab attention towards the Near East, Syria boycotted the Arab Summit in Amman in November. She doubled her military presence along the border with Jordan to discredit Iraqi President Hussein by exposing the military limitations of their alliance. But the USSR was not prepared to back Syria against Jordan, despite the Soviet–Syrian Treaty of Friendship and Co-operation which had been signed in October 1980. President Assad, after making his political point, gradually pulled back Syrian forces, mollified by funds from Saudi Arabia. Syria even allowed the renewal of the flow of Iraqi oil through the pipeline over her territory despite the continuing rupture between the two states, as economic incentives proved more powerful than ideological differences.

Another victim of the Arab divisions was the Palestinian Liberation Organization (PLO). Its efforts at mediation between Iran and Iraq failed, and the PLO felt reluctantly compelled to side with Syria, on whose goodwill its continuing activity in Lebanon largely depended. The Camp David process increased American opposition to international recognition of the PLO, and the Gulf events, together with the inter-Arab rivalries, removed both the Arab-Israeli issue and the role of the Palestinian Liberation Organization from the forefront of Arab attention.

The main beneficiaries of Arab disunity were Egypt and Israel. The overshadowing of the Palestinian issue by events elsewhere in the Arab world gave both states more time to reach a solution between themselves. Egypt, moreover, could take comfort from Saddam Hussein's failure in his bid for Arab leadership as the polarization within the Arab world deepened, and new alliances replaced the already weakened front nominally arrayed against Israel. President Sadat could point out that his policy had at least brought about tangible territorial gains, while the Rejectionist Front offered no alternative. Moreover, despite the Arab boycott of Egypt, both the PLO and Saudi Arabia discreetly maintained contacts with Egypt.

Israel also benefitted from the polarization in the Arab world in that she could postpone decision on the Palestinian question. Moreover, no matter how the war eventually ended, Iraq would have to devote more attention to her Eastern neighbour, thus constraining her commitments in the Arab world. Yet the respite was likely to be temporary; Arab politics had traditionally oscillated between unity and division, between emphasis on collective and more purely national interests, and the Palestinian problem was likely to again provide a focus for joint Arab action at some point in the future.

THE EGYPTIAN-ISRAELI IMPASSE

Both Egypt and Israel remained committed to the timetable stipulated by the Camp David Accords (CDA), signed in Washington in September 1978, but both continued to find it difficult during 1980 to make additional concessions in the peace process. They were constrained by opposition at home in the case of Israel, and abroad, in the case of Egypt, as well as by their basic differences over the interpretation of the agreements. The peace process was further complicated by the American Presidential elections and the approach of Israeli elections in July 1981. For President Sadat the Accords remained the basis of a comprehensive peace in the Middle East which would address the Palestinian question, and the agreed autonomy provisions for the Palestinians were the essential first phase. In contrast, for the Israeli Government of Mr Begin the agreement was essentially a separate peace between the two states, independent of the autonomy question, which Israel defined in very limited terms. Thus the chasm separating Egypt and Israel on this issue persisted.

Camp David Process
Yet, despite the impasse between them, both countries had reasons to want to sustain the momentum in the peace process. Sadat was eager to maintain his close ties with the United States, all the more so because the American interpretation of the Egypt–Israel Peace Treaty, signed in March 1979, was closer to Egypt's than to Israel's. Moreover, Sadat was not inclined to aggravate relations with Israel in case such an action would jeopardize the return of Egypt's territory in the Sinai as the Treaty stipulated. The Israeli government also had a clear interest in maintaining the Camp David process, while at the same time consolidating its hold on the West Bank and not straining relations with the United States. Thus, both parties were prepared to let the target date of 26 May (originally set for the conclusion of negotiations on autonomy) pass without an ultimatum and without prospects for an early compromise on the autonomy question.

Instead, the two governments concentrated on implementing those parts of the Treaty bearing on their mutual relations. On 26 January Israel withdrew her forces in the Sinai to the line stretching between Ras Muhammad on the Red Sea and El-Arish on the Mediterranean – the line her forces would hold until the full withdrawal scheduled for 26 April

1982. The evacuated area included Bir Gafgafa (Redifim), the largest Israeli airfield in the Sinai, as well as other military installations of strategic value. A month later Egypt and Israel established diplomatic relations and entered into economic talks, which soon resulted in the conclusion of an agreement for Israel to purchase Egyptian light crude oil from the wells she had relinquished in the Sinai.

Yet the normalization of bilateral relations aroused some opposition in Egypt. The failure of the Arab Rejectionist Front to produce a united force that could weaken the Egyptian regime externally clearly discouraged internal opposition, but latent opposition within Egypt gathered strength during the year as it became clear that no 'peace dividend' – economic advantages expected in the wake of the Treaty with Israel – would materialize and that Egypt's isolation in the Arab world would continue. A significant faction of educated Egyptians felt both humiliated by Israeli policies towards the Palestinians and exasperated with Sadat's regime for not pressing on with the promised democratization of Egyptian political life – although the only groups to articulate opposition to the peace treaty were on the Left ('Nasserites', and Communists, for example) or were among the fundamentalist Muslims.

However, the opposition's weakness was aggravated by its internal divisions as well as by its inability to articulate its criticisms in a popular idiom. And the differing tactical assessments that apparently existed within the Egyptian government did little to affect the President's authority. Vice President Husni Mubarak argued that formalization of relations with Israel should be conditional upon progress in autonomy and that links with the United States should be strengthened more gradually than Sadat favoured. Yet the deepening inter-Arab rivalries, the growing impatience with Israel in the West, and the political crisis in Israel all gave Sadat more time to produce the results he had promised.

With the completion of the bilateral part of the Treaty, Egypt again pressed Israel to move forward on the Palestinian aspects of the Camp David Accord, demonstrating her desire to assure the Arab world that she was not out merely to gain territory for herself but rather to safeguard broader Arab interests. Both Egypt and the United States persistently argued that the establishment of new Israeli settlements in occupied territories, especially the West Bank, harsh Israeli policies towards the Palestinians and frequent military action in Lebanon could only turn the Palestinians more against Israel, and thus reduce the chance that they might accept any form of autonomy. At the same time, the Carter Administration, embroiled in an election campaign, found it difficult to exert any real pressure on Israel. Following a sharp domestic and Israeli reaction, President Carter even disclaimed America's vote in support of the March UN Security Council resolution condemning Israel's settlement policy.

President Carter did make an effort to get the autonomy talks moving by inviting the two heads of state to Washington on 26 April. However, that meeting produced no more than a reiteration of earlier positions. Israel continued to insist that under the proposed autonomy she would bear the sole responsibility for the external and internal security in the West Bank (Judea and Samaria) and the Gaza district; that Israeli settlements established there after 1967 would continue to be subject to Israeli law during the five-year transition; that nothing could bear on Jerusalem's status as the capital of Israel; and that the powers of the proposed autonomy council be restricted to handling internal administrative matters, without legislative authority.

Egypt insisted that all the powers currently held by the Israeli Military Administration in the territories be transferred to the autonomy regime which would elect an administrative council with legislative powers; that the inhabitants of Arab (East) Jerusalem participate in the autonomy elections; and that during the negotiations Israel should stop building or expanding settlements whose future status would be subject to negotiation. Sadat was prepared to accept a first step of implementation in Gaza, a view shared by Israeli Defence Minister Ezer Weitzman as well as by some members of the Israeli Labour Party, contrary to the stance of the Begin government.

However, the obstacles to compromise mounted. There was an escalating cycle of violence and counter-violence on the West Bank between militant Palestinians and their Israeli counterparts. Neither the EEC initiative of 13 June, calling for the inclusion of the PLO in the peace negotiations, nor the resolution presented at the Fatah Congress in May, calling for the liquidation of Israel, made negotiations any easier. The difficulties were compounded on 30 July when the Israeli Knesset approved a law declaring all of Jerusalem as 'Israel's eternal and undivided capital'; the Begin government also revealed plans to move the Prime Minister's office to East Jerusalem. President Sadat could scarcely tolerate such an Israeli annexation of one of Islam's most venerated places and, after postponing the autonomy talks in May, he suspended them on 17 August. In September, after an intense mediation effort by US representative Sol Linowitz, Israel indicated that she would refrain from any real action with respect to Jerusalem, and the parties resumed cursory discussions, but it was clear that little progress could be made until the new US Administration's Middle East policies were defined and until the elections in Israel in July 1981 were over.

The Egyptian–American Connection
A central element of Sadat's strategy was close military and political links with the United States, both to indicate Egypt's strategic importance as a regional ally and to put pressure on Israel. This policy bore fruit quickly in the military sphere. Pointing to the danger of Soviet encroachment, Sadat was quick to offer to the United States air and naval facilities (such as Ras Banas, situated on the Red Sea facing Saudi Arabia). In January 1980 two American airborne warning and control systems aircraft (AWACS) carried out exercises in Egypt, in October a squadron of US *Phantom* aircraft left Cairo West airbase after 83 days of joint training with Egypt, and in November 1,400 US paratroopers held joint exercises with Egyptian soldiers in the Egyptian desert. Over all, Egypt received more than $1 billion in grants and concessional loans from the United States during the year.

There were, however, difficulties in US–Egypt relations. On the military front, after the Egyptian–Israeli Peace Treaty, the United States had embarked on a $3.5-billion programme of re-equipping the Egyptian military over five years. Yet it would take time for the Soviet-equipped Egyptian armed forces to shift from one set of weapons and doctrines to another, and in the interim Egypt's military capability would be limited, and she would remain heavily dependent on existing Soviet weaponry. Similarly, American economic aid could do little in the short run to re-build Egypt's shattered economy, which lacked sufficient infrastructure to absorb even the large financial injections from renewed oil production, from income derived from tourism and the Suez Canal, and from the remittances of Egyptians working abroad.

Yet, in spite of some dividends from the peace process and the absence of over-riding political pressure, it was still debatable whether Egypt could afford to wait until mid-1982 – when the remaining parts of the Sinai were to revert to her – for more tangible results. This would depend in large measure on American willingness to translate general support for Egyptian positions into concrete pressure on Israel. The prospects were further complicated by the arrival of the new American administration: would its emphasis on Israel as a strategic asset devalue Egypt's emergent role? Would its apparent insistence that Middle Eastern politics take second place to the strategic need to contain Soviet power lead to a departure from the Camp David formula and the pursuit of the 'Jordanian option' – seeking to bring Jordan into the peace process as the sponsor of the Palestinians – which remained far less attractive to Egypt?

Fragmentation in Israel
The politics of government survival dominated the approach of Menachem Begin's *Likud* administration on virtually every issue during the year. The credibility of Begin's policies was being eroded, but the opposition Labour Party proved too weak and divided to dislodge it. Ideological and personal rivalries were reflected in the contest for the leadership between Shimon Peres and former Prime Minister Yitzahk Rabin, which was settled only on 21 December with Peres' victory. Yet the Party emerged too bruised to present an immediate alternative to the present government, and if it were to return to power in the July 1981 elections, which appeared increasingly likely, it would be more a reflection of the failure of the Begin government, than of a clear determination to replace past policies. It remained to be seen whether a Labour government, with its internal divisions plus the constraints imposed by other coalition members and the opposition, would be able to

address itself more effectively to the acute economic and foreign-policy problems confronting Israel.

Entering an election year with inflation approaching 150%, Prime Minister Begin shifted attention from the persistent and politically unrewarding economic problems to security questions which remained at the core of the consensus within Israel, seeking to present Labour as a party less committed to the security of Israel than his own *Likud*. Begin also sought to restrain a future Labour government in a number of ways. One was the so-called 'Jordanian option' which was Labour's proposal for a territorial compromise between Jordan and Israel over the West Bank, bringing most of the Palestinians under Jordanian administration while continuing Israeli domination of regions deemed essential to Israeli security. Yet such a solution would mean the reversion of at least part of the West Bank to Arab control, a possibility firmly rejected by the *Likud*. To demonstrate that Jordan herself rejected such a proposal and to embarrass the Labour leaders, Begin divulged in June details of secret meetings between previous Labour-led governments and Jordan's King Hussein. Similarly, Prime Minister Begin encouraged a vote on the Jerusalem law which had been inititiated by the small and hawkish *Tekhiyah* (Revival Movement). This again demonstrated the indecision and divisions which were rife in the Labour Party. In the end, however, the law proved extremely damaging to Israel, as all thirteen embassies remaining in Jerusalem moved to Tel Aviv, and Israel was subjected to near-universal criticism on an issue which otherwise might have lain dormant. That bitter experience gave moderates within Israel the ammunition to oppose similar legislation with regard to the occupied Golan Heights, and, against its inclinations, the Begin government decided on 22 December to shelve the bill for fear of American repercussions.

Despite his dwindling popularity, Begin survived a number of political crises: charges of corruption levelled at a senior member of a coalition party (the National Religious Party); the desertion from the government of members of the crumbling Democratic Movement for Change; and finally the resignation in May of Defence Minister Weitzman in protest over Begin's policies on autonomy and the expansion of settlements. The Prime Minister maintained control of the Knesset with a small majority, aided by the support of small factions outside the government who were fearful of having to contest elections. However, the government was seriously affected by the resignation on 11 January 1981 of Economic Minister Hurwitz over economic issues. Deprived of the vital support of Hurwitz's three-man *Rafi* faction, the government faced the risk of a no-confidence vote, and in mid-January it called for early elections.

Once the Prime Minister had taken the defence portfolio, following Weitzman's resignation, Israeli policies towards the PLO in Lebanon and towards the Palestinians in the occupied territories took a tougher line. Rather than waiting for the PLO to act, the Israeli Defence Force (IDF) sought to forestall PLO terrorist action by attacking its bases in Lebanon. On 17–18 October the IDF mounted a four-pronged attack in different regions, destroying Palestinian installations north-west of the Litani River which served as staging posts for terrorist attacks against Israel. At the same time, Israeli support for the Lebanese Christian forces of Major Hadad, which controlled the enclave in southern Lebanon, contributed to the escalation between Israel and the PLO and to the worsening of relations between Israel and the United Nations monitoring force UNIFIL. As in the past, UNIFIL proved incapable of checking the vicious cycle of violence in Lebanon, and took more than 50 casualties over the year.

The PLO operated in the West Bank via the National Guidance Committee (NGC), a group led by the mayors of Nablus and Ramallah, which included prominent local politicians known to be affiliated with the Rejectionist faction of the PLO, but which excluded all supporters of King Hussein of Jordan. The NGC openly orchestrated opposition to Israeli occupation, leading to periodic outbursts of violence directed against Israeli settlers, especially those living in areas which were densely populated by Arabs. That militance was answered harshly by Israel and was accompanied by a new phenomenon: Israelis living in settlements took the law into their own hands to retaliate against the Palestinians. Thus, Palestinian radicalism led to government coercion and hardened Israeli positions, which in turn further radicalized the Palestinians.

On 3 May 1980 the Israeli government exiled the West Bank mayors of Halhul and Hebron as well as a religious leader, in response to a terrorist attack in which 5 Jewish settlers were killed. This fruitless attempt to weaken the NGC gave the mayors themselves new prominence as they continued their opposition to Israeli policies from abroad. Meanwhile, on 2 June the mayors of Nablus and Ramallah were seriously injured following bomb attacks on a number of mayors, allegedly carried out as reprisals by Israeli terrorists. At the same time the PLO and its supporters also used terror to deter any collaboration between Palestinian politicians and the Israeli authorities. In late November the Deputy Mayor of Jabiliyah in the Gaza Strip, one of Sadat's staunchest supporters, was murdered, and later that month there were assaults on six other Palestinians who were believed to have collaborated with Israel.

The indigenous Palestinian mayors managed to bolster their own position despite the strengthening of PLO influence in the occupied territories. They were helped by the Israeli decision to postpone indefinitely the municipal elections in the West Bank, scheduled for April. They became the focus of the struggle against Israel – as was demonstrated by the enthusiastic reception given the two wounded mayors when they returned to the West Bank in late December and early January 1981 – and potentially made them less aquiescent in PLO domination.

SOUTH AND SOUTH-WEST ASIA

The repercussions of the Soviet invasion of Afghanistan in December 1979 remained the dominant issue in the region. On the ground, the outcome was a stalemate: given the existing deployment of Soviet forces in Afghanistan, rebel forces posed no threat to basic Soviet control, yet they could not be eradicated; nor were there obvious signs of Soviet success either in re-building the shattered Afghan Army or in conferring legitimacy on the regime of Babrak

Karmal in Kabul. Events in Afghanistan affected security policies in South Asia, most obviously in Pakistan, but indirectly in India, even though the new government of Mrs Indira Gandhi seemed to acquiesce in the Soviet invasion. The events exposed Pakistan's weak strategic position to Soviet pressures and reinforced her motivation to seek a military nuclear capability as ultimate reassurance – which inevitably would raise concern in India.

AFGHANISTAN A YEAR AFTER THE INVASION

Soviet efforts to consolidate military and political control over Afghanistan after the December 1979 invasion met with mixed success. At the close of 1980 the Soviet force in the country stood at some 85,000 men, and it had reportedly sustained casualties of some 15,000 killed and wounded during the year. The invasion – the first large-scale use of Soviet troops outside Eastern Europe in the post-war period – had been an unqualified Soviet success only insofar as it had served to avert the imminent emergence of a hostile regime in Kabul.

Twenty months before the invasion, the People's Democratic Party of Afghanistan (PDPA) – a coalition of the *Khalq* (Masses) and *Parcham* (Flag) parties – had toppled the republican government of Mohammad Daoud in a military coup. This *Saur* (April) Revolution of 1978 had been accompanied by a major escalation in the Soviet Union's involvement in Afghanistan (for more detail, see *Strategic Survey 1979*, pp. 48–55). The two contending factions within the PDPA were in accord on the continuing primacy of the relationship with the Soviet Union, yet at odds over a range of other issues, including the sharing of power within the PDPA. Conflict between them quickly escalated in the weeks following the *Saur* Revolution. In July 1978, the *Khalq*-dominated government of Nur Muhammad Taraki moved against the *Parcham* wing of the party, either jailing of demoting its leadership. The *Parcham* leader, former Deputy Premier Babrak Karmal, was posted as Ambassador to

Prague, where he left his post and set up a dissident exile group.

At the time it seized power, the *Khalq* faction had between 5,000 and at most 10,000 members. It instituted a brutal domestic programme. Agricultural reforms, which had been promised within a period of two years, were hastily and carelessly carried out simply in order to win the peasantry over to the side of the government, but, despite this, by the middle of 1979 it was only in control of urban areas. The resistance movement, for the most part spontaneous, popular and varied, had virtually paralysed the country and appeared to be gaining the upper hand. It was at this point that the Soviet Union actively began to explore ways of halting the continued erosion of the Afghan internal situation.

There were suggestions that the initial Soviet plan was to oust Hafizullah Amin, *Khalq*'s unpopular Vice-Premier, and then blame him for the excesses of the Taraki regime as a prelude to reconstituting a more broadly based government, including leaders of the exiled *Parcham* faction. If this was the case, the execution of the plan in September 1979 went awry. Taraki was killed, not Amin, and the latter consolidated his control over the *Khalq* faction. This left the USSR with no other option than to underwrite the new regime, but she did give political refuge to those who had backed Taraki and increased her contacts with the *Parchami* exiles in Eastern Europe. The Amin government's reliance on Soviet military assistance to contain the growing insurgency movement, however, provided the Soviet Union with the pretext for stationing an increasingly large Red Army contingent within Afghanistan. Elements of this contingent prepositioned around Kabul (acting in conjunction with the main invasion force, which crossed the border at three points on 27 December) seized the presidential palace, deposed and killed Amin and installed the present *Parcham*-dominated regime under Babrak Karmal. The new Afghan leadership hailed the invasion in retrospect as marking 'the second phase of the *Saur* Revolution'.

Soviet Operations
In the initial period of the invasion Soviet forces quickly moved to secure the major garrisons, towns and communication lines, leaving the Afghan Army to shoulder the main burden of countering the insurgency threat in the provincial areas. In contrast to the pattern of American deployment in Vietnam, the Soviet Union did not attempt to cover the country with a large expeditionary force – a move which would have been both costly and probably ineffective. Nonetheless, her occupying forces still faced acute military problems.

In late January and early February reservists from the Soviet Central Asian Republics, the spearhead of the original invasion, were replaced by more experienced contingents of regulars. Then, in March 1980, an offensive was launched to eliminate insurgent resistance and gain control of key rural areas in the eastern provinces adjacent to Pakistan and in the north-eastern province of Badakshan. Operating in large armoured formations backed by air cover, Soviet combat units ran into severe difficulties in the mountainous terrain, and this brought about a change of tactics to combined operations involving motorized infantry, tanks and helicopter gunships; there were also charges that Soviet forces were using nerve gas and other internationally proscribed weapons, such as dum-dum bullets, against the Afghan armed opposition. The main impact of the spring 1980 offensive was greatly to increase the flow of refugees into Iran and Pakistan. In July Iran reported that she was caring for 500,000 refugees displaced by the war in Afghanistan, and on 6 August, a Pakistani census indicated that over a million Afghans had fled into that country.

Having been installed by the Red Army, the Karmal regime faced the need to enhance its fragile basis of domestic support. In March it announced a second phase of the land reform programme originally inaugurated by Taraki (including the continued break-up and redistribution of large landholdings) so as to generate peasant support. There was also a calculated appeal to Islam, so as to counter the religious appeal of the Muslim opposition groups, which involved *inter alia* the replacement of *Khalq*'s all-red flag by one incorporating a green stripe to represent Islam, and the sending of Afghan religious leaders to Soviet Central Asia to observe an ostensibly thriving Islamic culture operating in the context of state socialism.

The regime also tried to revitalize the Afghan Army and restore it to its pre-1978 strength of some 100,000 men, resorting to a number of expedients, which included financial inducements and forced recruitment. Desertion and defection to the insurgents continued to frustrate these efforts. In July the 14th Armoured Division, based at Ghazni, reportedly mutinied, and by September the Afghan Army was a demoralized and ineffective force estimated to number no more than 30,000 men.

The disarray of the Afghan armed forces compelled Soviet troops to assume an increasingly large share of the ground fighting. During the summer and autumn months fighting of varying intensity was reported in 12 of Afghanistan's 28 provinces: Ghazni, Paktia, Wardak, Parwan, Zabul, Baghlan, Konarha, Kunduz, Badakhshan, Nangarhar, Helmand and Kabul. In mid-November, Soviet forces moved into the strategically important Wakhan corridor adjoining Pakistan in the north-east. With the country divided into seven military commands (under the *de facto* control of Soviet generals, despite the presence of local PDPA leaders), the Red Army appeared to be preparing for an indefinite stay in Afghanistan and was building new airfields and permanent storage facilities.

The 'Sovietization' of Afghanistan in the military area was accompanied by the introduction of Soviet social and economic policies. Trade unions were organized along Soviet lines, and Afghan officials were reported to operate under the direction of Soviet advisers and experts who permeated every level of the bureaucracy and were involved in all major governmental decisions. The disruption of normal trade and aid resulting from the invasion led to the Afghan economy becoming almost totally dependent on the Soviet Union. (While this involved costs for the Soviet Union, it also implied some benefits – for instance, concessionary prices for natural gas exported to the USSR.) This dependence was most acute in respect of food, and the severe shortages caused by the war were a major cause of the flow of refugees into Iran and Pakistan – indeed there was speculation that starving the population in provinces where armed resistance was greatest might be a calculated element of Soviet strategy. Public disaffection with the pervasive nature of Soviet control over the Afghan government severely hindered the PDPA's efforts to expand its meagre internal base and made the domestic legitimacy sought by the Karmal regime more elusive than ever.

Armed Opposition

Although violent opposition to the Soviet occupation and to the Karmal regime spread to all regions of the country, it was concentrated along two major geographical lines: the first running east–west through the centre of the country from the border with Pakistan to the Hazarjat in the heart of Afghanistan, the second running north–south through the eastern half of the country. Outside these mountainous regions, which cover about half the country, there were further zones with large pockets of resistance – most notably around Kandahar and Herat. Although still primarily rural, tribal and divided, the Afghan armed opposition increasingly began to challenge Soviet forces for the control of major cities. During July and August 1980, for example, it was reported that the provincial cities of Jalalabad and Herat had come under partial opposition control.

The principal groups were basically those that had fought against the *Khalq* regimes led by Taraki and Amin since the April 1978 military coup. The headquarters of the six main resistance groups were located in Pakistan at Peshawar – an area whose native inhabitants, like the majority in Afghanistan, are ethnically Pushtun. Three of these organizations – the two contending factions of the Islamic Party led by Gulbuddin Hikmatyar and Mohammad Yunus Khalis, as well as the Islamic Society of Afghanistan headed by Burhanuddin Rabbani – were Muslim fundamentalist bodies. Slightly less doctrinaire in applying religion to political

programmes were the National Front for the Islamic Revolution of Afghanistan, headed by Ahmad Gailani, and the National Liberation Front, led by Sebgatullah Mojadedi. The sixth group, which was gaining in numerical strength, was the Revolutionary Islamic Movement (*Harakat*) under the leadership of Mohammad Nabi Mohammadi. Besides these main resistance movements, there were other small groups organized along ideological and ethnic lines – for example, the Hazaras and the Nuristanis, comprising some 12–15% and 3% of the population respectively, each had their own resistance organization.

The Afghan armed opposition movement thus remained multi-faceted, contradictory and confused. But perhaps most importantly, it did not yet represent an alternative to the *Parcham* regime but merely a rejection of it, and the expression of a desire to protect traditional ways against a centralizing state. In the political context of violent opposition to the imposition of 'socialism' by foreign tanks supporting a regime with no social basis, religious and national ideals represented the common resistance ideology.

Though the resistance grew more effective after the initial December 1979 Soviet invasion, it continued to suffer from two major problems: its political disunity, which lamed its challenge to the legitimacy of the Karmal regime in international fora, and a lack of modern heavy arms. Most of its equipment was acquired as a result of desertions from the Afghan Army, and from the traditional workshops of Peshawar. Despite the continuing demands of the resistance, outside supplies of military equipment were extremely modest, and the battle remained one between dispersed, under-armed guerrillas and a modern and well-equipped adversary. Soviet forces increasingly made use of weapon systems such as helicopter gunships, artillery and mines which tended to offset the guerrillas' advantage of mobility and against which they had few counters. Outside military aid was provided most discreetly – there were indications of some Chinese assistance and pledges of support from Egypt – not least out of consideration for Pakistan's precarious position, but there were signs that the new Administration in Washington would be more aware of the strategic value of such aid than its predecessor had been. Should the Afghan resistance receive man-portable anti-tank and anti-aircraft weapons, the human and material losses it could inflict on the USSR would increase, and so, too, might Soviet readiness to consider a negotiated settlement to the Afghan crisis which included the active participation of the principal insurgent groups.

In the end, however, the attitude of Pakistan would be crucial, for her support would remain the key to the military effectiveness of the armed opposition. As a result, Pakistan came under increasing pressure from the Soviet Union: pressure which, over time, could pose a serious challenge to her fragile domestic stability. In early 1981 there were signs – such as President Zia's proposal for tripartite talks between Pakistan, Afghanistan and Iran, made at the Islamic Conference summit meeting at Taif in late January – that Pakistan was attempting to distance herself politically from a stance of outright opposition to compromise. In Pakistan, unlike Iran, there was a clear recognition that, while these two countries were not currently threatened by Soviet forces in Afghanistan, the USSR was in the best possible position to exert influence on them if circumstances permitted.

Political Proposals

The international political response to the Soviet Union's December 1979 invasion of Afghanistan was both immediate and critical. In early January a draft resolution deploring the intervention and calling for the immediate and unconditional withdrawal of foreign troops was vetoed by the Soviet Union in the UN Security Council, but it was subsequently passed by an emergency session of the General Assembly on 14 January by 104 votes to 18, with 18 abstentions. Two weeks later, a hastily convened meeting of the Islamic Conference in Islamabad condemned the invasion in similar language and called on all member states to withhold recognition of the 'illegal' regime. At around the same time two high-ranking US missions (headed by National Security Adviser Zbigniew Brzezinski and Presidential emissary Clark Clifford) were sent to Pakistan and India respectively, where they sought to discuss the regional implications of the Soviet move, although they did not bring any of the undertakings expected in the region.

The search for a political solution leading to a Soviet withdrawal from Afghanistan remain-

ed the subject of diplomatic discussions throughout 1980. On 19 February, the EEC Foreign Ministers, meeting in Rome, approved a proposal sponsored by the British Foreign Secretary, Lord Carrington, for the neutralization of Afghanistan under international guarantees in return for a Soviet withdrawal. Nine days later India expressed her opposition to neutrality 'in the technical sense' and sought consultations with the countries adjacent to Afghanistan in the hope of a 'regional solution' to the crisis. This effort foundered, however, on Pakistan's rejection of India's mediating role. In late March, Cuban President Fidel Castro, in his capacity as chairman of the Non-Aligned Movement, similarly offered his 'good offices' to work towards a regional settlement of the Afghan crisis.

On 17 April the Karmal regime formally proposed separate bilateral discussions with the governments in Tehran and Islamabad to 'discuss questions pertaining to the normalization of Afghan-Iranian and Afghan-Pakistani relations'. Less than four weeks later, Kabul Radio and Tass broadcast an additional set of Soviet-backed proposals from the Afghan leadership for a negotiated political solution, including the suggestion that the United States and the Soviet Union should provide guarantees against external interference. On 15 May US Secretary of State Muskie dismissed the Afghan proposals as 'cosmetic and ambiguous' rather than 'a serious response to our demand for the withdrawal of Soviet troops'. Less categorical in his criticism was Lord Carrington, who commented that the fact that the USSR was 'prepared to talk about a non-aligned Afghanistan is not discouraging'. A meeting of Islamic Conference Foreign Ministers, held in Islamabad on 17–22 May, resulted in the creation of a Standing Committee (consisting of the Iranian and Pakistani Foreign Ministers and the Secretary-General of the Islamic Conference Organization) to work for a resolution of the crisis, and at its first meeting in early June the Committee decided to seek talks with the Soviet and Afghan Governments, as well as with the Afghan resistance movement.

On 14 October, during his extensive visit to the Soviet Union, and again on 28 December, after his return, Babrak Karmal renewed the PDPA's call for separate bilateral negotiations with Pakistan and Iran. One month later, at the

Islamic Conference summit meeting in Taif, President Zia ul-Haq, citing 'intimations of flexibility' by the Soviet Union and the regime in Kabul, proposed that the UN Secretary-General convene a three-sided meeting between Pakistan, Afghanistan and Iran, significantly failing to mention the Muslim insurgent groups fighting the Kabul government. In fact Secretary-General Waldheim had already named a representative, who, in accordance with the 20 November General Assembly resolution (passed by an even larger majority than the initial one of 14 January), was to seek negotiations for 'the immediate withdrawal of foreign troops from Afghanistan'.

There were, however, no signs that the Soviet Union was willing to enter into any serious negotiations. She maintained throughout the position first formulated in January 1980 that the sole reason for the presence of her forces was provocation by outside powers – China, Pakistan and the United States – and that those troops would only withdraw if these provocations (for which no evidence was provided) stopped. Similarly, she refused to consider seriously any of the multilateral diplomatic initiatives made during the year: the bilateral negotiations with Pakistan and Iran called for by the Karmal government would have the double advantage of excluding the Afghan armed resistance and implying recognition for the regime in Kabul. In October a joint Soviet-Afghan communique and speeches by both Brezhnev and Karmal called the links between Afghanistan and the USSR irreversible. Even the more modest suggestions of mediation with UN participation were rejected by the USSR in early 1981.

Clearly, the Soviet Union deemed the consequences of withdrawal still unacceptable and the costs of the continued military presence tolerable. With a limited military involvement she was able to maintain the Karmal government in power, if not in authority; and there was a clear expectation, not entirely discouraged by the events of the year, that sooner or later the other countries in the region, and in particular Pakistan, would move towards a recognition of the *status quo* created by the Soviet military presence.

PAKISTAN

As 1980 began, Pakistan was confronted by four serious crises. Her economy was in difficulties. Her political system was unstable. Her relationships with powerful neighbours and distant allies were cool at best. And Soviet troops were approaching the Durand Line, her common frontier with Afghanistan. By the end of the year most of these crises were at least stabilized, and some were being gradually resolved. Nonetheless, Pakistan's internal stability would remain powerfully influenced by her foreign relations, within the region and beyond it.

The Threat from Afghanistan
In the first weeks of 1980, three interpretations of the Soviet invasion of Afghanistan were debated in Pakistan. Some saw it as a new manifestation of historic Russian designs on South Asia that had opened the route to Karachi and the Indian Ocean. Others, a much larger group, saw the Soviet move as primarily defensive: an attempt to retain Afghanistan within the Soviet sphere of influence. Yet others viewed the invasion as part of a broader encirclement of the Persian Gulf and as a way of putting pressure on Iran. The weight of informed opinion was that Pakistan herself was not in immediate danger from the USSR but might become so if she appeared to be vulnerable to Soviet threats and resistant to important Soviet interests.

Pakistan therefore entered into discussions with the United States about the renewal of military and economic assistance – the former had been cut off many years earlier, the latter in 1979 because of US assertions that Pakistan was seeking a military nuclear capability. The rhetoric of the American reaction to the Soviet invasion, as well as Mr Brzezinski's posturing on the Khyber Pass during his visit at the head of the US mission in February, raised Pakistani expectations of a major military and economic assistance effort by the United States. Such expectations were disappointed, however. The Carter Administration had ruled out the supply of the very weapons systems which would make a military difference to Pakistan's defences (high-performance aircraft and armour) and was only prepared to supply 'defensive' arms – anti-tank weapons, radars and other equipment – designed to counter a threat along the Durand Line. Neither the magnitude of the proposed American 'aid' package ($400 million over two years) nor the terms (credit at 11% interest) could satisfy Pakistan's need for more substantial reassurance. President Zia ul-Haq dismissed the Carter offer as 'peanuts' and held out instead for a stronger political commitment from the US to supplement not only the 1959 agreement to defend Pakistan against armed aggression but also the 1963 assurances that she would consult Pakistan in the case of aggression by India; this was not forthcoming.

Pakistan held fast to her historical analysis that the challenges to her security emanated not only from the Soviet Union but also from India, and it seemed to her that, after three years of Carter diplomacy emphasizing human rights, nuclear proliferation and regionally preponderant powers (in this context, India), American diplomacy was unable to adjust quickly to a more strategic approach to regional developments. She did continue to receive US assistance in the form of debt relief and continued to buy arms from the US (acquiring two *Gearing*-class destroyers in November 1980). However, such measures were in the final analysis marginal to the central strategic issues confronting Pakistan on her frontiers and inadequate to provide the backing she would need in order to resist pressure from her more powerful neighbours at a time when she was already sheltering a million Afghan refugees. On her western frontier, Soviet movement towards the Durand Line was seen as limited probing coupled with threats of worse to come. Soviet Foreign Minister Gromyko in mid-February and Babrak Karmal in November warned Pakistan against providing any support for the Afghan *Mujaheddin*. In September and October 1980 Soviet helicopter gunships attacked Pakistani pickets along the Durand Line and an undefended refugee camp, and overflights of Pakistani territory occurred repeatedly from the time that Soviet troops first entered Afghanistan. Moreover, Soviet and Afghan hints suggested that Pakistan's vulnerability in Baluchistan might be exploited. That economically depressed province, with its largely tribal and nomadic population, remained disaffected from the central govern-

ment in Islamabad, and assistance from Soviet-occupied Afghanistan to promote the country's fragmentation remained a potential threat which clearly affected Pakistani calculations.

While taking care not to invite Soviet attacks and considering a plan to move refugee camps away from the immediate frontier area, Pakistan therefore raised a seventh corps headquarters in Baluchistan. Like those of the corps based in Peshawar, its divisions were under strength and under-equipped, but it could provide the command needed if divisions should be moved from the Indian border to the Durand Line.

Domestic Politics and Security

The complexity of Pakistan's security policy reflected the diverse and conflicting elements of her national self-image. The first was the conception of Pakistan as inheritor of the passes of the North-west Frontier and Baluchistan, on guard against Soviet encroachment. A second was that of a nation geographically and culturally embedded in South Asia, sharing a language, frontier and – most importantly – a history with India. The third, the view of Pakistan as an Islamic state, was the country's *raison d'etre*; militant Islam would provide both a justification for the survival of the state and a renewed opportunity to expand ties with a variety of increasingly powerful Muslim states to the west. A fourth element was Pakistan's role as a member of the Non-Aligned Movement.

As in the previous three years of military rule, political debate in Pakistan during 1980 continued to centre on the quest of President Zia's government for acceptance. Before the Soviet invasion of Afghanistan, Zia, under attack for his authoritarian ways, had felt obliged to hold out the promise of free elections, but after the invasion this public pressure abated. However, the domestic scene did not calm down for long. Attempts to establish a federal cabinet and a substitute parliament without holding elections failed when Ghulam Mustafa Jatoi, a prominent figure in the late Zulfiqar Ali Bhutto's Pakistan People's Party (PPP), rejected an invitation to assume the premiership under pressure from Bhutto's widow Nusrat and daughter Benazir, who now led the party. To guard against unrest, the country's universities were closed once again in February 1981, and in the same month nine political parties, including the PPP, announced the formation of a united opposition alliance, the Movement for the Restoration of Democracy.

The hijacking of a Pakistani airliner on 2 March 1981 again highlighted the relationship between domestic politics and security. While the hijacking was under the apparent control of Murtaza Bhutto, the late Prime Minister's son, much of its long-term implication will depend on the extent of the involvement of the other Bhuttos. While the episode demonstrated Zia's vulnerability, it could also provide him with a popular excuse to crack down on his opposition.

The surface stability of military rule was reinforced by the strong performance of the economy in 1980. Food production remained at a high level and remittances from Pakistanis working abroad – a vital source of foreign exchange – reached a record $2 billion for the year. The regime's 'Islamization' programme secured the support of another important domestic constituency – in particular, the *Jamaat-i-Islami* fundamentalist party – but it also brought the possible danger of renewed sectarian tension, since Shi'ite Muslims (some 15–20% of the 70-million population) feared that the programme would further enhance the power of the dominant Sunni sect at their expense. On balance, however, the President and his military-backed regime seemed to have drawn greater strength at home from the challenges they faced abroad.

The regime re-committed Pakistan to the policy of military self-reliance, originally forged during the Bhutto period, including the indigenous production of conventional, and eventually nuclear, weapons. The conventional weapons programme was concentrated in the region north of Rawalpindi, where several major production and repair facilities had been established at Kamra, Wah and Taxla. One plant at Kamra enabled Pakistan to overhaul her 700 Chinese-supplied T-59 tanks (a serviceable weapon but with a gun inferior to the 105mm in equivalent Indian tanks), while another, built in 1979, could strip and over-

haul the *Mirage* III fighters flown by Pakistan and other Middle Eastern and Asian air forces. A facility at Attock, commissioned in November 1980, could overhaul Chinese-supplied F-6 (MiG-19) fighters. By 1980 factories at Wah produced a nearly complete range of explosives, shells, small arms and other weapons, and engaged in a thriving export business. These efforts in indigenous arms production remained small in comparison to their Indian equivalents, but they reflected Pakistan's strong determination to be self-reliant in arms supplies.

The military nuclear programme appeared to be motivated by essentially the same concern. Encouraged by the highest levels of the army, Pakistani strategists also argued that an indigenous nuclear-weapons capability would enhance rather than undermine regional stability, pointing out that the only actual use of a nuclear weapon to date had occurred when one state possessed it and another did not. The evidence available in 1980 seemed to indicate that Pakistan was indeed pressing ahead with her own nuclear programme for the production of both enriched uranium and plutonium. Construction of a large uranium enrichment plant continued at Kahuta, about 24 miles south of Islamabad. (For a background discussion of the programme, see *Strategic Survey 1979*, pp. 15–20.) In June it was reported that, following the purchase of vital components from Switzerland and the Italian subsidiary of a French firm, she had clandestinely resumed construction of a plutonium reprocessing facility near Rawalpindi (work had been abandoned in the summer of 1978 when the French Government, after consistent prodding from the Carter Administration, had cancelled its licence for the sale of this equipment). This plant was widely regarded as a major breakthrough in the Pakistani nuclear weapons programme, and the resumption of work on it, coinciding with reports of large-scale financial backing for the project from Saudi Arabia and the preparation of a desert test site in Cholistan, revived Western and regional anxiety over the possibility of an 'Islamic bomb' in Pakistani hands before long.

INDIA

The beginning of 1980 was marked by two events, the domestic and foreign policy repercussions of which were to dominate the Indian political scene over the course of the year: Mrs Indira Gandhi's return to power after her party's stunning electoral victory, and the extension and consolidation of the Soviet hold on Afghanistan after the invasion of 27 December 1979. After two-and-a-half years of relative stagnation under *Janata* coalition rule, Mrs Gandhi's campaign pledge of 'a government that works' matched the pervasive public desire for decisive and effective political leadership. And yet, in the realm of foreign policy, the Gandhi government's relatively relaxed, even understanding, attitude to the Soviet occupation of Afghanistan generated new internal divisions and added fresh impetus to the long-standing debate on the nature of India's 'legitimate role' in regional politics. Abroad, India's refusal to condemn the Soviet invasion outright seemed to run counter to any claim, after Tito's death, to provide new leadership for the Non-Aligned Movement.

Reactions to Afghanistan

The Soviet invasion of Afghanistan occurred during the final days of Charan Singh's caretaker Government. In sharp contrast with his hard-line, anti-Soviet position on the crisis, Mrs Gandhi, who took office on 14 January 1980, sought to project what was described by Foreign Ministry officials as a more 'balanced position'. In keeping with her desire to avoid 'one-sided condemnation', India abstained on 14 January when the UN General Assembly passed a resolution calling for the 'immediate termination of armed intervention in Afghanistan', and in the politically charged atmosphere which followed the invasion her ambivalent stance was widely taken to indicate tacit support for the Soviet position – an impression strengthened by her recognition in August of the Vietnamese-imposed, pro-Soviet Heng Samrin regime in Kampuchea.

In late January, President Carter's emissary Clark Clifford visited New Delhi to explain the $400-million assistance package which the US offered to Pakistan in immediate aftermath of the Afghanistan invasion. He also brought the offer of renewed US military sales to India – a departure from previous American policy. Mrs Gandhi, taking a position repeatedly echoed over the ensuing months, reportedly told Clifford that the United States had taken 'disproportionate measures' in response to the crisis in South-west Asia. She further affirmed that her Government could not regard Soviet moves in Afghanistan in complete 'isolation'. This was an implicit reference both to the expansion of American facilities in Diego Garcia (part of US plans for increased military preparedness in the Gulf region) and the evolving Sino-American security relationship. While not condoning the Soviet occupation of Afghanistan, Mrs Gandhi refused to discount moves by 'the other super-power' which had heightened Moscow's perception of encirclement. Indian policy concerns thus centred less on the immediate regional implications of a Soviet presence on the Durand Line than on the dangers of an American over-response which could extend the East–West rivalry into south Asia. Indeed, Mrs Gandhi claimed that, to the extent that Pakistan allowed herself to be transformed into the anti-Soviet 'arsenal' that the US and China envisaged, these dangers would be increased. On 17 April, during discussions with President Zia held in Salisbury during Zimbabwe's independence celebrations, Mrs Gandhi reportedly asked the Pakistani leader to distance his country politically from the United States so as to facilitate a 'regional solution' to the Afghanistan crisis.

Foreign Minister Andrei Gromyko's visit to New Delhi in mid-February was the Soviet Union's first high-level contact with the Gandhi government since its return to power. The purpose of the visit was reportedly twofold: to gain Indian understanding, if not support, for Soviet policy in Afghanistan, and to reassure New Delhi that the USSR would not permit the rearming of Pakistan to pose any threat to India. In language as emotive as that employed by Mr Clifford a month earlier, Mr Gromyko baldly warned Pakistan of grave consequences if she continued to be used as a 'springboard for aggression' against Afghanistan. During the private sessions with him, Mrs Gandhi and the Indian External Affairs Minister, Narashima Rao, pressed for a timetable for Soviet withdrawal from Afghanistan in return for certain, not fully specified, international guarantees; though he rejected this initiative Mr Gromyko did assure India that it was unlikely that the Soviet Government would despatch *additional* forces to Afghanistan.

On his departure, Indian officials asserted that Mr Gromyko had privately indicated Soviet willingness to withdraw from Afghanistan under the 'proper conditions', and on the basis of this hitherto unexpressed 'flexibility' in the Soviet position, India entered into informal exploratory discussions with the United States, Afghanistan and Pakistan in the hope of engineering a 'regional solution' to the crisis. This initiative foundered on President Zia's swift rejection of the Gandhi government's mediating role – a rebuff which clearly reflected Pakistan's suspicion of India. Though periodic discussions continued – for instance during Pakistani Foreign Minister Agha Shahi's visit to New Delhi in mid-July – these hopes for a regional solution were stifled by the divergent Indian and Pakistani perceptions of the implications of the invasion of Afghanistan. At the time of Soviet President Leonid Brezhnev's state visit to India in December, officials in New Delhi argued that the intensity of international criticism against Moscow, coupled with the persistence of the Afghan armed resistance movement, had hardened Soviet attitudes and thereby made the withdrawal of its forces less likely.

Internal Stability
Mrs Gandhi's return to power on 14 January 1980, after the sweeping electoral victory of her Congress Party (I) earlier in the month, was all the more striking because the electorate, angered by the governmental abuses of the emergency period, had overwhelmingly voted her out of power only a little less than three years before. Two factors were primarily responsible for her remarkable comeback: the economic failure of the Desai and Singh Governments and the incessant leadership conflicts within the *Janata* Party. The election results which gave Mrs Gandhi her two-thirds parliamentary majority also brought about the virtual eclipse of the *Janata* party and of the major parties of the Right, the *Lok Dal* and the Official Congress, and for the first time in Indian history the Left alliance of Marxist and Socialist parties became the dominant opposition grouping. However, as had been the case with the *Janata* coalition in the late 1970s, it appeared to have no programmatic basis for continued unity other than opposition to the Gandhi government.

With an inaugural pledge to continue her 'interrupted task', Mrs Gandhi moved quickly to consolidate her domestic power base. In mid-February, following a questionable precedent set by the *Janata* government in 1977, she dissolved nine state assemblies on the grounds that their composition no longer reflected popular opinion in the wake of her party's electoral victory. This caused an intensification of regional attempts to challenge the central government's authority.

In Assam, the oil-producing state at the centre of India's troubled north-eastern region, militant students protesting at the continued influx of Bengali immigrants effectively blocked the flow of oil to the rest of the country between March and November. The importance of Assamese oil, which accounted for about a third of domestic production, was heightened by the shortages stemming from the Iran–Iraq war (India having been one of Iraq's main clients). This forced the Government's hand and prompted it to order the army into the state to restore both order and the flow of oil. The latter aim was achieved, but the student opposition group continued to enjoy widespread popular support and maintained its paralytic hold over the state's civil apparatus. In the neighbouring states of Manipur and Tripura, too, violence erupted in similar campaigns against Bengali and Nepalese immigrants (in June some 450 deaths were recorded in clashes between indigenous tribespeople and Bengali immigrants in Tripura alone). Equal in significance to this intensification of ethnic conflict was the sporadic resurgence of Hindu–Moslem violence across the northern half of the country. At the end of 1980 it was clear that the Government's ability to meet the challenge of ethnic and sectarian fragmentation would be a major test of Mrs Gandhi's leadership – a leadership which was also weakened in June by the death of her son and political heir apparent, Sanjay Gandhi, in a flying accident.

Military Modernization
The decision to build major new weapons systems under license marked a further signi-

ficant advance towards India's goal of self-reliance in arms production. India became the sixth nation to make a successful satellite launch when the 77-pound *Rohini-I* went into orbit on 18 July. Though Mrs Gandhi discounted the security implications of this event, the *Times of India* concluded that the Indian Space Research Organization was 'growing a potentially strong tooth for the nation's defence'.

India's military modernization programme accelerated as 1980 defence spending reached its highest level ever, some $5.5 billion, accounting for over 30% of total government spending (3% up on 1979) and roughly 8% of the nation's GNP. One of the principal causes of the increase was the fact that India was entering a cycle of major military equipment replacement. The primary emphasis of this effort was to build under licence a modern generation of combat aircraft to replace her obsolescent MiG-21 and *Hunter* fighters and *Canberra* bombers and to build a new main battle tank to replace the *Vijayanta*. And, together with the launching of the *Rohini-I*, it also served to underscore broad and sophisticated nature of her military-industrial base, clearly now one of the most advanced in the Third World.

The modernization programme received a major boost in June with the conclusion of an arms agreement with the Soviet Union, completed in the wake of India's assiduous efforts to block the flow of Western arms to Pakistan after the Soviet invasion of Afghanistan. The massive size of the deal and the extraordinarily favourable terms which the USSR granted to India ($1.63 billion on 17-year credit at 2.5%

interest) stood in sharp contrast to the $400 million military assistance (at 11%) which the US had offered to Pakistan. The package enabled the Gandhi government to build under licence two major weapons systems as part of the replacement cycle: the MiG-23 fighter-bomber, as a successor to the MiG-21 (to be built in the three factories already building the MiG-21) and an unspecified number of T-72 tanks (to be built at Avadi) to succeed the *Vijayanta*. Following President Brezhnev's four-day state visit to New Delhi in December, it was further reported that the Soviet Union had offered to supply India with an undisclosed number of Mach 3.2 MiG-25s – presumably for reconnaissance and as a replacement for the MiG-21bis interceptor.

Despite the Indo-Soviet arms deal, Mrs Gandhi did not officially eschew the policy of acquiring weapons from a diversity of sources. This was reflected in the Government's approval of a contract with West Germany for two submarines, as well as in Defence Secretary K. P. S. Menon's October visit to Washington to discuss the possible purchase of certain types of specialized American military equipment (e.g. night vision devices) with Carter Administration officials. The future of the proposed purchase from Britain of 40 *Jaguar* fighter-bombers, and the co-production in India of a further 110, remained uncertain. However, President Brezhnev, during his December visit, expressed 'dismay' that India might be spending her declining foreign exchange reserves on material for which the Soviet Union would have gladly accepted payment in rupees.

EUROPE

For the security of Europe and perhaps beyond, the most significant event of the year was the crisis of the Communist regime in Poland which led to a workers' movement not controlled by the Communist Party, *Solidarnosc* (*Solidarity*), obtaining status as an independent trade union. By early 1981 the outcome of this crisis was still uncertain. If the Polish experiment were to succeed, the impact on Communist regimes all over Europe would be profound. If it were to be suppressed by Soviet military force, the repercussions could provoke a conflict within Eastern Europe which could pose a major threat to security in Europe as a whole.

Other worries receded into the background under the impact of the Polish events. In Yugoslavia, the death of the founder of the post-war state, Marshal Tito, did not lead to the challenges from within and without that many had predicted. And the serious rift between the United States and her European allies – which had appeared after the Soviet invasion in Afghanistan, raising serious doubts about the ability of the Western alliance to react coherently at a time of deteriorating East–West relations – was at least superficially healed in late 1980, when concern over Poland produced a common resolve among Alliance governments. But just as the evolution of events in Poland remained uncertain, so too did the future ability of the West to maintain a co-ordinated and effective policy towards the Soviet Union.

CRISIS IN POLAND

Post-war Poland had seen more manifestations of civil opposition to Communist power than any other of the Soviet Union's East European client states. In 1956, strikes and unrest had removed the Stalinist leadership and replaced it with what seemed, at the time, a more pragmatic and nationally minded Politburo under Wladyslaw Gomulka. In 1970, again following a wave of labour unrest in the country, Gomulka was forced to resign and Edward Gierek, a popular Communist district leader from the south-western mining area of Katowice, suceeded him. In 1980, Mr Gierek himself fell victim to the new crisis in Poland.

The immediate cause of the crisis was the decision by the Warsaw government to increase meat prices and to free the Polish budget from the heavy burden of food subsidies, which in 1979 amounted to 25% of the national expenditure. Since this was compensated neither by increased wages nor adequate supplies, a punishing wave of strikes erupted all over the country. When the shipyard workers of Gdansk and Szczecin joined in, that brought the country to the edge of economic and political disaster.

The communist hierarchy, surprised by the vehemence of the protest and weakened both by international indecisiveness and the lack of effective responses, finally acceded to the workers' demands, and an agreement was signed between government and workers' representatives in Gdansk on 31 August. In return for an end to the strikes and an acknowledgement of the leading role of the Communist Party, the workers won the legal right to strike, independent trade unions free of direct Party control, and greater access to the media for both the new unions and the Roman Catholic church, a commitment to revise the censorship laws, and a series of concessions on pay and social benefits.

On paper the Gdansk agreement, by sanctioning the formation of autonomous trade unions, pushed back the boundaries of economic and political change in Eastern Europe further than had been thought possible since 1968, when Soviet troops had abruptly terminated the reforms which had been contemplated in Czechoslovakia in 1968. The Gdansk concessions were wrung from a reluctant Communist Party at a moment of political weakness. Following Mr Gierek's sudden illness, the political leadership was taken over on 6 September by Stanislav Kania, the former Party Secretary in charge of State

Security, and with him came many of those who had earlier opposed Mr Gierek's policies, among them General Moczar, the former Interior Minister in the Gomulka regime. The challenge for the Party under Mr Kania was twofold: to give in to the demands of the Gdansk agreement would not only weaken its authority within the country but also its credibility outside it, and particularly *vis-à-vis* the Soviet Union; and honouring the agreement, while strengthening the regime's internal support, would scarcely remedy Poland's pressing economic problems in the short run, and these would provide a constant source for potentially decisive unrest.

The Polish leadership therefore pursued two related courses of action, one internal and one external. Internally, while warning of the need for economic austerity, the Party sought to cede as little as possible to the new trade union force, while attempting to regain the initiative. In a ham-fisted attempt in October, a Warsaw court sought to insert into the union's statute a clause explicitly recognizing the political supremacy of the Communist Party. This was overruled by the Supreme Court on 11 November, thus avoiding a nation-wide general strike. But even with this legal victory, Union representatives claimed in early 1981 that only 3 out of the 21 provisions of the Gdansk agreement had yet been met. Mr Kania's government continued with its rearguard action, trying to claw back from the unions concessions made earlier. Externally, the new leadership sought above all to reassure the Soviet Union, and to receive in return the economic support of the USSR and other Warsaw Pact countries, as well as a modicum of military and political pressure which might help to promote compromise at home. In September, Mr Kania visited Moscow and appeared to have received President Brezhnev's support. In December the Soviet Union pledged a total of $1.1 billion in hard currency credits to Poland, and food supplies were received from her and from Poland's other socialist neighbours. (At the same time, Poland negotiated loans from West Germany of $150 million in January 1981, plus credits from other Western nations, and sought the renegotiation of her massive foreign indebtedness, some $7.5 billion of which was due to be paid in 1981.) Amid mounting criticism from the East German and Czech Communist Parties, an extraordinary summit

meeting of the Warsaw Pact was held on 5 December in Moscow; it appeared to conclude that the Polish leadership should be given more time to sort out the problems of the country.

The Soviet Perspective

There was reason to believe that the Soviet leadership, like its Polish counterpart, only gradually began to realize the potential seriousness of the Polish crisis. But when it did, it saw the danger above all in ideological terms. At the centre of the Soviet perception was the fact that an ideologically unacceptable group, the free trade unions, had achieved a degree of real power in Poland. Somehow or other this situation would have to be changed, the group weakened or emasculated, and full Party control acceptable to the Soviet Union re-established over the Polish industrial class.

The Soviet Union took an early decision to demonstrate her resolve and increase her options by a large-scale military build-up in and around the country. Most Soviet forces in the area remained at high levels of readiness after the Autumn Warsaw Pact exercises, especially those in East Germany and the western military districts of the USSR, as well as the two tank divisions stationed in Western Poland. Existing units were further strengthened, and exercises were held in East Germany, Czechoslovakia and the western USSR. By mid-November, a force of 25–30 divisions had been prepared to a high state of readiness in case the order should be given to invade Poland. Moreover, General Ivanovski, the former C-in-C of Soviet forces in East Germany, and one of the Soviet Army's most experienced senior commanders, was put in charge of the Belorussian military district, from where an invasion into Poland might be directed.

The option of invasion remained open, but it was clearly one that the Soviet leadership would choose only as a last resort. The risks would be considerable and, even if military success were assured, the political problems of post-invasion Poland would have to be met – under worse conditions than before. Among the most obvious risks was the possibility that the Polish armed forces would resist, or at least not co-operate – and this was clearly in the mind of the Soviet C-in-C of Warsaw Pact forces, Marshal Kulikov, who visited Warsaw in January 1981, probably to promote closer co-operation between Polish and Soviet forces. The Polish military leadership had for many years sought to portray the Polish Army as a national, not a Party institution, and during the events of the summer it had reportedly warned against any attempt to suppress the strike movement by military force. What if the Polish forces, with well-equipped and trained divisions, were, at least in part, to fight back against a Soviet invasion? The conflict could spread through Eastern Europe, or at least there would be manifestations of unrest and opposition elsewhere.

Even if a Soviet invasion were to overcome these difficulties, the subsequent military occupation would face overwhelming problems. As *Solidarity* leader Lech Walesa bluntly put it: 'Soviet tanks can occupy the country but they will not get it to work again'. The political leadership would be profoundly discredited, the Communist Party would be exposed as incompetent, and the economic problems would be even more intractable than before. If post-invasion Poland were to disintegrate politically, administratively and economically, how long would the Warsaw Pact be able to survive as an effective military and political organization?

Quite apart from implications for relations with the West, these were the risks that the Soviet leadership would have to weigh. It would also have to assess what risks would follow if the gains made by a non-Communist representative force in Poland were to be consolidated and the *de facto* sharing of power as it emerged in 1980, between the Party, trade unions and the Church, were to be legitimized through the passage of time. The dilemma for the Soviet Union was profound. There was little doubt that, if all other measures to re-establish Communist control in Poland should fail, she would not flinch from the option of military occupation. But it was equally clear that all other options would be exhausted before such a momentous and dangerous step. In the meantime, therefore, she would demonstrate rather than use her military power, in the hope that this might strengthen Mr Kania's efforts and instil in the Polish nation a respect for the limits of what could be tolerated by the Soviet neighbours. The Polish crisis was therefore likely to fester for some considerable time – and it would demand from the West more than a response to the possibility of invasion.

East European Uncertainties

While many features of the Polish crisis were peculiar to Poland's history and experience, others were of more general relevance to Eastern Europe as a whole. All the East European economies, not excluding that of the Soviet Union, had experienced bouts of economic unrest – including occasional strikes – in recent years. And, after a period of relative economic prosperity during the 1970s, in the 1980s all faced the prospect of reduced economic growth and steadily rising inflation – a phenomenon previously associated exclusively with the capitalist world. If the assumption was true that in the past political stability in the region had been bought with increasing economic prosperity, then all the East European regimes faced an uncertain future.

Not surprisingly, with the exception of Hungary, which gave a cautious welcome to the prospect of limited reform of the Polish economy, the rest of Eastern Europe took every precaution to prevent the spread of the 'Polish disease'. Both Soviet and Eastern European leaders began to pay more public attention to the role of the trade unions and the needs of the consumer in an obvious attempt to head off any potential dicontent in the work force. And in the months immediately following the Gdansk agreement Poland's neighbours, East Germany, Czechoslovakia and the Soviet Union, took measures to restrict travel to and from Poland, applied increasing pressure on Mr Kania to curtail the concessions made at Gdansk, and were soon promising full 'fraternal assistance' should the new Polish leadership not be up to its task.

But the roots of Eastern Europe's political and economic crises run deep, and can be traced back to the imposition on all these countries of an essentially Soviet model of a centrally planned economy and a monopolistic political system. Defending the power of the Communist Party has always had to take precedence over economic rationality. The result is a set of political systems more preoccupied with maintaining their own authority than with managing change in increasingly complex societies.

Whatever the outcome of the current crisis, Poland's economic plight, which sparked the political unrest, again placed the issue of economic reform in Eastern Europe on the political agenda. Despite national variations, like the Hungarian model of a semi-market economy, central planning has invariably resulted in inflexible production quotas, slowness in technological innovation and inefficient use of manpower and materials (Soviet figures admit that the Council for Mutual Economic Assistance (CMEA) countries use 40% more fuel and energy resources per comparable national income unit than the EEC countries). The result has been poor quality output and periodic scarcity of essential goods, particularly foodstuffs. Yet at the same time, and throughout the region, the regimes in power were coming under increasing pressure to deliver the fruits of 'developed socialism'. Attempts at radical reform, however, were bound to run into opposition from two very different directions: internal limitations and social concern.

On past experience (for instance, the Soviet Union in the 1960s and Poland in the 1970s), simply tinkering with the levers of central planning would not improve its workings significantly. Yet to go further and dismantle some of the political controls on the economy, risked challenging the monopolistic powers of the Communist Party – indeed this was one of the accusations levelled at Dubcek in 1968 and was thought to be one of the reasons for the retrenchment of the East German economic reform of the late 1960s and early 1970s. New Polish plans for the limited decentralization of economic decision-making and increased worker participation were likely in the end to suffer the same fate. So far only Hungary has managed to strike a happy medium, but her reform programme has also suffered periodic readjustment. It was this combination of economic timidity and political inertia which produced periodic bouts of acute instability in the region. And, as in Poland in 1980, inept economic mismanagement could fuel the flames of discontent.

Attempts in the 1970s to use imports of Western technology to evade the issue of economic reform, leap the technology gap and meet rising consumer demands did little in the short term to enhance economic efficiency, and instead added a heavy financial burden to already creaking economies. By the end of 1979 the CMEA's total external debt to the West

Table 1: CMEA Total External Debt

	Net Debt ($ m)	Debt service ratio
Bulgaria	3,356	58
Czechoslovakia	2,975	27
East Germany	9,891	36
Hungary	7,029	46
Poland	20,665	79
Romania	6,921	43
USSR	14,918	18
	65,755	

SOURCES: 'Euromarkets – 1980' *International Herald Tribune,* November 1980.

had exceeded $68 billion. Even before the 1980 upheavals, Poland, in particular, had run up against the practical limits of the credit Western financial institutions could prudently extend. In an attempt to reduce this burden all the European CMEA economies made considerable efforts in the late 1970s to rebalance their trade with the West. But this meant above all curtailing still needed imports.

The combined impact of slow economic growth and heavy external debt was exacerbated by Eastern Europe's growing energy crisis. With the exception of Romania, all the CMEA countries were heavily dependent on Soviet oil imports. Between 1975 and 1980 the cost of Eastern Europe's oil imports more than doubled (and by 1985 the price was likely to double again). This inevitably resulted in (a) a greater share of Eastern Europe's export capacity being diverted to meet the energy bill; (b) the obligatory commitment of scarce investment resources to help finance energy and raw materials extraction projects in the Soviet Union; and (c) fewer export goods being available to earn hard currency in the West. The Soviet Union informed her allies that she could not meet their growing demand for oil in the 1980s (already the CMEA can only meet 65% of its energy needs from its own sources; by the end of the decade the figure will be down to 50%), and the East European states would have to compete for their extra oil supplies on the yet more expensive world market.

As a result of these burdens, economic growth throughout Eastern Europe in 1979 fell

Table 2: Growth of CMEA Net Material Product 1979

	Actual (%)	Planned (%)
Bulgaria	6.5	7.0
Czechoslovakia	2.7	4.3
East Germany	4.0	4.3
Hungary	1.4	3–4
Poland	–2.0	2.8
Romania	6.2	8.8
USSR	2.0	4.3

SOURCE: Compiled from official figures.

below expected targets. Even the more successful economies, such as that of East Germany, would find it increasingly difficult to sustain even modest levels of growth over the coming decade. Hungarians were warned by their government to expect a halt, or even a decline, in living standards over the next few years, and while Romania and Bulgaria were still reporting respectable growth rates, they were the two countries with by far the lowest standards of living in Eastern Europe. On this basis, further bouts of economic discontent cannot be ruled out.

The Soviet Stake

The Soviet stake in Eastern Europe has grown, not diminished, with the passage of time. Eastern Europe's traditional role as the Soviet Union's security buffer has been enhanced, both symbolically and ideologically. The Sino-Soviet dispute and instability along her southern borders has reinforced the USSR's need for security in the West. But more importantly, the growing attraction of the Chinese and Euro-communist models of development, at the expense of the Soviet path, means that Eastern Europe is now the only region where the Soviet model has taken root, however inadequately.

The assumption in the 1960s that a more relaxed East–West relationship would induce the Soviet Union to tolerate the increasing independence of individual East European regimes underestimated this ideological and strategic stake. The invasion of Czechoslovakia in 1968 did not so much change the rules as make them more explicit: any potential change striking at the core of the political systems of Eastern Europe would run up against a Soviet veto. Yet although the Soviet Union will continue to wield ultimate power within the Warsaw Pact, Eastern Europe is not invulnerable to change. Some degree of flexibility is necessary to absorb political and economic strains and head off the kind of crisis which challenges the political authority of the Communist Parties in power, and which all but engulfed Poland in 1980.

Indeed, notwithstanding any 'resolution' of the Polish crisis, a glance back over the past decade of Soviet–East European relations shows that since 1968 Soviet efforts to re-establish a greater degree of discipline and control in Eastern Europe have met with only limited success. Renewed and largely successful Soviet pressure to promote integration at all levels, both within the CMEA and the Warsaw Pact, has not prevented the East Europeans from resisting the call to help finance Soviet foreign policy in the Third World, to increase defence spending and military integration, and to extend the commitments of the Warsaw Pact. And the differing East European responses to the Soviet invasion of Afghanistan likewise suggest divergent interests and perspectives within the Pact: East Germany, Bulgaria and Czechoslovakia fully supported the Soviet action, but Hungary and Poland, the two states most closely dependent on good relations with the West, were silently critical. Romania called openly for the withdrawal of Soviet troops.

Some degree of internal economic and political flexibility would, therefore, be essential to keep the growing problems within Eastern Europe from exceeding the limits of Soviet tolerance and thus threatening security in Europe as a whole. As the Polish events of 1980 underlined, the combination of economic inefficiency, ideological inflexibility and Soviet security concerns makes Eastern Europe a security concern for the continent.

YUGOSLAVIA AFTER TITO

While President Tito was alive few doubted that under his leadership the Yugoslav regime would vigorously resist not only an armed attack by a foreign power but also any attempt from within to undermine the system. But there were fears that without Tito, the charismatic, authoritative leader, the country could be threatened from within by a resurgence of nationalistic, separatist discontent and from outside by a Soviet armed attack or KGB-inspired plot to return Yugoslavia to the Soviet sphere of control which she left in 1948. When Tito died on 4 May 1980 these fears certainly did not come true; all the same the departure of the founder of post-war Yugoslavia did raise the question of whether the state and the political system he left behind would be able to hold together in the longer term.

Externally, the country's position remained good – in fact a good deal better than that of pre-war Yugoslavia had been. Communist Yugoslavia had established good relations with her three non-Communist neighbours, Austria, Italy and Greece, and, further afield with West Germany, France, Britain, the US and other Western states. President Carter spoke for all of them when, after the Venice summit in June, he visited Yugoslavia and pledged American support for her independence and territorial integrity. And the threat of a Warsaw Pact attack on Yugoslavia, always remote, seemed even more so after the Afghan and Polish crises. It was hard to imagine that, for the moment at least, the Soviet Union would want to open yet another difficult political front, this time in the Balkans. But the post-Tito leaders were taking no chances. The country's armed forces were being modernized, and the army was trying to diversify its sources of supply, among which the Soviet Union was still pre-eminent. While remaining vulnerable to Soviet attack, Yugoslavia traditionally has aimed to compel the Soviet Union at least to consider the cost of an invasion in casualties and in diplomatic damage done to East–West relations, plus the risk of an extension of the conflict. The latter, even more than the prospect of prolonged Yugoslav resistance, is probably the real deterrent against a Soviet attack (It remains an unanswered question whether, if attacked, the consumer-oriented

Yugoslavia of today would adapt to guerrilla war in quite the same way as the country's predominantly peasant population, which had little to lose anyhow, in 1941 and 1942).

Yugoslav–Soviet relations improved after Tito's death, largely because of the Soviet leaders' wish to do nothing that would alienate the still insecure collective leadership in Belgrade. This Soviet desire for good relations was probably also reflected in the improvement in Yugoslav–Bulgarian relations during 1980. (Bulgarian territorial aspirations in Macedonia, now part of Yugoslavia, give the Soviet Union a lever to use against Yugoslavia). Yugoslav foreign minister Josip Vrhovec visited Sofia in November 1980, and Bulgarian politburo member Alexander Lilov held talks with the (Macedonian) president of the Party Praesidium, Lazar Mojsov.

The Soviet bloc became of increasing economic importance for the hard-pressed Yugoslav economy – which faced inflation of nearly 40%, unemployment of 13% and persistent shortages. Real income fell by 7% in 1980, but Yugoslavia managed to reduce her huge $7.4-billion foreign trade deficit to $6 billion during the year, albeit mainly by increasing her exports to the USSR and other CMEA countries. In the autumn of 1980 the Soviet Union and Yugoslavia concluded a trade agreement which envisaged an increase in the value of their total trade from 16 billion roubles in 1976–80 to 26 billion in 1981–85. In September, the Soviet Union contracted to buy 96 ships, worth $1.3 billion, in the 1981–85 period. The general deterioration in East–West relations and the polarization in the Non-Aligned Movement made it more difficult for the country to maintain its middle position as a Communist but non-aligned nation.

The post-Tito collective leadership maintained cohesion, and the state Presidency and the presidency of the Party Praesidium were both rotated on schedule in May and October, although there was the beginning of a public debate over the Tito principle of rotating the top jobs annually among the Yugoslav republics. Paradoxically, the lack of an overt Soviet threat encouraged pressures for political liberalization, but there was little evidence of willingness by the leadership to make significant reforms. The hard economic times and choices ahead – over what economic liberalization actually meant – implied the risk of serious worker discontent. But in Yugoslavia, unlike Poland, that discontent appeared likely to re- main fragmented and without focus for the near future. Only if it coincided with a new out- break of serious divisions between national minorities would it pose a threat to the country's stability.

NUCLEAR WEAPONS IN EUROPE

Nuclear weapons have been in Europe, at Europe's request, throughout the post-war period, and France and Britain, with their national deterrence forces, have been the only modern nuclear weapon states in addition to the two super-powers. Yet familiarity has not meant wholehearted acceptance, and as new procurement decisions on nuclear weapons were taken in a climate of deteriorating East-West relations, so the controversy over nuclear issues surfaced again in European politics. The controversy had begun with the ill-fated hand- ling of the 'neutron bomb' issue in 1977–8, and had gained intensity with the debate on the state of the theatre nuclear balance and with the NATO decision of 12 December 1979 to proceed simultaneously with a major pro- gramme of modernizing its long-range theatre weapons and with a parallel arms-control effort. Meanwhile both Britain and France made clear their continuing interest in pre- serving their own 'independent' capabilities.

Britain

The British decision to purchase the *Trident* C-4 submarine-launched ballistic missile (SLBM) from the United States, announced on 15 July 1980, had been widely expected. It was known that the four existing nuclear-powered ballistic-missile submarines (SSBN) of the British strategic missile force would be show- ing their age by the 1990s, that only limited support and replacements for the *Polaris* mis- sile they carried could be forthcoming from the United States once her own *Polaris* force was phased out, and that it would take a decade or more to prepare a successor. The Conservative Government, which came to power in May 1979, had made clear its commitment to replace *Polaris*, and preparatory work on the alternative options had been undertaken dur- ing the previous Labour Government. The basic decision to opt for *Trident* was probably taken by late 1979, with agreement in principle

on the deal reached at the Summit meeting bet- ween President Carter and Prime Minister Thatcher in December 1979. From then on it was a question of working out the technical details, financial arrangements and the appro- priate timing of the final decisions and announcement.

The issue for Britain had long been 'how minimum can a minimum deterrent be?' Given her precarious economic position and lack of room for manoeuvre in spending on conventional forces, Britain needed a capabi- lity that was cheap as well as credible. She had spent less on her force than the other declared nuclear powers, by benefiting from American developments in delivery vehicles and concen- trating her efforts on one particular type of system. This approach had paid off. The *Polaris* force was not expensive to maintain (under 2% of the annual defence budget), and the boats on station at sea remained virtually invulnerable to surprise attack. This second- strike capability remains a primary virtue of a submarine-based force and Britain was not likely to trade it for any alternative launching platform. There was some interest in maintain- ing the existing *Polaris* missile, but it was felt that this would only delay the question of a long-term replacement while the short-term savings would be slight.

Despite its obvious attractions of adapt- ability and low unit cost, the submarine- launched strategic cruise missile never really presented a serious challenge to the ballistic missile. The main concern was that sub-sonic cruise missiles would have to face extensive Soviet defences, which were expected to be built up in response to American programmes, and a serious British cruise missile force would have to be able to saturate these defences in order to provide a credible deterrence. This would raise the numbers required, which would in turn raise the submarine require- ment. Taking into account ship-building capacity and submarine patrol patterns, the Ministry of Defence estimated that providing a capability equivalent to five SSBN with 16 *Trident* missiles each would require 11 cruise missile submarines, each carrying 80 missiles. The cruise missiles' shorter range and the length of time needed to fire them all would make the submarines vulnerable to interception, and the total force would be more expensive.

By contrast, ballistic missiles were the more attractive because defences against them remained circumscribed by the 1972 Anti-Ballistic Missile Treaty, at least so long as the Treaty remained in force. Even so, the limited Soviet ABM deployment around Moscow was considered sufficiently worrisome for a new warhead, known as *Chevaline*, to be developed for *Polaris* missiles. This system aimed to swamp the defences with a mixture of real warheads and decoys. Its existence, and the expenditure of £1 billion on it, was revealed by Defence Secretary Francis Pym in a Parliamentary debate in January 1980. The programme indicated both a belief that a minimum deterrent must at least be able to threaten Moscow and a clear preference for a ballistic delivery system.

The requirement for SLBM of proven capability, able to penetrate the Moscow defence and available for purchase from the United States made *Trident* the obvious choice. Even so, there was concern that the cost of a four-boat force (£4.5–5 billion, with another £600 million if a fifth boat were to be authorized) would represent a major additional strain on a defence budget already under severe pressure. The arrangement entered into by the British and the US Governments in July 1980 was, in financial terms, an attractive one for Britain. As with the 1963 *Polaris* agreement, she would receive American missiles and re-entry vehicles, building only the warheads herself; she would pay a 5% surcharge on the cost of missiles and re-entry vehicles as a contribution to American research and development costs. The cost of the entire programme was estimated in July at £5 billion, plus £600 million if a fifth boat were built. And yet, as the year progressed and Britain's economy entered its most severe crisis since the 1930s, the new programme, despite its attractions, came under increasing criticism. This underlined the view of many outside observers that the real ques-

tion was whether Britain could continue to afford the current range of her conventional contributions to Western defence and also maintain a modern and credible nuclear force of her own. The *Trident* programme thus looked likely to become increasingly controversial in the British political debate. While Labour governments in the past had supported the strategic nuclear programme, the support of future Labour governments was now much more uncertain, and so was the future of Britain's nuclear deterrent if Mrs Thatcher's Conservative government should lose power at the next elections.

France
France took a number of decisions to modernize her nuclear forces during the year, and these ran into few of the difficulties experienced in Britain. Rather, there seemed considerable agreement among the country's major political forces that French independence in nuclear matters should be maintained and the price of modernization paid. France had never accepted dependence on a single system for her nuclear deterrent, though like Britain she had come to rely heavily on her SSBN force. Her fifth boat entered service in 1980, and a sixth (carrying the new M-4 missile) was expected in 1985. The *Mirage* IV medium-range bomber force, which had provided one pillar of the French deterrent since 1963, was due to be phased out. This would leave the 18 intermediate-range ballistic missiles (IRBM) in Haute Provence as the only back-up to the SSBN force. In 1980 the first battery of nine IRBM received the new S-3 missile, with a longer range and higher yield, (3,000 km and 1 megaton) than the existing S-2 (1,000 km and 150 kilotons); the second battery was to replace the remaining nine S-2s in 1982.

Despite this modernization, there was increasing concern over the vulnerability of these fixed-base missiles to a surprise attack, particularly with the advent of the Soviet SS-20 and its accurate warheads. On 26 June President Giscard d'Estaing suggested that the most likely response to this problem was to introduce a new generation of mobile missiles in the early 1990s, though there were doubts whether France's defence resources would stretch to cover such a programme. The probable candidate for this role was a ballistic missile, designated S-X, with a range of some 4,500 km and three warheads of 50 kilotons each; about 100 of these would be carried on mobile trailers in reserved zones in suitable areas of the country. There appeared to be far less support for an alternative option, a cruise missile similar to that being developed in the United States. As in Britain, there was concern over the demands that likely Soviet air defences would impose on a cruise missile system and over whether France could independently develop and operate the requisite *Tercom* guidance system without inordinate expense.

On 26 June, President Giscard announced that work was well advanced on an enhanced radiation weapon (neutron bomb) and that a decision could be taken on production in 1982–3. This announcement came after a lively debate between his own party, the Union pour la Democratie Française (UDF) and the Gaullist Rassemblement pour la République (RPR). The Gaullists were supicious that neutron bombs, with their short range and battlefield role, represented a move to re-integrate France into NATO's military command, with its strategy of graduated response, instead of relying on the threat of massive and automatic nuclear retaliation to deter the Soviet Union from trespassing on French territory. However, the Gaullists would not find it easy to oppose neutron weapons, having long ago accepted the principle of tactical nuclear weapons by countenancing the short-range *Pluton* missile and its successor, *Hades*, currently under development.

Long-Range Theatre Nuclear Forces

In December 1979, after much debate, the North Atlantic Council had approved the deployment from December 1983 of 108 *Pershing* II medium-range ballistic missiles and 464 medium-range cruise missiles under American control in a number of West European countries. At the same time, the Council invited the Soviet Union to enter into bilateral negotiations with the United States to seek agreement on a mutual ceiling for medium-range nuclear forces in Europe. Developments in the Soviet arsenal during the year emphasized further the need to modernize existing nuclear systems in Western Europe, since they were rapidly becoming vulnerable to a Soviet pre-emptive attack. This in turn threatened NATO's doctrine, which, given the asymmetries of conventional forces in favour of the East,

had long envisaged the possible first use of nuclear weapons to underpin deterrence. Soviet nuclear deployments continued across the board: the SS-20 mobile IRBM, with its 3 150-kiloton warheads and 5,000-km range, was deployed at a rate of about one every five days, the *Backfire* bomber force grew by 25 during the year, and the introduction of new shorter-range theatre nuclear weapons (SS-21, SS-22 and SS-23) was well under way, each with greater range and accuracy than its predecessor (*Frog*, SS-12 and *Scud* B, respectively).

Yet the NATO programme was affected by both technical and, more important, political problems. The *Tomahawk* ground-launched cruisemissile encountered difficulties in test flights, particularly in the guidance and command-and-control. The December 1983 introduction date for the first of these systems was still likely to be met but could be pushed back further by technical problems. But it became clear that the full implementation of the programme would take up virtually the whole decade. While the 108 *Pershing* II missiles were expected to be in place by 1986 (all in West Germany), only 160 of the planned cruise missile force would be operational by then – and in the meantime Soviet deployments were likely to continue significantly beyond the 1979 level, to which this NATO programme was intended as a response.

But however serious the military aspect, the political problem – how to maintain support for the NATO modernization programme in European countries – seemed even more serious. At the outset, Belgium and Holland had been reluctant to accept the stationing of the new weapons on their soil. In December 1979 Belgium had promised a decision after six months, but a continuing government crisis caused delay, and a statement eventually issued in September was still equivocal, linking any eventual decision closely to progress in arms-control talks. In Holland, the domestic opposition that had led the Government to put off its decision until mid-1981 showed no sign of abating. Moreover, towards the end of the year opposition had also grown in those countries which had supported the programme. In October the annual conference of the British Labour Party passed resolutions which opposed the siting of cruise missiles in Britain and said that any party manifesto 'must include a

firm commitment opposing British participation in any defence policy based on the use
or threatened use of nuclear weapons'. And in
West Germany political forces on the left of the
ruling Social Democratic Party increasingly
voiced reservations about a programme which
the SPD congress in December 1979 had supported with an unprecedented 85% majority.

Two factors, above all, were behind this renewed controversy. The first was the traditional nuclear sensitivity of Europeans. This
had been allayed by the emphasis that nuclear
weapons were intended for deterrence and not
for use, but it broke out afresh in July when the
United States announced Presidential Directive No. 59, a nuclear doctrine which, though
underlining deterrence as the objective, described the need for more selective, limited
options in the use of nuclear weapons. There
were questions about some aspects of this doctrine for purely strategic reasons (discussed on
pp. 12, 44); but there was no doubt about its
adverse effect on European political sensi-
tivities. Soviet propaganda did not fail to pick
up the card which the Carter Administration
had handed to it. The second factor was the US
Senate's failure to ratify the SALT II agreement
and the success in the presidential elections of a
candidate who did not hide his suspicions of
arms-control talks with the Soviet Union. It
was feared that these developments would
leave only one part of NATO's December 1979
decision intact – the nuclear modernization –
while the parallel search for negotiated constraints on theatre nuclear forces would be
abandoned. It became clear once again how
much arms control, or at least the readiness to
negotiate, is, for good or ill, a condition for
pursuing nuclear arms programmes in the
European environment.

Arms-Control Soundings

Initially, the Soviet Union had pointedly
refused to consider the arms-control proposal
which accompanied NATO's modernization
decision. Her reaction had been outlined
before that decision: there could be negotiations on medium-range delivery systems only
if the West first cancelled or deferred its own
programme. Furthermore, since these negotiations would be between the United States and
the Soviet Union (and thus part of the SALT III
process), she argued that it was pointless to
negotiate while SALT II still had not been

ratified by the US Senate.

At the start of July, during Chancellor
Schmidt's visit to Moscow, the Soviet position
was substantially modified. The Soviet leaders
now agreed to new talks which, as required by
NATO, were to be bilateral with the United
States and within the SALT context. The talks
could start before ratification of SALT II, although this would still be a precondition for
the implementation of any new accord.

Three motives for this change in the Soviet
position seemed likely. First the original position was not tenable over the longer term.
Witholding consent to talks would not only fail
to slow the Western programme, it would also
allow the West to gain the moral high ground as
promoters of arms control. Secondly, the
USSR may have wanted to give a boost both to
Chancellor Schmidt, prior to his October
elections, and to the cause he had come to
represent of preserving detente in Europe
despite the deteriorating situation elsewhere.
For Schmidt had earlier demonstrated his
desire to get some arms-control effort under
way, both to ease pressure from Western European opponents of the December NATO
decision and to offer some glimmer of light in
the gloom over East–West relations. In April
he made an ambiguous call for a three year
moratorium on new missile deployments,
which touched off a minor row with Washington. Schmidt's language could be interpreted
either as a serious departure from the NATO
position or merely as pressure on the Soviet
Union to freeze her deployment while NATO
prepared its own programme, a move aimed
primarily at his own domestic political
audience. This proposal was initially rejected
by the Soviet Union.

The third motive, and one shared by many in
Western Europe, was keeping the United
States attached to some arms-control process.
This may explain the urgency with which the
Soviet Union moved to get the new talks under
way after July. In August President Brezhnev
wrote to NATO leaders complaining that they
were dragging their feet on the matter; in
September President Carter confirmed agree-
ment to open unconditional talks; and on 16
October the talks began at Geneva.

Nonetheless, even if the talks were under
way, there were still few indications of how,
once the American political situation had
settled, they could be brought to a successful

conclusion, broadly satisfactory to either side. (The negotiations are discussed in more detail on pp. 109–10.) Both sides agreed that the talks should be bilateral, within the framework of SALT III and should cover medium-range missiles. But beyond that the conceptions of the two sides diverged; in particular the Soviet Union returned to her long-standing insistence that talks on missiles had to be 'organically' combined with discussions of American forward-based systems (medium-range aircraft and perhaps missile-carrying submarines based in and around Europe and capable of hitting Soviet territory). So, while the opening of the talks confirmed that the USSR now accepted that her medium-range nuclear systems,

which could hit America's allies in Europe but not the US homeland, could no longer remain outside the framework of negotiation, progress would be slow and agreement difficult. Moreover, Ronald Reagan's victory in the US presidential election caused additional uncertainties. The new Secretary of State, Alexander Haig, made it clear that the new Administration would not want to be seen to turn its back on negotiated arms control, and this was reassuring to European governments. On the other hand, it was unlikely that the Reagan Administration would attach to the talks on theatre nuclear weapons the priority that the left-of-centre political forces in Europe were demanding.

CONFERENCE ON SECURITY AND CO-OPERATION IN EUROPE

Events in Poland and Afghanistan cast long shadows over the Madrid Conference held to review the implementation of the Helsinki Conference on Security and Co-operation in Europe (CSCE). The Review Conference opened one day later than scheduled on 12 November, but it seemed remarkable that it opened at all, given the bitter procedural wrangling which had taken place during the preparatory phase over the preceeding two months. The disputes had centred on the agenda and timetable for the Review Conference and on the commitment to a further Review Conference in due course.

The preparatory phase began on 9 September, and it became clear at the outset that the Western, neutral and non-aligned CSCE signatories all wanted a full review of past performance in implementing the Helsinki Final Act before going on to discuss any new proposals. By contrast, the Soviet Union and her allies suggested only a week to ten days for review. Despite forecasts of complete breakdown, a compromise put forward by a number of neutral states (Sweden, Austria, Cyprus and Yugoslavia) was accepted – but not until the Conference had resorted to stopping the clock at three minutes to midnight on 10 November. This compromise, which was largely regarded as a modest success for the West allowed for six weeks of review but with new proposals permitted to be tabled in the fifth week and 'explained' in the sixth. On the issue of the next

conference, the compromise reached was that the Main Conference should not close as planned on 5 March 1981 without a consensus to hold a further review meeting – probably in Romania in 1983.

Long before the Main Conference convened it had become clear that, although far from Europe, Afghanistan would come to dominate the first phase. In the words of American Secretary of State Muskie: 'This is a way for us to raise the Afghanistan issue and to challenge the Soviets' performance'. Nor, when the Conference did convene, did the Western group lack solidarity. Delegate after delegate cited the Soviet invasion of Afghanistan in their plenary statements. The Soviet Union, though clearly embarrassed, continued to assert, in the words of her chief representative, Leonid Ilychev, that 'Afghanistan has nothing to do with this Conference' and fell back on the unconvincing technical defence that CSCE was not a treaty, so there was no legal obligation to abide by the undertakings given at Helsinki. Though issuing no ultimata, the Co-Chairman of the US Delegation, Max Kampleman, argued that Soviet proposals for military detente in Europe would only be considered if there were clear signs of a Soviet withdrawal from Afghanistan. Since few believed that the Soviet Union would give such undertakings, this seemed a recipe for stalemate. Yet no party – and certainly not the Soviet Union – wished to be the cause of total breakdown. Moreover, so long as the Conference was in session, a Soviet military move against Poland was less likely. It would considerably increase the costs to the USSR of intervening militarily in Poland's affairs if she was at the same time discussing in Madrid how to lessen tension in Europe.

By the Christmas recess, some 70 proposals had been tabled, but there were few signs of convergence. There had been a number of statements from all sides beforehand that confidence-building measures (CBM) should be extended in scope, and there appeared to be a superficial identity of view as to the directions in which they should be developed. However, there remained very wide differences over where and how this should be done. The Eastern side, via the Polish Delegation, tabled the Soviet favourite: a Conference on Military Detente and Disarmament in Europe, to be held in Warsaw in October 1981 (and, it was assumed, outside the CSCE process). France then tabled a proposal which had been widely circulated among Western participants in the preceeding months and more or less accepted, even if the US was less than enthusiastic. This emphasized the extension of CBM in a first phase and conventional arms reductions in a susequent phase. It differed from Eastern proposals in three important respects: it would be closely tied to the CSCE process; it would make CBM binding and more verifiable; and it would include all of the western USSR up to the Urals, instead of a narrow 250-km strip along her western borders. A third proposal was tabled by Yugoslavia. This had a pronounced nuclear emphasis and called for both more CBM, military 'disengagement' and a zonal approach to reductions. Under it nuclear weapons would be removed from Europe, and, like the French proposal, it was tied to CSCE. Romania argued in favour of declarations 'to refrain from the use of force', but the West indicated that it had little use for rhetorical statements, seeking instead concrete ways of reducing the dangers of surprise attack.

In spite of this plethora of proposals for 'military detente', it was doubtful whether another conference would advance matters significantly in the field of arms control. Nor was it likely to satisfy those who, while sceptical about any substantive progress, nevertheless hoped that creating new fora for the East–West dialogue would re-establish the much weakened detente in Europe. Rather, these proposals seemed to belong to an earlier period when political detente was widely assumed and military constraints appeared to be a natural follow-up. It was clear that this underlying assumption would have to be re-examined, although President Brezhnev's announcement in February 1981 that the Soviet Union would accept the extension of the CBM to all of the European part of the country, in exchange for unspecified extensions on the Western side removed one obstacle to the convening of a new conference.

AFRICA

The emergence and relatively peaceful evolution of the new state of Zimbabwe in 1980 brought a degree of stablity to southern Africa which it had not known for a decade. As the Mugabe government moved promptly to deal with its most critical problems, the chances of effective armed intervention in its internal affairs rapidly faded. The advent of peace denied both the Soviet Union and South Africa an important source of leverage over southern African developments. Moreover, since Zimbabwe's geographic and economic position made her a keystone of the region, her independence provided the impetus for a regional development plan bringing the black-ruled countries of southern Africa closer together.

Namibia remained the region's most serious unresolved issue. The collapse of the four-year-old Western peace inititaive early in 1981 left the opposing parties generally agreed on the terms of a future settlement; but South Africa was as yet unwilling to risk Nambia's moderate internal parties in a free election with the Namibian nationalist group, SWAPO.

Elsewhere in Africa, the Horn continued to experience chronic tensions and long-term instability, despite the success of Col. Mengistu's ruling *Dergue* in consolidating its power in Ethiopia. Soviet- and Cuban-supported military campaigns in Eritrea and the Ogaden largely succeeded in pacifying both areas for the time being, but national aspirations there were only temporarily dampened. Somalia, despite military defeat in the Ogaden and staggering economic and refugee problems, had yet to renounce her irridentist claims against both Ethiopia and Kenya. In the Sahara, Libya's sudden lunge into the conflict in Chad sharply increased tensions in an already unstable region. Chad, inherently important as a possible source of uranium, had been a major buffer state between the Arab north and the more important French client states, like the Ivory Coast. Nigeria, with her own dissident Muslim problem in the north, was also alarmed by Libya's expansionist moves, but Franco-Nigerian co-operation to meet this threat had yet to emerge.

SETTLEMENT IN ZIMBABWE

The 'miracle at Lancaster House' – the December 1979 Rhodesian peace settlement which ended seven years of increasingly bloody guerrilla war – was followed by a series of minor miracles no less remarkable. A fragile cease-fire held; some 30,000 armed guerrillas gathered peaceably in specified assembly camps; 2.7 million black voters (over 93% of those eligible), brought an air of goodwill and patience to a remarkably quiet election. Moreover, despite the shock among whites generally, and among Robert Mugabe's political opponents, at his sweeping victory in the polls, there was no move to overturn the election results. No coup was attempted, none of the disparate armed groups tried to reopen hostilities, and, with few exceptions, Zimbabwe's remaining 220,000 whites decided to stay on and give the new government a chance.

The transition itself was surprisingly smooth. Mr Mugabe moved swiftly and easily to form a coalition government, drawn from his own ZANU(PF) party and the PF party of his main electoral adversary Joshua Nkomo, and to tackle the problems awaiting him. From a number of early policy statements and key personnel appointments it was evident that he had chosen a path of moderation and conciliation internally, although he made no secret of his mission ultimately to bring about deep changes in Zimbabwean society. Moderation was also the keynote in foreign affairs, with conciliatory statements on policy toward South Africa. Indeed, Mr Mugabe's declaration of non-alignment, and his move to strengthen Zimbabwe's links with Britain, the EEC, the Commonwealth and the world market, left only one group out in the cold: the Soviet bloc, to whom he and his ZANU(PF) party owed nothing.

The new government faced a series of severe and inter-related problems, however. First, it had to keep the smouldering hostility between the followers of Mr Mugabe and Mr Nkomo from flaring up. This was all the more important because the government coalition included two opposing political parties with armed guerrillas loyal to each. Second, places had to be found in the economy or the new national army for these ex-guerrillas (more than 30,000 of them), most of whom were idle and increasingly bored with life in the camps where they had been assembled since the beginning of 1980. Third, more than a million Zimbabwe civilians displaced by the war had to be re-settled, and jobs had to be found for those seeking work. Fourth, the economic and social infrastructure – particularly in the devastated countryside, where over 80% of Zimbabwe's people had lived and worked before the war – had to be restored. This implied, among other things, large initial injections of foreign assistance if the new state were to succeed economically and so gain time to resolve its other problems. Fifth, the exodus of skilled whites had to be minimized. Such a catalogue of problems was bound to tax both the internal structure of the young state and the capability of Mugabe leadership over the next few years.

The Cease-fire
On 28 December 1979 a cease-fire took effect, and a Commonwealth Monitoring Force (CMF) of 1,500 troops – drawn from Britain, Australia, New Zealand, Kenya and Fiji – began overseeing the arrival of guerrillas at reception points and their conduct into 16 assembly camps scattered through the country. The guerrillas, suspicious of the idea of being concentrated in camps, were slow in responding, but within a few days after the 4 January assembly deadline 18,500 had reported, bringing little but their weapons. This placed a tremendous strain on CMF logistics: food, blankets, utensils and clothing were required ultimately for a substantially larger number of guerrillas than had been expected.

Meanwhile Lord Soames, who had assumed colonial authority as Governor-General on 21 December, grew concerned over reports of mounting lawlessness and large guerrilla concentrations hiding in the bush near the Mozambique border. On 6 January he announced that he had authorized the Rhodesian Army to keep law and order. This move, together with the continuing presence of South African military units inside Rhodesia, led to a rift between the Colonial administration in Salisbury, on the one hand, and the two guerrilla movements and some of the five 'Front-Line' states (Angola, Botswana, Mozambique, Tanzania and Zambia) on the other.

This rift widened as campaigning got under way for the three-day elections due to begin on 27 February. Lord Soames' office reported an alarming rise in political intimidation and cease-fire violations, and charged Mr Mugabe's forces with prime responsibility. By mid-February the situation appeared sufficiently serious for the Governor-General to threaten to ban candidates and meetings, to forbid parties to campaign, and to call off elections in any district where he felt intimidation had made free elections impossible.

But Mr Mugabe and the Front-Line leaders, particularly President Nyerere of Tanzania, also had serious complaints. They objected to the freedom of movement allowed to the Rhodesian forces and the auxiliaries loyal to Bishop Muzorewa and his UANC party, while the Patriotic Front guerrillas were confined to assembly camps. After two attempts on his life, Mr Mugabe threatened to renounce the cease-fire unless the Rhodesian forces were confined to barracks. And Mr Nyerere threatened to break relations with Britain because of her alleged violations of the Lancaster House agreement. The Governor-General held his ground, however, and even issued a massive call-up of Rhodesian troops and police to keep the peace during the voting. By the time the Commonwealth force began its phased withdrawal on 3 March Lord Soames had fielded some 24,000 Rhodesian soldiers and police, plus 90,000 territorial and police reserves.

The Elections
Elections for the white seats in Parliament took place on 14 February and gave Ian Smith's Rhodesian Front a clean sweep and control of all twenty. Elections for the eighty black seats were a more complex matter and fraught with danger, particularly for Lord Soames, who would have to decide whom to ask to form the new government. While it was generally conceded that Robert Mugabe's ZANU(PF) would win more seats than either of the other two major parties – Joshua Nkomo's PF and Abel Muzorewa's UANC – Mugabe was widely perceived as a radical Marxist and the least accept-

able leader to Rhodesian whites and moderate blacks. There were fears that his selection as Prime Minister would lead to a massive white exodus, if not to civil war or a South-African supported coup. In the event, Lord Soames was saved an agonizing decision: Mr Mugabe's ZANU(PF) swept 57 of the 80 black parliamentary seats to the PF's 20 and the UANC's 3. The results astonished almost everyone, including Mr Mugabe's political opponents, most white Rhodesians, and South Africa. Even Mr Mugabe himself seemed to have expected a narrower victory.

The elections were remarkably peaceable, helped in no small part by exemplary planning and logistics and the presence at polling sites of British police constables in uniform. Some people had to walk miles to polling-stations and wait several hours in long queues to vote, yet a 'holiday atmosphere' was widely reported. The final word lay with an eleven-member Commonwealth Observer Group, which spent seven weeks in Rhodesia observing the organization and conduct of the elections. Though critical of many aspects, it sympathized with the Governor-General, who 'had supreme authority but few instruments of his own'. In the circumstances, the Group's overall assessment was a clear endorsement of the process:

> Overall there was a very substantial level of peaceful political activity by all the parties, and sufficient freedom of movement, assembly, and expression to enable the parties to put the case to the electorate. We were satisifed that the people would be going to the polls with an appreciation of the positions of the various parties, confident for the most part in the secrecy of ballot and thus capable of making an informed choice according to their best judgment.

Independence: the First Year

On 5 March – the day after the election results were announced – Mr Mugabe invited Mr Nkomo to join forces with ZANU(PF) in a coalition government. He also asked General Walls, commander of the Rhodesian security forces during the war, to take charge of integrating guerrillas and regular Rhodesian forces into a Zimbabwe National Army. Within a week he had named his cabinet, applied for Commonwealth membership, pledged to uphold the constitution, and promised there would be no victimization or nationalization of private property. He also asked Britain to help train the army and air force.

Whites were stunned by these moderate and conciliatory moves and reassured by his appointment of three respected whites to important cabinet posts and the retention of Gen. Walls. The Prime Minister's black political opponents had less reason to be pleased. Of 23 cabinet portfolios, 17 went to Mr Mugabe' party, along with 11 out of 13 deputy ministerial posts, while four, mostly minor, ministries went to Mr Nkomo's (Mr Nkomo himself was given a somewhat emasculated Ministry of Home Affairs). Bishop Muzorewa and his party were left out in the cold.

By independence day, 17 April, Zimbabwe was settling down to normal peacetime pursuits. But already the inheritance of seven years of war had emerged as a serious and long-term problem for the new government. More than 250,000 families – a million people – displaced by the war had fled, either to neighbouring countries or to squatter settlements around the country's cities. Land resettlement for this (largely agricultural) mass of people therefore became a first priority. But this would require large inputs of foreign aid, because, although Zimbabwe had the necessary conditions to make herself more than self-sufficient in food production, she lacked the wherewithal to get started: money for the purchase of seed, fertilizer, tools, cattle and (above all) land. A third of black-owned cattle, including oxen needed for ploughing had been lost during the war, and the rural infrastructure was a shambles, with the destruction of cattle dips and the cessation of spraying during the war leading to a resurgence of cattle and crop diseases.

Other priorities were job creation and the restoration of medical and educational services. Between 1976 and 1979, as sanctions finally began to bite, black unemployment grew by 225,000, and over half the regular black work force was jobless. Yet, while the country's high birth rate (over 3.5%) meant sharp increases in the number of school age children and in the labour force, the number of jobs available had shrunk and three-quarters of the schools had been destroyed or closed by the war. Medical services, which had been good before the war, had virtually collapsed except in urban centres, and malaria, tuberculosis, bilharzia and other diseases had risen sharply.

In facing these problems Mr Mugabe tried to strike a careful balance between excessive black expectations and Zimbabwe's limited capacity to respond. Early successes were encouraging, and the enactment of a variable minimum wage, together with government efforts to reorganize the country's splintered trade unions, led to a tapering off of the labour unrest that had accompanied independence. Other measures included a sharp cut in the sales tax on necessities and a programme to build 167,000 housing units. Most important was the government's plan, announced in November, to take over vacant and unused white farmland, estimated to amount to some 6 million acres, for resettlement by black farmers. Since the government had no funds with which to compensate former owners, it was looking to foreign aid donors to help out – an expectation based on Britain's undertaking at the Lancaster House talks to help promote a multi-national fund for this purpose – and by October 1980 foreign aid commitments for the next two or three years (excluding military assistance) totalled roughly $150 million.

Additional economic measures have been taken to strengthen domestic market forces and to link Zimbabwe closely to the Western world's economic system. The government has declared that it will repay its foreign debts, apparently including those due to South Africa for its aid to the Smith regime.

A rise in the government's support price for grain led to a large increase in the acreage planted and a 1981 crop estimate of up to half a million tons. In September Zimbabwe joined the International Monetary Fund, and in November she signed the Lomé Convention, thus gaining preferred access to EEC markets for her sugar, tobacco and beef. By the middle of the year manufacturing was operating almost at full capacity, output was expected to rise by 15%, and employment probably grew by 50,000 during the year. Economic growth, originally forecast at 4% looked more like reaching 6% as the year drew to a close, and the 1980 maize crop was up by 56% and cotton by 10%. The buoyant domestic economy was accompanied by an impressive 36% rise in exports and growing foreign private investment.

What posed the gravest threat to Zimbabwe's peace and stability, however, was the growing antagonism and armed violence between ZANLA and ZIPRA – the ex-guerrilla armies of Mr Mugabe and Mr Nkomo respectively. Still heavily armed, increasingly restless with nothing to do in their separate camps throughout the country, both forces were ready for a fight, and Mr Nkomo's forces held the added grudge of seeing their party largely excluded from the spoils of victory. In mid-September factional fighting broke out in several of Salisbury's black townships. In November, scuffles occurred during an inflammatory ZANU(PF) political rally deep inside Nkomo country near Bulawayo, after which ZIPRA forces opened a mortar and rocket attack from their camp against the ZANLA camp half a mile away. By the time the new national army had restored order three days later, 55 people had been killed and over 500 wounded, most of them civilians caught in crossfire. The most serious violence broke out in mid-February 1981, after Mr Nkomo's demotion to a lesser cabinet post. Fighting between ZIPRA and ZANLA members of an integrated army battalion broke out in a beer hall, and the situation quickly deteriorated. Disgruntled ZIPRA soldiers in three of Zimbabwe's twelve amalgamated army battalions took up arms against ZANLA troops. Regular units of the Rhodesian African Rifles restored an uneasy calm a week later; but there were 300 dead and at least as many wounded. Fighting was largely confined to several army camps on the outskirts of Bulawayo and Gwelo, but Bulawayo was closed down for a couple of days. Fractious ZIPRA groups were disarmed and sent to separate encampments.

Mr Mugabe and Mr Nkomo recognized the dangers of escalating violence. Both publicly reaffirmed their support for the coalition, and both took steps to calm their followers. A serious problem for Mr Nkomo, however, was the flaking away of his support among ZIPRA followers, who seemed to be split into those still loyal to him and those disaffected by his failure in the struggle for power.

The ZANU(PF)–ZIPRA violence was closely tied to two basic problems facing Mr Mugabe. The first was the programme to merge the two ex-guerrilla forces into the new national army. By mid-summer a new mixed battalion was being formed every few weeks, and some 10,000 men had been integrated by early 1981. Troubles in three of these battalions (one of which split completely apart during the February violence) undoubtedly slowed the amalgamation and raised serious doubts about the process itself. His other urgent problem was to establish greater control over his own party. He had recently taken steps to muzzle several radical ZANU(PF) officials and cabinet ministers whose threatening and inflammatory statements had alarmed Zimbabwe's white population and infuriated Mr Nkomo's supporters. Although such outbursts did not reflect current government policy, they struck a sympathetic chord among the ZANU(PF) rank and file.

Two specific incidents were particularly damaging: the Tekere case, and the resignation of General Walls. In July General Walls, who had commanded Rhodesia's counter-insurgency effort during the war, unexpectedly resigned as Commander of Zimbabwe's armed forces. In an unfortunate television interview, he not only expressed his disquiet at 'present political conditions' but also acknowledged that he had urged Mrs Thatcher to annul the March election results when it had become clear that Mr Mugabe had won. His resignation added to white apprehensions, and his public remarks seriously embarrassed Mr Mugabe. In August Edgar Tekere, Minister of Manpower and Secretary-General of ZANU(PF) admitted murdering a white farmer while leading a punitive attack on some former ZIPRA guerrillas. After an acrimonious trial, during which the outspoken Mr Tekere largely succeeded in portraying his case as a blacks-versus-whites issue, he was acquitted on a technicality. His followers saw the verdict as a triumph while whites regarded it as ominous.

Prospects

In spite of the outbreak of factional violence in February, the prospects for political stability during 1981 looked reasonably good. Frictions between the Mugabe and Nkomo parties and their constituencies would remain, however, and the coalition would be delicate. From recent African experience, the existing political mix – a single majority party in coalition with the most important minority party – seemed a more stable arrangement than a shifting coalition among many small parties, *provided* the dominant party allowed its minority partner a proportionate share of offices and other rewards. Whether the Mugabe Administration would find ways gradually to win the support of the Nkomo people, or whether it would allow them to remain a disaffected minority, remained one of the key questions in Zimbabwe's future.

Zimbabwe's rapid economic recovery gave the government at least a breathing space in which to demonstrate progress in the longer-term economic and social transformation to which it is pledged. No political figure had yet emerged to challenge Mr Mugabe's programme for building a multi-racial society on the basis of a mixed economy and close economic and military ties to the West. Whether in time Mr Mugabe would be forced towards a more radical position would depend on his skills as a political leader, and on how far Western countries and international institutions supported Zimbabwe in the urgent task of reconstruction.

STALEMATE IN NAMIBIA

In 1980 the South African Government continued its diplomatic balancing act in Namibia. It seemed to be convinced, both for internal and external reasons, that it must get rid of the Namibia problem and that – if South Africa was to avoid an escalation of guerrilla warfare – the solution had to be acceptable to the outside world. An internal settlement would not do. Yet the South African leadership was also convinced that a free election would almost certainly lead to a victory for the South-West African People's Organization (SWAPO): a result which neither the South African government nor the white population, and particu-

larly not the whites in Namibia, were as yet prepared to accept.

The Western powers and many African states had long wanted to avoid a showdown in the UN Security Council over sanctions against South Africa. Both groups also wanted to see an end to the fighting which, though so far at a fairly low intensity, clearly had the potential for erupting into a larger conflict involving outside countries. Pretoria correctly judged that these factors made the West and the UN eager to get South Africa's signature on a peace settlement and to avoid the collapse of their painstaking initiative. South Africa therefore seemed to be in a position to control the pace and direction of talks in Namibia during the past three years while she pursued a three-pronged strategy. The first prong was to stretch out preliminary talks and postpone as long as possible the hard negotiations over UN Resolutions 385 and 435, which called for a cease-fire, a transition period and the election of a constituent assembly, all under UN supervision. The second, was to move rapidly to strengthen those political forces in Namibia opposed to SWAPO and to produce greater unity and political consensus among Namibia's diverse ethnic groups – a goal which had hitherto proved elusive. The third prong was to weaken SWAPO militarily, and hence politically, in the hope of forcing it to settle on terms more favourable to South Africa.

Despite its successful diplomacy, the South African leadership had so far failed in a larger sense. For, although the Mugabe victory in Zimbabwe and the crushing defeat of the internal parties there apparently convinced South Africa's leaders that a SWAPO electoral victory in Namibia was inevitable, they had yet to face up to this contingency. Hard decisions had been put off, and nothing had been done to prepare South Africa's white electorate for a SWAPO-dominated government in Namibia.

During the first part of 1980 proposals and counter-proposals centered on the issue of establishing a demilitarized zone (DMZ), sixty miles wide, straddling the Namibia-Angola border. The idea of a DMZ, first suggested by the late President Neto of Angola, was acceptable to both sides in principle, but each had reservations. South Africa felt that the proposed UN force of 7,500 was too small to monitor a cease-fire in a zone 60 miles wide and 700 miles long. She also wanted to keep 40 of her military bases in the DMZ and called for the UN to monitor SWAPO bases in Angola and Zambia during the cease-fire – a demand which both countries flatly rejected. SWAPO, for its part, demanded the right to have military bases inside Namibia.

By the summer the gap had narrowed substantially. SWAPO, under pressure from Angola and Zambia, dropped its demand for bases inside Namibia, and South African Prime Minister Piet Botha agreed to only 20 bases in the DMZ, and dropped his demand that SWAPO should be monitored in its sanctuaries. UN Secretary-General Waldheim responded in a letter of 20 June, acknowledged South Africa's remaining reservations (chiefly on the question of the UN's impartiality) and spelled out ZambNan and Angolan assurances that no SWAPO infiltration would be allowed during a cease-fire. A few days later South Africa said that she was pondering Mr Waldheim's letter – and there matters sttood for the next two months.

Meanwhile a dramatic rise in military and political activity had occurred inside Namibia. SWAPO infiltration suddenly increased in early 1980. Attacks on power lines had blacked out Namibia a half-dozen times by April, and in May a SWAPO mortar attack destroyed several military aircraft at the South African base at Ondangwa. South African forces reportedly killed 90 guerrillas a month inside Namibia, as against 13 a month in 1979. The deaths of Europeans, civilian and military, each week, and the need to move oil tankers across the country in armed convoys, had brought the 'operational zone' to the suburbs of Windhoek by summer.

South Africa responded by intensifying her counter-insurgency. A major attack by mobile ground units was launched inside Angola on 9 June. In four days of fighting and mopping up South Africa calimed to have destroyed SWAPO's operational headquarters and to have killed 200 SWAPO personnel and captured 100 tons of equipment; 16 South African troops were reported killed. This attack was undoubtedly a serious setback for SWAPO.

Taking to heart the lesson of the defeat of Muzorewa's 'do-nothing' government in the Zimbabwe elections in March, South Africa's leaders also accelerated the pace of political change inside Namibia. The Botha government placed all its bets on kthe multi-racial Democratic Turnhalle Alliance (DTA) becoming the dominant force in Namibian political life and facing SWAPO in the future struggle for power. But if the DTA were to avoid the fate of the Muzorewa government, it must, at the very least, be seen to represent a broad political consensus,and to be capable of running the territory's affairs independently of Pretoria. Accordingly, South Africa's Administrator General for Namibia announced on 30 May that executive powers would be granted to the National Assembly – the DTA-dominated legislature whose members had been chosen in a December 1978 general election (in which SWAPO did not take part). On 1 July a Council of Ministers chaired by Dirk Mudge, head of the DTA, was nominated and sworn in. It was to administer some 20 government departments, including a Department of Defence to be established in Windhoek, and its first act was to promulgate a law establishing compulsory military service to begin in 1981. In practice, however, defence and foreign affairs remained under South African control, as exercised by her Administrator General, who was also commander of all troops operating in Namibia. In July racial discrimination in public accommodations and urban residential areas was made illegal and punishable by fine. And on 1 September control of the police passed to the Namibian National Assembly.

Diplomatic activity resumed on 30 August, when South Africa's Foreign Minister finally responded to Mr Waldheim's letter of 20 June. South Africa was prepared to discuss the composition of the UN Transition Assistance Group (UNTAG) and the status of forces, on two conditions: the UN must first demonstrate its impartiality on Namibia, and the internal parties must be included in all subsequent talks. A UN team, headed by Brian Urquhart, Deputy Secretary-General, visited Pretoria in late October ot discuss these terms.

As she had done on previous occasions when she was about to make concessions, South Africa bared her claws, and on the day the team arrived South African forces launched a heavy attack against SWAPO bases inside Angola – the first since June. This show of aggressiveness was probably designed as much to impress Mr Botha's right-wing opposition to a UN settlement as to demoralize SWAPO and its supporters. The UN team offered to end UN financial support for SWAPO's political and propaganda activities, and to terminate the ambivalent position of Mr Martti Ahtisaari as both the (neutral) UN Special Representative for Namibia and the Commissioner for Namibia (a post which, South Africa felt, tilted towards SWAPO). South Africa reiterated an earlier demand that the Secretary-General should dissociate himself from the long-standing UN recognition of SWAPO as the sole and authentic representative of the Namibian people. After a week it was clear that the talks, which officially totalled only 4–6 hours, had failed. However, a new deal appeared to be in the making: South Africa offered (secretly) to accept March 1981 as the starting date for implementing the UN

plan and to meet with SWAPO to work out details. But these concessions were dependent on SWAPO's agreeing to all-party talks at which the internal Namibian parties would play an active role (presumably as a separate delegation from South Africa's, although this was not clear).

In the late autumn South African policy suffered two setbacks, one of them serious. The so-called 'second-tier' elections, to the largely powerless ethnic legislative assemblies in Namibia, took place in mid-November. The white Legislative Assembly had long been dominated by AKTUR, the party of right-wing Afrikaners opposed to a multi-racial Namibia. The elections were therefore seen as a test of public opinion which, if the multi-racial DTA won, would demonstrate white support for a unitary state and the principle of one man, one vote. In the event, however, AKTUR won 56% of the vote, and, despite its vigorous electoral campaign, the DTA ended up with 7 seats to AKTUR's 11: exactly what it had held before. A second, less serious, setback was Foreign Minister Roelof Botha's failure to win support for South Africa's position during his brief tour of major European capitals in early November. By his own admission, he met with tough talking from Britain, West Germany and France, all of whom told him South Africa must stop stalling and get on with implementing the UN plan.

On 24 November Mr Waldheim announced that 'pre-implementation talks' would take place in January 1981, with delegations from SWAPO, the DTA and the South African Government taking part, and the 'Front-Line' states, the 'Western Five' Contact Group and the Organization of African Unity sending observers. Even before the conference opened it was clear that there were wide differences over how it would function and what it was to accomplish. South Africa failed in her bid to have the internal parties recognized as a separate delegation and to assume an observer role for herself. When the conference opened in Geneva on 7 January 1981 Dirk Mudge, leader of the internal DTA group, nonetheless played an active role for the South African side of the table. Reiterating the South African charge of UN bias in favour of SWAPO, he set out seven conditions which the UN would have to fulfil to 'regain the confidence of the Namibian people'. These included rescinding the General Assembly resolution naming SWAPO as the sole and authentic representative of the Namibian people, withdrawing SWAPO's permanent observer status at the UN, and ending UN financing of SWAPO activities. SWAPO, in contrast, was conciliatory, and stated its readiness to sign an immediate cease-fire.

The failure of the Conference was sealed at a special meeting on 11 January at which the 'Western Five' asked Mr Mudge if he would agree to a UN resolution which would authorize $400 million for the UN peace-keeping force, rescind SWAPO's special UN status and commit the UN to treat all parties equally in an election. His reply was to ask for a delay of 18 months. Three days later the head of South Africa's delegation formally put paid to the Conference with a brief statement that it was 'premature' to start implementing the UN plan. This meant that, for the first time in nearly four years, there was no machinery in motion in the search for an international settlement in Namibia. It left South Africa with an elusive 'internal solution' and the prospect of intensified guerrilla war in Namibia – a war that had little popularity among her own population, which provided most of the troops for the counter-insurgency effort.

Despite the deadlock, however, the contours of a possible final settlement had become clearer – and in large part accepted. South African objections appeared to be not so much to the substance as to the atmospherics and imminence of the UN plan. Whether South Africa would soon decide to run the risk of accepting a settlement under which SWAPO would probably win power remained to be seen. In time, the internal Namibian parties might decide to risk an election, thus taking the decision (and blame) out of her hands, but in the meantime, with a general election scheduled for the spring of 1981, South Africa was unlikely to give much attention to Namibia before the middle of the year.

THE HORN OF AFRICA

As Ethiopia's ruling *Dergue* and its leader, Col. Mengistu, entered their seventh year in power in September, it was clear they had consolidated their internal position and had successfully contained both secessionist and Somali pressures. By the middle of 1980 Mengistu was the unquestioned 'strong man' of Ethiopia, exercising powers comparable to those wielded by the late Emperor Haile Selassie. Widespread smouldering discontent was reported, yet organized opposition in the capital was to all appearances crushed, and the illegal political parties active only a year or two before had been reduced to underground cabals. Despite the continued detention of numerous political prisoners, the atmosphere in Addis Ababa was far more relaxed than during the 'Red Terror' of 1977–8. Government policy favoured the establishment of a monolithic nation-wide socialist party; but by the end of the year this was still only in the planning stage. Relations between Ethiopia and the Soviet Union remained cordial, as the *Dergue* lent diplomatic support to the Soviet invasion of Afghanistan and negotiated with a high-level Soviet naval delegation over greater accommodation for Soviet vessels at Ethiopia's ports.

The Somali regime of Maj.-Gen. Mohamed Siad Barre, though smarting from its earlier defeats and the forced withdrawal of its forces from Ethiopia as well as the resultant massive influx of refugees, still survived. Economic problems were increasingly pressing, police repression continued, and a state of emergency was imposed on 21 October. Yet President Barre had not relinquished his country's commitment to a greater Somali state (to incorporate Somali-populated areas of eastern Ethiopia, northern Kenya and most of Djibouti), and so support for Western Somalia Liberation Front (WSLF) military operations in the Ogaden area of Ethiopia was maintained. But Somali irredentist policies, which ran counter to the Organization of African Unity's position on the sanctity of national boundaries, left Somalia with little diplomatic support on the continent throughout much of the year. Deepening tensions between the Great Powers unleashed by Soviet action in Afghanistan had their impact, however. The United States, interested in obtaining bases for military deployment around the Arabian Sea, finally agreed to supply Somalia with military assistance to replace that received from the USSR before the

SUBSCRIBE TO IISS PUBLICATIONS

Three alternative forms of annual subscription are available, covering publications issued during the year from subscription commencement date to be filled in on the Subscription Card (for prices, see Subscription Card below)

Combined covering 1 issue of *The Military Balance*, 1 issue of *Strategic Survey*, 8–10 Adelphi Papers and 6 issues of *Survival*.

Special covering 1 issue of *The Military Balance*, 1 issue of *Strategic Survey* and 8–10 Adelphi Papers.

Survival covering 6 issues of *Survival*.

If you would like to take out one of these subscriptions, please fill in and mail the tear-off subscription card below.

Subscription Card

Please enter subscription ticked below for 1 year from . . . .
(date)

Combined ☐ £26.00 ($60.00)
Special ☐ £22.00 ($52.00)
Survival ☐ £8.50 ($20.00)

I am a **new** subscriber ☐
I already have a Combined subscription ☐
    Special subscription ☐ *(please enclose IISS*
    Survival subscription ☐ *mailing label)*

Please print name and address clearly

Name . . . .

Address . . . .

City . . . . **Country** . . . .

☐ **Payment enclosed** ☐ **Bill me** SS 80–81

Strategic Survey 1980–1981

The IISS offers further copies of **Strategic Survey 1980–1981** at the following rates per copy (prepayment is required)*

1–10 copies £4.00 ($9.00); 11–100 copies £3.40 ($7.65; 101 copies and over £3.00 ($6.75)

Please send . . . . copies of **Strategic Survey 1980–1981** at . . . .
(date)

Name . . . .
(please print)

Address . . . .

City . . . .

☐ **Payment enclosed** ☐ **Bill me** SS 80–81

Rates apply to 1980–81 edition only. For other editions, tick 'Bill me' box.

THE INTERNATIONAL INSTITUTE FOR STRATEGIC STUDIES
Sales Department
23 Tavistock Street
London WC2E 7NQ
England

THE INTERNATIONAL INSTITUTE FOR STRATEGIC STUDIES
Sales Department
23 Tavistock Street
London WC2E 7NQ
England

the 1977–8 war in exchange for facilities for her ships and aircraft at the port of Berbera (previously built and used by the Soviet Union).

The Ogaden and Eritrean Conflicts

Despite the official withdrawal of the Somali army from the Ogaden in 1978, guerrilla warfare there continued almost unabated for another eighteen months. Fighting intensified significantly in April 1980 but later subsided into a stalemate. Ethiopia's army – 60,000 men, mainly militia, assisted by perhaps 6,000 Cuban soldiers (according to some estimates as many as 12,000) – remained in control of the three principal towns of Harar, Dire Dawa and Jigjiga, while mastery of the air by her small but efficient air force and the use of convoys heavily guarded by armoured cars enabled Ethiopian forces to move throughout the area at will. On the other hand, Somali guerrillas were stiffened by logisic support and 'volunteers' from the Somali army – estimated to number three battalions – and were liberally equipped with Soviet-made rifles, machine-guns and grenade-launchers. For much of the year they exercised effective control over about half the countryside. They were, however, badly beaten in the autumn, and the WSLF ceased conducting visiting journalists far into Ethiopian territory. The Ethiopian air force meanwhile carried out numerous bombing operations, and on several occasions dropped a dozen or so bombs across the Somali frontier. The potential for a renewal of major hostilities between the two countries remained.

In Eritrea, as in the Ogaden, Ethiopia held the upper hand throughout 1980. The two liberation organizations, the Eritrean Liberation Front (ELF) and the Eritrean People's Liberation Front (EPLF), both dispirited since their failure to capture the Eritrean capital of Asmara in 1978 and suffering from diminished external support, were on the defensive. They were further weakened by armed clashes with each other and by desertions. Ethiopian forces some 120,000 strong, consisting of both regular army units and militia supported by the air force, had a decisive edge over the guerrillas, who numbered perhaps 20,000 in the EPLF and 5,000 in the ELF. Ethiopia was in effective control of all Eritrean towns with the exception of Naqfa, an EPLF-held settlement in mountainous territory near the Sudanese border, after a 'reconquest' apparently achieved against the advice of the Soviet Union, which had favoured concessions towards the Eritrean nationalists and a 'political solution'.

Despite Ethiopian military superiority, including complete control of the sky, Eritrean guerrillas, particularly those of the EPLF, obliged the Ethiopian regime to commit considerable forces to the area. In June the EPLF opened a branch in the Somali capital of Mogadishu so as to forge an Eritrean-Somali axis against the Mengistu regime. However, during the year the EPLF, blocked in its main aim of liberating Eritrea, also became increasingly involved with secessionist rebels in the adjacent Tigre province. The Tigre People's Liberation Front (TPLF) was thus able to take the offensive against Ethiopian forces on a number of occasions, notably in the Aksum-Adowa area. EPLF units also sought to encourage and train Galla (Oromo) dissidents of the Oromo Liberation Front which was active in the south-eastern province of Bala, adjoining the Ogaden. But these other secessionist movements did not appear to offer a serious threat to the Addis Ababa regime. On the other hand, there was growing Eritrean interest, especially in the ranks of the ELF, in seeking a 'people's peace' with the Ethiopian Government. Advocates of this policy favoured a 'face-saving' formula which would guarantee local autonomy in Eritrea while ensuring Ethiopian unity and access to the sea for the central provinces.

External Relations

Ethiopia and the Soviet Union remained outwardly close. There was no slackening in Soviet military support to the *Dergue*; in July Admiral Gorshkov, Commander of the Soviet navy, visited Ethiopia and inspected the ports of Assab and Massawa; he later described the visit as fruitful, but whatever deal may have been concluded was not made public. However, Soviet influence on internal Ethiopian matters did not seem to be decisive – for instance, Ethiopia delayed creating a Soviet-style party. Moreover, the leadership in Addis Ababa seemed to be determined to keep lines open to the West. Ethiopian Airlines, for example, continued buying American aircraft, and Addis Ababa University went on recruiting much of its expatriate staff in the West. Col. Mengistu, though a self-styled Marxist, seemed to be increasingly adopting the posture of an

Ethiopian nationalist, and he was thought to have proved a tough negotiator with the USSR.

For Somalia, the major external development was the completion of negotiations with the United States on her request for arms in exchange for the use of the former Soviet naval facilities at Berbera and Mogadishu. This led to protracted talks between the two countries, and negotiations were at one time deadlocked for several months. Gen. Barre, hoping to obtain massive aid comparable to what he had previously received from the USSR, began by demanding $2 billion spread over ten years, as well as a commitment of American diplomatic, political and economic support. The US at first demurred, reluctant to encourage, or become involved in, an Ogaden war which had never really ended, and anxious to avoid giving offence to either the OAU or Kenya, or pushing Ethiopia into further reliance on the Soviet Union. She offered to supply only 'defensive' weapons, and insisted that they should not, like other Somali arms, be handed over to guerrillas fighting on Ethiopian territory. Somalia subsequently agreed to settle for a much smaller package than she had originally sought, and the aid package signed on 21 August provided her with $2 million in military sales credits in 1980 and a like amount in 1981, plus $5 million in budgetary support. The US also agreed to develop Mogadishu port and to complete the unfinished Soviet-built installations at Berbera (which include a 15,000-foot concrete all-weather runway). The Somali Government gave 'firm assurances' that weapons supplied under this agreement would not be used to fight in Ethiopia, and declared that Somali regular troops would not be allowed across the frontier. American officials conceded uncertainty as to how much weight could be

attached to the latter assurance in view of Somalia's past record of involvement in the WSLF struggle, but in January 1981 the State Department pronounced them credible, and the deal was completed.

As anticipated, this agreement evoked strong opposition not only from Ethiopia but also from Kenya. The former pointed out that Berbera was only 117 miles from the Ethiopian frontier, where fighting was still in progress. The Kenyan reaction, though more restrained, revealed that the Government of President Daniel Arap Moi, Washington's staunchest ally in black Africa, was far more concerned about Somali claims on Kenya's northern province than about the presence of Russians and Cubans in Ethiopia.

Like Kenya, the Sudan also began to normalize relations with Ethiopia. In part this shift may have reflected President Numeiry's conclusion that the *Dergue* had a firm grip on power and was there to stay, but it reflected other, more direct, Sudanese interests as well. For one thing, Sudan had lost her former enthusiasm for the Eritrean secessionist movements as these came under increasing domination by young Marxists from the Christian highlands. (Saudi interest in an independent Eritrea had also shown a marked decline, for the same reason.) In addition Sudan was deeply concerned by the economic burden, and the potential political problem, posed by the 330,000 Eritrean refugees who had taken up apparently permanent residence on her soil. Sudanese policy in 1980 therefore turned increasingly to seeking a peaceful solution to the Eritrean question. Gen. Numeiry closed the Sudanese-Eritrean frontier, and repeatedly urged the Eritreans and Ethiopians to reach a political solution.

LIBYA AND THE SAHARA

The most important threat in North Africa during 1980 stemmed from the ambitions of one country – Libya. Col. Gaddafi's vague announcement of a 'union' with Chad in early 1981 was only the most striking manifestation of his country's role in the whole Saharan region, which also included growing support of the Western Saharan rebellion and penetration into Niger. These events occurred in the con-

text of the power vacuum in the Sahara and the peculiar image that Libyan leaders had of their country's role.

The newly independent states of the Sahara had traditionally suffered from sparse population and inhospitable terrain. The region seemed to require little defence, since it was an unattractive prey, and French policy had been to supply the minimum military insurance needed to supplement local armies and support the fragile sovereignties of Saharan states, all of which (except the Spanish Sahara) had been her former colonies. Thus, the French army had responded to a call from the government of Chad for help against rebellion in mid-1968, to a request by the Mauritanian government in late 1977, and to that of the Tunisian government when Libyan-backed rebels seized the town of Gafsa in January 1980. In so doing, France was also seeking to provide a buffer for her more important client states, such as Senegal and Ivory Coast, where her intervention forces were actually stationed. Libya regarded the area as attractive, however, and she was sufficiently strong to pose a security threat in the Saharan region around it.

Involvement in Chad

Col. Gaddafi's new emphasis on a Saharan vocation dated from his visit to Mauritania in 1972, when he discovered that Mauritanian tribes spoke the same Hassaniyya Arabic as his mother's tribe in Libya. Before that, Libya's role in the Sahara had been as mercurial and indecisive as any other aspect of its foreign policy. The Libyan monarchy had offered sanctuary, but little active support, for the Muslim rebellions that occurred in Chad after 1964. The revolutionary military regime that overthrew the monarchy in 1969 did little more, but it provided sporadic training to the various branches of the Front de Libération Nationale (FROLINAT), and it was implicated in FROLINAT's raid on Chad's capital, Ndjamena, in August 1971. Chad's President Tombalbaye, reversing his earlier policies, visited Libya a year later, received Libyan financial support, broke off relations with Israel and sent home the French army. In 1974 he accepted Libyan occupation of the 300-km-deep Aouzou strip along the border, which had been ceded to Libya in a 1935 Franco-Italian treaty that had never been ratified. The Aouzou strip is believed by some to contain uranium, but that is unproven.

Tombalbaye's regime was overthrown by the army in 1975. His successor, Gen. Felix Malloum, went to Libya to sign a cease-fire with FROLINAT, but the FROLINAT leader, Goukouni Oueddei, with Libyan support, called for an end to the 'dictatorial neo-colonial regime' and continued his guerrilla war. In February 1979 Malloum's government fell, and Goukouni set up a national coalition the following month which was broadened to include Chad's 11 different factions by the Lagos agreement of August 1979. This Transitional Government of National Unity, however, was an unstable coalition, and by January 1980 it fell apart, challenged because of its Libyan domination by Defence Minister Hissène Habré, a northerner from Tibesti province.

The ensuing civil war among northern factions devastated the capital and destroyed any pretence of national authority, completing the political vacuum. In May 1980 the force of French soldiers – which had maintained a *de facto* division of the country into French and Libyan zones of influence, in the south and north respectively, in accordance with an alleged 1978 agreement between Giscard d'Estaing and Gaddafi – was withdrawn. In June, Goukouni signed a defence agreement with Libya. Repeated attempts by the Organization of African Unity, particularly during and after its July summit in Freetown, brought no agreement between the Goukouni and Habré factions, and in mid-October Libya began moving troops into Ndjamena and the north in response to an appeal from Goukouni. By early December about 5,000 troops, 50 tanks and supporting aircraft had arrived in the capital area, having pushed back the forces of Habré along the way. A month later Col. Gaddafi announced the union, though, under pressure from OAU members, he subsequently declared that it would be subject to a referendum.

The northern part of Chad is populated by mountain and Saharan people restive under any government. Their various rebel movements had on occasion welcomed Libyan support, but they had also fought against it when it became overbearing, and they were unlikely to welcome the Libyan dominance that union would bring. And President Goukouni himself was cool in his statements about the Libyan military presence in December, despite the assistance Libya had given him, and he did not welcome the demotion inherent in union. Finally, it was not clear whether the union would cover all the country, including the portion of the country south of 12° N – which was negro and Christian/animist – or whether it would consecrate the Franco-Libyan division of 1978; if included, the South would be subjected to domination from the Arab and Muslim north. Beyond these purely Chadian reasons suggesting instability lay Libya's record of failed mergers: she had already declared mergers with four countries (Tunisia, Egypt, Sudan and Syria) – some of them twice (Syria and Egypt) – and, although the union with Syria was formally still in force, it was in practical terms a dead letter.

Action in North Africa

There were other Libyan activities in the Saharan region, besides those in Chad. Libyan troops were also reported in northern Niger, where the north-east corner of the country – which is twice as far from its state capital as the northern strip of Chad – was also the subject of an unratified 1935 treaty of cession to Libya. Apart from Chad, however, Libya's activity was strongest at the Western end of the Sahara. Her support of the Popular Front for the Liberation of Saguia el-Hamra and Rio de Oro (POLISARIO) had been as uneven as her support for the factions of FROLINAT. After Spain's 1975 withdrawal from her former colony of the Spanish Sahara, Libya had supported POLISARIO both out of a common revolutionary feeling and out of opposition to the Moroccan monarchy and its claims to the territory. But she suspended aid at one point in 1977 in deference to Mauritania (which also claimed the territory) and did not recognize the Saharan Arab Democratic Republic, POLISARIO's government in exile, until April 1980, because of her opposition to 'balkanizing the Arab nation'.

Figures on Libyan and Algerian support for POLISARIO are hard to obtain. Soviet arms from Libya (including SA-7 and SA-9 ground-to-air missiles) began to flow in quantity in 1978 as POLISARIO tried to move from guerrilla to conventional war. There were indications that in 1980 Algerian support primarily involved sanctuary and politico-diplomatic assistance, while the continuing flow of up-to-date Soviet arms to the western Sahara came from Libya via Ghadames, Tassili and Hoggar in Algeria, and Taodeni in Mali. The more Algeria moved towards efforts at a political solution, the more POLISARIO moved towards the harder Libyan position; and the more dominant the Libyan faction seemed to become, the more Algeria had reason to support a political settlement – although its terms were not yet discernible. However, notwithstanding this competitive aspect of their relationship, Algeria and Libya

were linked by a treaty of friendship 'for the defence of the revolution', signed at Hassi Messaoud on 28 December 1975 and several times reaffirmed, and both were members of the Arab Steadfastness Front. Algeria was embarrassed by, but did not disavow her complicity in, the Libyan raid on Gafsa in Tunisia in January 1980, and she did not seek an open break with Libya.

Besides Morocco, two other countries served as counterweights to Libya in the region. One was Nigeria, which has the continent's largest population and GNP, its largest army apart from Egypt's, and a growing sense of continental leadership. Nigeria had been the organizer of the 1979 Kano and Lagos conferences on Chad and had sent a force of 800 to Ndjamena in early March 1979 to maintain the cease-fire. But three months later her forces were withdrawn at the request of the Chad government for acting 'like an army of occupation'. Nigeria then passed the African responsibility in the conflict to an OAU committee of Congo, Guinea and Benin, chaired by Togo, which was to send an Inter-African Force and arrange reconciliation of the factions; only Congo sent troops, in January 1980, and they were soon withdrawn. Nigeria was, however, shaken by the Libyan military presence in Chad and by a number of other incidents. In late 1980 Libyan planes landed in Maidiguri to resupply and refuel with the agreement of the Nigerian state of Bornu. Libya also recruited northern Nigerian Muslims for her Islamic Legion, and at the end of the year the Libyan Embassy in Lagos was taken over by a revolutionary committee. Nigeria closed the embassy, joining Senegal, Ghana, Niger, Gambia and Gabon which had already broken relations with Libya. However, apart from leading African diplomatic opposition to the merger with Chad, Nigeria had limited means of redressing the situation. The OAU emergency summit at the beginning of January 1981, attended by only 12 heads of state, condemned the merger, but this was to be followed by more efficient measures.

The other state with interests in the region, France, was directly affected by the year's events. Both Libya and Nigeria had agreed that African problems must have African and not post-colonial solutions, and this view dampened the prospects for Franco-Nigerian cooperation against Libya. And French troops were withdrawn from both Mauritania and

Chad in May 1980 on the orders of the host governments. The Libyan military presence in Chad finally drew a vague French warning in mid-December. It was followed by a French decision to cancel an oil exploration agreement with Libya on 7 January 1981 and to increase the French intervention forces stationed at Bangui in the Central African Republic. But this was a response dictated by the limited options at France's disposal and by the difficulties of assuring more stability in the region through military action. On the other hand, Libya's actions could only increase resentment against her in the continent, and her position remained vulnerable in spite of her wealth and large stocks of Soviet military supplies: a country of three million, with a government that had repeatedly been the object of attempted *coups* by the armed forces, was unlikely to be able to continue to impose her will on other regional states if seriously challenged.

EAST ASIA

South-east Asia, though troubled, did not see a major outbreak of war during the year. The Heng Samrin government in Kampuchea consolidated its position with Vietnamese help, but it continued to be challenged in parts of the country by the *Khmer Rouge*. There was no repetition of the previous year's Chinese 'punitive' attack on Vietnam. Yet the region was hardly tranquil. Most notably, Vietnamese forces crossed the Thai border from Kampuchea in June in an effort both to disrupt the repatriation of refugees and to demonstrate to Thailand the cost of tolerating the camps which have served as sanctuaries for the *Khmer Rouge* on her territory. In the wake of the Vietnamese invasion, American military supplies to Thailand were speeded up, and the states of the Association of South-East Asian Nations

(ASEAN) closed ranks her, calling the incursion 'an act of aggression by Vietnam'.

The tension between Asia's largest Communist states, China and Vietnam, did not abate, even if it did not flare into war, and Sino-Soviet relations, too, remained bitter. The Korean peninsula, like Indochina, was notable for what did not happen, and internal turmoil in South Korea in the wake of President Park's assassination was contained. China appeared preoccupied with internal questions: on the surface by the trial of the 'Gang of Four' – including Mao's widow, Jiang Qing, who defiantly pointed to Mao as the real architect of the Cultural Revolution – while beneath the surface, a range of questions about ideology, domestic politics and economics, about foreign policy and defence remained unsolved.

CONTINUING CONFLICT IN INDOCHINA

In 1980 the familiar cycle of warfare in Indochina – major engagements in the dry season (late October to May) and guerrilla war in the wet – was not fully repeated. An anticipated dry-season offensive by the Vietnamese expeditionary force of approximately 200,000 in Kampuchea against the *Khmer Rouge* resistance did not materialize. The dispersion of the *Khmer Rouge* – estimated at 30,000 in June – with its ready access to sanctuaries across the border in Thailand, combined with the difficult terrain, made a major military operation far from easy. In the early months of the year the Vietnamese forces and the Heng Samrin government sustained intensified counterinsurgency operations and attempted to exercise greater control along the border with Thailand. The Vietnamese forces returned to positions that they had conceded during the wet season of 1979.

The military outcome was a measure of stalemate. The heavy concentration of Vietnamese forces along the border with Thailand curtailed major wet season operations by the *Khmer Rouge*, which was reduced to small scale guerrilla raids directed at exposed targets in Kampuchea such as communications. Viet-

namese forces undertook only limited operations, for example in the thick jungle of the Malai hills in Battambang Province adjoining the Thai border, and barely penetrated the much more extensive Cardamom Mountains further south, which served as a forward bastion for the insurgents giving them access to the heartland of Kampuchea.

Politically, the continuing conflict did not pose any immediate challenge to the Vietnamese-maintained government in Phnom Penh. The *Khmer Rouge* military threat did not seriously obstruct the slow return of the tormented country to some semblance of normality: for instance, the 1980 harvest was up to 65% of pre-war levels. However, major troop deployments – not only in Kampuchea but also in Laos – were a continuous drain on Vietnamese resources at a time when Vietnam's own internal economy and administrative system appeared to be seriously weakened. The *Khmer Rouge* thus served as a lever for both China and Thailand in sustaining political pressures on the government in Hanoi. Another source of pressure was the repeated threat of a second 'punishment' from China, which necessitated the sustained mobilization of seasoned regiments along Vietnam's northern border. To underscore this threat, in June China formally suspended the negotiations with Vietnam begun after their border war in 1979 and adjourned in March 1980.

Incursion in Thailand

Thailand continued to tolerate refugee camps close to the border with Kampuchea. That at Sa-Khao, in particular, served as a sanctuary where battle-weary *Khmer Rouge* could receive rice, clothing and medical treatment as beneficiaries of international relief operations. In addition, military equipment of Chinese origin reached insurgent quartermasters through Thailand. In June the Thai Government announced a policy of 'voluntary repatriation' of refugees, which meant in practice that up to 4,000 male *Khmer Rouge* who had enjoyed sanctuary during the dry season were returned to Kampuchea with the formal endorsement of the United Nations High Commission for Refugees only to return to battle. The government in Phnom Penh described the Thai policy as 'a plot to enable the Pol Pot bandits and other reactionary gangs to harass the People's Republic of Kampuchea during the rainy season', and Vietnam took military action in the early hours of 23 June, when Thai forces along the border were being rotated. One company, with artillery support, attacked across the border near Ban Mak Moon in Prachinburi Province, and other raids were mounted further south at Ban Non Sao E and at Ban Nong Chan, the terminus of the international relief 'land bridge'. Since the attacks did not extend near Sa-Khao, the main victims of these two-day limited assaults were authentic refugees, not soldiers.

The immediate objectives of the Vietnamese incursions seemed to be to drive refugees deeper into Thailand, to end the practice of 'voluntary repatriation', and also to persuade international relief agencies to reconsider their land bridge operation and to concentrate their efforts on direct dealings with the government in Phnom Penh. Beyond that, Vietnam clearly hoped to drive home to Thailand the cost of Thai involvement with the *Khmer Rouge*. Vietnam may also have hoped to add conviction to her claim that the only real conflict was along the border with Thailand, and that this could be resolved by the establishment of a demilitarized zone and

recognition by Bangkok of the Heng Samrin regime in Phnom Penh. Yet while the operations brought 'voluntary repatriation' of refugees to an end, they did not achieve other objectives.

Vietnam's action against Thailand took place only two days before the annual meeting in Kuala Lumpur of the foreign ministers of the ASEAN states – Thailand, Indonesia, Malaysia, Singapore and the Philippines. If one of her objectives had been to drive a political wedge between the ASEAN partners, it was not successful. The ASEAN governments closed ranks in support of Thailand and reaffirmed their common position on the Kampuchean conflict, reiterating their demand for the total withdrawal of Vietnamese forces from Kampuchea. On 25 June the five foreign ministers expressed their serious concern over 'the act of aggression by Vietnam'.

This concern was shared by the United States, Thailand's chief ally. Using emergency powers, President Carter authorized a four-day air-lift to Thailand in early July of machine gun ammunition, howitzers and recoiless rifles; and 18 armoured personnel carriers were delivered by sea in early August. In addition, the US provided training in the use of a newly delivered *TOW* anti-tank missile system and Congress approved the sale of an additional 35 M-48A5 tanks, regarded as a match for Vietnam's Soviet-built T-54s. These tanks, together with additional automatic rifles and ammunition, arrived at the end of September. Other American arms supplies included 3 C-130 transport aircraft, 14 helicopters and 5 patrol aircraft.

The continuing tension in South-east Asia, coupled with increased Soviet naval activity, prompted an Australian initiative for the revival of the Five-Power Defence Agreement with Malaysia, Singapore, Britain and New Zealand; preliminary discussions took place at the September meeting of regional Commonwealth heads of government in New Delhi. The five agreed to consider holding a combined military exercise similar to the *Bersatu Padu* operation they had held off the east coast of Malay in 1970. Australia's increased commitment to regional defence was underlined in September by the visit to Singapore of the aircraft carrier *Melbourne* and its task group.

Vietnam's dependence on Soviet military supplies deepened, and a major resupply operation was reported, beginning in August, with Soviet freighters being discharged in the Kampuchean port of Kompong Som. In October, Vietnamese troop concentrations along the Thai border were increased from 8 to 10 divisions in a major rotation of units with new equipment. However, while Vietnam's dependence on Soviet military supply gave the USSR easy access to Vietnamese naval facilities, Soviet units did not have total freedom in operating from them; (there were accounts during the summer of Soviet annoyance at continuing limitations imposed by Vietnam). Nonetheless, the 43,000-ton Soviet aircraft carrier *Minsk* was sighted at Cam Ranh Bay in September, and at the end of October it also appeared in the Gulf of Siam, within a hundred miles of the Thai naval base of Sattahip, at the end of the visit to China by the Prime Minister of Thailand.

The heightened intensity of conflict in the region also undermined the precarious *modus vivendi* reached between Thailand and the Vietnamese-sponsored government in Laos in January 1979. In June 1980 one Thai was killed and two wounded when two Thai river patrol boats on the Mekong came under fire from the Laotian bank. When the Laotian Government refused to accept responsibility or to apologize, Thailand retaliated by sealing the 1,760-km common border at all key crossing points, thus highlighting Laotian economic dependence on Thailand. The border was reopened at the end of August after a conciliatory gesture from the Laotian Ambassador, but the earlier relaxed atmosphere was replaced by mutual suspicion and accusations of bad faith.

Laos remained well within Vietnam's sphere of influence, with some 50,000 Vietnamese troops still deployed there, but had to confront a measure of both internal dissent and external pressure. It was revealed in September that a so-called Lao People's National Liberation United Front directed against Vietnamese domination had been set up in Champassak Province. Although the Lao party newspaper *Siang Pasason* referred to outside enemies and counter-revolutionary remnants who sometimes 'even cause our people loss of life and property', there was no evidence to suggest that the new Front posed a serious threat to the basic stability and control exercised by the government in Vientiane.

The Quest for Negotiated Solutions

Attempts continued during 1980 to fashion a political compromise to the Kampuchean problem, but to little avail. Vietnam held to her long-standing position that the situation in Kampuchea was irreversible, and the ASEAN states to their demand for implementation of the UN General Assembly's November 1979 solution calling for the immediate and total withdrawal of Vietnamese forces from Kampuchea. Malaysia's Foreign Minister, Tengku Ahmada Rithaudeen, obtained a mandate from his ASEAN colleagues to approach Vietnam, but discussion did not produce dialogue, either in Hanoi early in the year or in Kuala Lumpur in May, when Vietnam's Foreign Minister, Nguyen Co Thach, returned the visit. In a visit to Bangkok that same month Thach pointed out: 'The solidarity of the Indochinese nations is as important to Vietnam as is the solidarity of ASEAN to Thailand ... We cannot accept the premise that an Indochinese country be made a buffer zone between these [two] groups of countries'.

In March, Thailand appealed to the United Nations to dispatch an observer team to the Thai side of the border with Kampuchea, establish a safe haven within Kampuchea for refugees and convene an international conference on the conflict. The Indochinese countries under Vietnam's tutelage advanced a counter-proposal in July, following a meeting in Moscow earlier in the month between the Soviet and Vietnamese leaderships at which Kampuchea's Foreign Minister, Hun Sen, was present. It called for the establishment of a demilitarized zone in the border area between Kampuchea and Thailand and a joint commission to implement an agreement guaranteeing peace and stability; Kampuchean–Thai co-operation to find a solution to the refugee problem and, in particular, to negotiate a settlement for the repatriation of Kampuchean refugees in Thailand; discussions between Kampuchea and the international relief agencies to ensure the most effective relief operations on the basis of respect for the independence and sovereignty of Kampuchea; and direct negotiations between Kampuchea and Thailand to solve questions outstanding between them. This initiative was rejected by Thailand, whose foreign minister described it as a political trick to lure his government into negotiations with the Heng Samrin regime.

The diplomatic deadlock underlined that behind the narrower issues between Thailand and Vietnam lay the harder question of relations between Vietnam and China. There were, however, indications of limited flexibility by both Vietnam and China. In July, Vietnam offered a partial troop withdrawal from Kampuchea in return for the establishment of a demilitarized zone along the Kampuchean-Thai border and negotiations between Bangkok and Phnom Penh. In September, China's Premier Zhao Ziyang indicated that a complete withdrawal of Vietnamese troops was not a precondition for his government's participation in an international conference over Kampuchea, although such a withdrawal would have to begin before the meeting were convened.

All the same, Vietnam continued to focus on the Chinese threat. As Radio Hanoi said in October: 'to create favourable conditions for Vietnam's armed forces to withdraw from Kampuchea, a necessary and urgent thing to be done is to strive by all means to rule out the reason for its presence, that is the Chinese threat against the security of Kampuchea and Vietnam'. From Vietnam's perspective that threat comprised not only Chinese support (both rhetorical and material) for the *Khmer Rouge* and the tension along the border with China , but also the Radio Peking broadcasts by Vietnamese defectors which called on the Vietnamese people to unite in struggle to overthrow 'the Hanoi ruling clique'.

In October, Vietnam challenged the report of the credentials committee of the UN General Assembly, which had recommended seating the delegation from Pol Pot's ousted Democratic Kampuchean Government. Despite their distaste for the savagery of the Pol Pot regime, most nations regarded the Heng Samrin government, the People's Republic of Kampuchea, as imposed by outside military force and therefore illegitimate. The Vietnamese attempt was consequently defeated, by 74 votes to 35 with 32 abstentions, and the Democratic Kampuchean delegation continued to represent Kampuchea at the UN. Later in the month the ASEAN governments secured passage of a resolution, by 97 votes to 23 with 22 abstentions, which recommended the convening of an international conference on Kampuchea to arrange a monitored total withdrawal of foreign (i.e. Vietnamese) troops by a set deadline and the holding of free elections under UN supervision. This resolution was categorically rejected by Vietnam which endorsed the public position of her client in Phnom Penh that there was no Kampuchean problem and thus no need to search for political solutions. The diplomatic impasse continued into 1981 when the ASEAN governments rejected an initiative by their Indochinese counterparts for a regional conference.

DOMESTIC CHALLENGES IN CHINA

For China 1980 was a year of suspended judgments. On the surface the triumph of Vice-Chairman Deng Xiaoping seemed complete: the posthumous rehabilitation of Liu Shaoqi, former State Chairman and principal victim of the Cultural Revolution, was completed in February, and at the very end of the year the appearance of the first volume of Zhou Enlai's selected works was announced. China appeared set on the path of the Four Modernizations, and the end of the 'Gang of Four', their allies and their policies was symbolized in the great show trials which ended in December. Below the surface, however, many questions of economics, defence and foreign policy remained unsettled, creating the prospect of internal disruption.

The Myth of Mao

The reasons for this state of affairs were not hard to find. All autocratic systems, whether of Right or Left, that have been too long dominated by one man, face the problem of how to adjust the myth of the great leader once he has gone from the scene. China seemed to avoid the shocks of de-Stalinization, continuing to revere Mao while revising his policies. What are now called the disasters of Mao's last ten years – from 1966 to 1976, the decade of the Cultural Revolution – proved, however, to be too traumatic to suppress.

The key figures of the present leadership were both victims and survivors of the Cultural Revolution. They have neither forgotten those who did not survive nor come to trust those who not only survived but prospered from its turmoil. Chief among the latter was Chairman Hua Guofeng, whose political eclipse seemed complete by the end of the trial of the Gang of Four, who were convicted in December. Jiang Qing, Chairman Mao's widow, was sentenced to death in January 1981 but the sentence was deferred for two years. Her defiance at the trial added an element of unexpected drama to the public spectacle, as did her insistence that all she did was done with the approval of Chairman Mao and the Central Committee. Ironic mock slogans became widespread in China in a way unthinkable twenty-five years earlier, when the Chairman's simplest utterance was treated as a revelation from on high. The Gang of Four – Jiang Qing, Zhang Chunqiao, Yao Wenyuan and Wang Hongwen – served as scapegoats for the excesses of the Cultural Revolution. But that inevitably bred insecurity among the cadres who had risen in the hierarchy, or even joined the Party since 1966. And millions who had achieved prominence in pre-1978 China doubtless feared retribution.

By 1980 politics in China were supposed to be conducted according to different norms, and with a new emphasis on legality and stability. However, there was no sign that China would suddenly be transformed into a pluralist state. The famous slogan 'let a hundred flowers bloom, let a hundred schools of thought contend' reappeared for a while in the middle of the the year, yet in January the leadership had announced a decision to delete a part of Section 45 of the State Constitution which refers to the right to 'speak out freely, air views fully, hold great debates and write big-character posters'. In defence of this deletion, it argued that the Constitution still protected basic democratic rights and that poster politics had been the cause of many abuses, from the anti-rightist campaigns of the 1950s to the Cultural Revolution itself. Yet no-one hearing these arguments could forget that Chairman Mao himself had encouraged the posters and defended the right of rebellion. It was far from clear whether the new leadership could erase this memory, prevent further factionalism and sustain a smooth bureaucratic style of politics, a task made harder still by economic problems.

The Four Modernizations

Despite their constant reiteration, similar doubts hung over the programme of four modernizations: agriculture, industry, science and technology, and defence. How were they all to be achieved, given China's limited resources, even by the end of the century? And if they could not be achieved simultaneously, which were to be given priority? Since the disasters of the Great Leap Forward in 1958, agriculture had headed the list of priorities. But modernizing Chinese agriculture through large scale investment in mechanization would lead to a great reduction in the numbers of agricultural workers. How could the rest of the economy absorb such a vast transfer of manpower? There were similar problems with industry, where rapid modernization would mean a further squeeze on hard-currency resources and further dependence on foreign investment. There were also the issues of whether the industrial focus should be moved further away from heavy industry towards light consumer industry; of how much market forces should be permitted to determine industrial directions; and of how China's scientific and technological base could be rapidly developed without unprecedented investment in education and much greater importation of foreign skills. All these questions had clear implications both for the internal debate and for China's approach to foreign policy. Yet 1980 provided few hints that any of them were close to resolution.

Defence had remained last on the list of modernizations, and there was no evidence during 1980 that its priority increased, notwithstanding the demonstration of China's military shortcomings in the war against Vietnam. On the contrary, despite apparent hopes that increased defence spending might be possible, the budgetary discussions of the National People's Congress in September 1980 suggested that little growth in defence outlays was in prospect. China faced a large unplanned budget deficit, in part due to defence expenditures that outran plans by 10%, and it was announced that the 1980 defence budget would be cut back by the equivalent of two billion dollars (13.2%) compared with 1979.

The September Congress did not make clear how the cut would be allocated – a question which affected the larger debate about the relative priorities of the nuclear and conventional programmes of the People's Liberation Army (PLA). On one hand, China's most spectacular military event of the year was the successful launching on 18 May of her first full-range ICBM, the CSS-X-4. (This, with a range of 12,000 km, was described by China as solid-fuelled, though other reports suggested it was liquid-fuelled.) That launching, and other missile tests during the year, suggested that China might be giving nuclear programmes greater priority. On the other hand, there were strong grounds for believing that conventional force improvements continued to be the focus. Given her foreign-policy orientation, China had little interest in targeting the United States with nuclear weapons, and therefore little real need for a full ICBM. The missile tests probably represented the delayed recovery of the missile programme from earlier turmoil and suggested China's interest in steady nuclear development. Concentration on a greater professionalization of conventional forces, therefore seemed more plausible, and the civilian Chief of Staff was replaced by a military man. But the military requirements for improving China's conventional strength would be enormous. The cost of modernizing one of her 400 armoured divisions illustrates the order of magnitude. The estimate in the table is based on the current, relatively austere, Chinese division structure. A more powerful organization, with

Cost of Modernizing a Chinese Armoured Division

Equipment	No.	Unit Cost* ($ m)	Total Cost ($ m)
Tanks	300	1.0	300.0
Other armoured vehicles	107	0.5	53.5
Artillery	42	0.2	8.5
Vehicles	2,500	0.05	125.0
Air defence	36	0.2	7.2
Miscellaneous			50.0
Communications			20.0
Ammunition			100.0
Total			664.0

* Estimates of the costs of US equipment in international trade, not of what it might cost China to produce her own equivalent.

SOURCE: 'Organization of a Chinese Armoured Division' (chart), *The Military Balance 1980-1981* (London: IISS, 1980), p.100.

adequate self-propelled artillery, more mechanized infantry, improved logistic backing, more helicopters and the like, would push the estimate towards $1 billion per division. Moreover, a greater emphasis on military efficiency in the PLA would have to be sustained against the resistance of vested interests in favour of maintaining the size and political weight of the armed forces, particularly if large cuts in manpower were involved.

China and the Super-powers

There was little evidence of change in China's perception of her strategic environment. She continued to see the world as highly unstable, with the expansionist policies of the Soviet Union a constant threat to peace. The other super-power was no longer seen as the threat it had been, and was at least a tactical ally in many respects.

In April a symbolic event of some note passed without much comment – the formal end of the Sino-Soviet treaty of Friendship, Alliance and Mutual Assistance, which had come into effect in 1950 but had been a dead letter for many years. One Soviet spokesman described the Chinese decision not to extend the treaty as a 'rash and myopic act'. And China was one of the 65 countries to boycott the Moscow Olympics. Nonetheless, despite continuing tension with the Soviet Union, China proposed that state-to-state negotiations continue between the two countries on outstanding issues. These were not resumed, but all the same there did seem to be a deliberate scaling down of the rhetoric of attacks on the Soviet Union by Chinese leaders. In November Deng Xiaoping called on the USSR to take 'concrete action' towards improving Sino-Soviet relations and gave as an example the reduction of Soviet troops along the Sino-Soviet and Sino-Mongolian borders to the numbers maintained there under Khrushchev (which would imply a startling reduction from 46 divisions to roughly 10). But whether such suggestions were prompted by greater trust in Soviet intentions was doubtful; more likely they reflected Chinese caution in the light of the Soviet willingness, demonstrated in Afghanistan, to use military force against neighbours, coupled with the realization of China's military weakness.

China's links with the West continued to develop during 1980. In May, Hua Guofeng became the first Chinese head of state to visit Japan in several millenia. The continuing parallelism between Chinese and American policies was underscored by US Defense Secretary Brown's visit to Peking in January, when he declared that China and the United States shared similar strategic assessments and would broaden the contacts between their defence establishments. In the wake of his visit, the United States announced that she was prepared to provide China with information from a ground station for the *Landsat-D* earth resources satellite (which had some military relevance). The US also announced that she was prepared to sell China so-called 'non-lethal' military equipment - trucks, communication equipment and the like. This was a significant departure from the previous American position that she would supply no militarily relevant equipment to China.

In 1980 it was hard to see developments that might force China's internal debates to a conclusion or lead to changes in her external orientation. One imponderable, of course, lay in the policies of the Reagan Administration, and Vice Presidential candidate George Bush visited China in August to try to quiet the row caused by Mr Reagan's expression of readiness to establish some official relations with Taiwan. It was, however, hard to imagine that, given its sharply competitive approach towards the USSR, his team would not come, sooner rather than later, to take an interest in closer Sino-American relations.

JAPAN: GROWING SECURITY CONCERNS

In June Japan went to the polls, an occasion made more dramatic by the death of Prime Minister Ohira ten days earlier. The result was a landslide victory for the governing Liberal Democratic Party, its best result since 1969. National security featured in the campaign, and, although there was no clear evidence that it influenced the voters' decision to any marked degree, opinion polls and subtle changes in the platforms of most opposition parties did indicate strong public support for the existing Self-Defence Forces and the Mutual Security Treaty with the United States. The new government of Zenko Suzuki moved cautiously to implement security policies that had begun to emerge in the previous administration, amidst the deteriorating world situation and under pressure from its US ally.

Japanese Security Perceptions
The Ohira government had at first reacted hesitantly to the Soviet invasion of Afghanistan, anxious to safeguard bilateral economic relations with the Soviet Union. In the end, Japan joined the Olympic boycott, though not before waiting to see how other Western countries acted. She also took economic sanctions against the Soviet Union in the wake of Afghanistan, although some joint economic ventures continued.

Normal Japanese–Soviet contracts continued throughout the year, but Soviet actions did little to dispel Japanese concerns about a growing security threat to Japan. Soviet forces on the Northern islands claimed by Japan reached divisional strength, and for the first time included ground forces on Shikotan, one of the small islands close to the Nemuro Peninsula of Hokkaido. In this context Japan responded coolly to President Brezhnev's call in August for closer economic ties between the Soviet Union and Japan. On 23 August, the USSR towed a disabled nuclear-powered submarine through Japan's territorial waters, having asked for permission but without waiting for formal clearance. After a brief flurry about the violation, Japan recognized this as 'an instance of innocent passage'.

The general atmosphere of international crisis – tensions in South-east Asia, reports of Soviet bases in Vietnam, the dispatch of units of the US Seventh Fleet to the Indian Ocean and the crisis in the Gulf – fed the debate on security in Japan. In the wake of Afghanistan there was also an increase in US pressure on Japan to do more for her own defence, and after Mr Ohira's visit to Washington at the beginning of May there was a marked increase in the government's emphasis on defence. Both houses of the Diet established special committees on security affairs for the first time, and Mr Ohira set up a Special Advisory Group on Comprehensive National Security under the Chairmanship of Masamichi Inoki. This group reported in July and recommended increasing the defence budget by 20%, raising defence expenditure to 1.1% of GNP, increasing the proportion of the defence budget devoted to equipment from 20% to 30% and research and development expenditure five-fold to 5% of the defence budget. The Suzuki government later implemented one of the report's suggestions by establishing a cabinet-level Comprehensive Security Council as a forum for the discussion of a wide range of security issues.

Future Policy

More authoritative expositions of the government's views emerged from the 1980 Defence White Paper, published on 5 August, and the Foreign Ministry's Blue Book for 1980, published shortly afterwards. The White Paper listed some of the deficiencies in military equipment – such as the inadequate number of tanks (most of them obsolete), the shortages of anti-missile and anti-aircraft capabilities in the Maritime Self-Defence Force, and the inadequacy of the Air Self-Defence Force's base infrastructure – but was less specific about the measures to be taken to remedy them.

The Blue Book called for efforts 'to improve the self-defence capability on an appropriate scale'. It dropped the previous stress on an 'omnidirectional' policy and instead it suggested a more active role for Japan as a member of the Western World and the need 'to face a hard choice and even make some sacrifice'.

The defence budget for Fiscal 1981, which the Suzuki government decided at the end of the year, called for an increase of 7.6% over 1980 spending. For the first time in post-war history the defence increase exceeded that of all major budget items (including welfare, education and science, and public construction). The budget was designed to make possible completion of the existing modernization programme perhaps a year earlier than scheduled, as the US government had been demanding. Yet defence spending would still remain at 0.91% of GNP and would remain a point of contention between the US and Japan.

Yet if Japan's security policy seemed to move towards a greater emphasis on defence, it was not only as a result of American prodding. Rather, it followed from a gradual recognition that security could no longer be taken for granted. For one thing, there were doubts about the United States' ability to come to Japan's assistance in future crises. (Prime Minister Ohira expressed these in a casual aside in April, when he said that the United States was 'not a superpower anymore. The days are gone when we were able to rely on America as a deterrent'.) Second, the weight of Soviet political and military pressure in the region was growing, and the Soviet leadership repeatedly warned Japan in the year not to abandon her hitherto 'reasonable' policies. Finally, there was a growing realization in Japan of the need to promote stability in third-world regions, exemplified by Japanese economic assistance to Thailand, Pakistan and Turkey, and the discussion over Japanese arms exports. All this did not, as yet, amount to a comprehensive security policy but, as elements of insecurity became more marked and the debate in Japan more articulate, the basis for such a policy was being put in place.

THE KOREAN PENINSULA

The main question for 1980 was the internal stability of South Korea after the assassination in October 1979 of President Park Chung Hee, who had governed the country since 1961. On that score the worst possibilities did not come true – internal unrest in the South did not tempt North Korea to launch an invasion – but the future of South Korea remained in some doubt, with economic woes feeding political turmoil.

A brief period of liberalization after Park's death, led by caretaker President Choi Kyu Hah, was cut short by a junior officers' coup in December 1979. In April 1980, with inflation running at 28% and rising rapidly, strikes broke out in the provincial capital of Kwangju, and by mid-May the economic protest had become a popular uprising involving as much as a fifth of the city's population. South Korean troops moved in to quell the riots on 27 May, but as many as 400 people died in the subsequent fighting. In August President Choi resigned, and General Chun Doo Hwan, previously head of security, became President.

Elections, largely a formality, confirmed General Chun in power on 25 February 1981.

The internal unrest affected South Korea's relations with her two closest allies, Japan and the United States, who together account for more than half of her foreign trade. The most serious issue was the fate of Kim Dae Jung, the country's most prominent opposition leader, who was arrested during the Kwangju disturbances and sentenced to death for subversion on 17 September. Japan threatened to cut $100 million worth of aid to Korea, and US Secretary of State Muskie expressed 'deep concern' that South Korea was 'moving away from liberalization policies ... essential to its long term health.' Under pressure, the Seoul government commuted Kim's sentence to life imprisonment on 22 January 1981. Looking both to his allies and to the forthcoming elections, President Chun, while continuing a 'purification' campaign that virtually eliminated political opposition, also announced an end to martial law and several economic reforms.

There was little evidence that North Korea tried to exploit the turmoil in the South, despite some allegations by officials in Seoul that the Pyongyang government was responsible for riots in Kwangju. North Korea apparently felt, with considerable justification, that any major move would only frighten the competing South Korean factions into patching up their differences in the face of a common enemy. The United States also warned North Korea several times during the year, reaffirming that she would 'react strongly in accordance with ... obligations to the Republic of Korea to any external attempt to exploit the situation'. In 1979 the Carter Administration's plan to withdraw American ground forces from South Korea had been deferred until 1981, and probably shelved indefinitely, in response to concerns in Korea and Japan and to new intelligence indicating that total North Korean strength was over 700,000 (and not 600,000, as had been believed). American troop strength in Korea remained at 38,000 during 1980 and during Chun's visit to Washington in January 1981, the Reagan Administration announced that no withdrawals would take place.

For her part, North Korea was too weak economically and lacked strong support from either China or the Soviet Union to sustain a long war against the South. With the military taking 11% of the work force, her industrialization programme had been set back, and economic growth was enjoying a higher priority than at any time since the reconstruction after the Korean War. She continued to balance her relations with her two patrons, China and the USSR, with the latter continuing to be the principal source of material support. Both countries had reason to restrain North Korea from any move towards the South and to prefer the *status quo* of the North–South division: a North Korean adventure would complicate the external relations of both (especially relations with the United States) and might well lead to war, while any effort to push the North towards either reunification or acceptance of formal division ran the risk of driving the Pyongyang government into the arms of the other patron.

Both South and North Korea made proposals for unification talks during the year, though they seemed to be made mostly for propaganda purposes, but in February they did manage to re-open telephone lines between their capitals which had been closed since 1976. In January 1981 President Chun offered to go to Pyongyang, or to have North Korean President Kim Il Sung visit the South, but that seemed to be a gesture addressed more to the South Korean electorate than to Pyongyang.

As 1981 began President Chun and his government faced the double task of consolidating a tolerable degree of political stability and tackling the equally pressing problems of the economy. South Korea had been hard hit by higher oil prices coupled with the cumulative distortions of her years of extremely fast growth; her GNP actually fell by 5.7% in 1980. Economic growth had served President Chun's predecessor as a political stabilizer, but this safety valve was more questionable even though the outlook for 1981 was relatively bright. With the new Administration installed in Washington, South Korea could look to stronger support and less criticism from her American ally, and this would be important in continuing to deter the North; Chun was the first head of state to visit President Reagan in Washington. But the central test for future security lay in internal stability, which repressive measures could not assure for long.

ARMS CONTROL

It was hardly an auspicious year for arms control. The second Soviet–American attempt to limit strategic nuclear weapons, the SALT II Agreement, which had been signed in June 1979, fell victim to growing US anxiety over Soviet policies and began the year in a parlous condition, at least when viewed as a formal treaty which had to be ratified by the American Senate. By early 1981 it looked dead beyond recall. Other arms-control negotiations remained moribund, with the limited exception of some movement in the Mutual and Balanced Force Reduction (MBFR) talks in Vienna, which had long ceased to occupy the place on the East–West arms-control agenda to which the importance of their subject would appear to entitle them. Equally ominously for the future, 1980 was a discouraging year on the nuclear non-proliferation front. The International Nuclear Fuel Cycle Evaluation (INFCE) – a 1977 initiative of the Carter Administration which had served at least to defuse several major nuclear disputes by deferring them – ended in a very scant success that might be overshadowed by the fact that the end of the evaluation meant that the disputes underlying it could no longer be postponed. The second review of the Non-Proliferation Treaty (NPT) broke up with no consensus. Meanwhile, events suggested that several would-be proliferators were continuing their progress towards nuclear-weapons capability.

If the results of 1980 were meagre for arms control, the year also provided few signs that the situation would improve. In some cases, such as the talks about reducing outside presence in the Indian Ocean, 1980 seemed to confirm that the attempt had been doomed from the beginning. In the case of the Strategic Arms Limitation Talks (SALT), the growing American scepticism about arms control was more and more apparent, bringing with it a real possibility of strain between the United States and her European allies. As the Reagan Administration came to office, it pledged to continue the SALT process, but it would certainly be well into 1981 before the new team knew what it wanted out of future negotiations.

STRATEGIC ARMS LIMITATION TALKS

As 1981 opened, the future of SALT remained uncertain. President Ronald Reagan and the Republican majority in the US Senate accustomed themselves to the reality of government, while the Soviet Union warily assessed the meaning of the change in American leadership. The new Administration made clear that it would not seek the ratification of SALT II in its existing form but that it wanted the SALT process to continue, perhaps even soon. What the Administration might seek in the realm of SALT, however, remained open, and the new Defense Secretary, Caspar Weinberger, suggested it would be mid-1981 or later before the new team was prepared to make proposals to the Soviet Union.

For the time being, neither side seemed willing to foreclose the possibility of reviving SALT II in some form. Officially, the United States said she would take no action to defeat the purpose of the treaty. Though the Soviet Union did not take a parallel position and insisted that an unratified agreement is not binding, she reaffirmed her desire to have the treaty ratified by the United States, implying that she will not act against the principles of the agreement while some prospect of its coming into force remains. As 1981 began both sides were acting so as not to prejudice future implementation of SALT II's terms. That meant, for example, that both refrained from flight-testing intercontinental ballistic missiles (ICBM) with more warheads than the treaty would permit if ratified.

By contrast, while both the United States and the Soviet Union were continuing to dismantle submarine delivery vehicles under the terms of the 1972 Interim Offensive Weapons Agreement, neither side was moving to meet the 1979 treaty's ceilings on strategic nuclear delivery vehicles and tests. This would have required reductions of 254 delivery vehicles by the USSR and 33 by the US, to a final ceiling of 2,250 each. However, this omission would not undermine the treaty, since the dismantling could always be done later.

The long postponement of ratification vitiated the SALT II Protocol, which was to expire at the end of 1981. The Protocol, intended temporarily to restrain new technologies until more lasting agreements could be reached, included bans on deployment and flight testing of mobile ICBM launchers and the deployment of land- and sea-based cruise missiles with ranges in excess of 600 km. However, with the June 1979 US decision to deploy the MX mobile missile after 1985 and NATO's December 1979 decision to deploy land-based, medium-range cruise misiles in Western Europe in 1983, the Protocol constraints had come to have little more than symbolic value. The other programmes deferred by the Protocol appeared not to be under serious consideration by either party.

The important provisions of SALT II – the overall ceilings and sub-ceilings, the counting and classification rules, the aids to military surveillance and verification, and the expanded role of the Standing Consultative Commission – thus remained in suspense. This was likely to continue until a new agreement was fashioned to replace SALT or one of the signatories indicated that it no longer intended to become a party to the treaty.

If the Reagan Administration were actively to pursue an arms-control effort, then – so its early statements suggested – it would want to do so only after strengthening America's strategic forces. It would insist on making progress in arms control dependent on Soviet behaviour being generally compatible with essential American security interests (the notion of 'linkage' which Mr Carter had sought to avoid until late 1979); and its strategic arms-control objectives would include much lower aggregate ceilings on delivery vehicles (a position reminiscent of Carter's March 1977 'comprehensive proposals').

The basic SALT options open to the Reagan Administration are:

1. To abandon SALT II while accelerating existing strategic programmes and initiating new ones to correct perceived strategic imbalances.

2. To continue observing the central features of SALT II while seeking to renegotiate only those aspects of the treaty it regards as particularly unacceptable – such as the provision that only the Soviet Union may deploy 'heavy' missiles or the exclusion of the Soviet *Backfire* bomber from the numerical ceilings of the treaty proper.

3. To continue not to foreclose implementation of SALT II while seeking to do better in SALT '2½' – a new agreement that would have lower ceilings on strategic forces, and a longer duration and would generally conform more to the Administration's view of an equitable accord.

Decisions about the future of SALT will be influenced by the fact that few, if any, American weapons initiatives taken now would affect the strategic balance in the near term. Even if existing programmes – such as the MX ICBM, the *Trident* SLBM, or even air-launched cruise missiles – were accelerated, the systems would not by 1985 be available in such numbers as to have much impact on the balance. Even the 'quick fixes' mentioned by Reagan advisers – like random basing of *Minuteman* ICBM among an increased number of silos, or the deployment of cruise missiles aboard attack submarines – would be expensive and would take time to accomplish.

The Soviet Union, on the other hand, could affect the balance simply by continuing to deploy more of the current generation of missiles, the SS-17, -18 and -19. Moreover, while in theory the United States could initiate strategic programmes that would violate the qualitative provisions of SALT II (for instance, the limits on warheads per missile) to do so would be less in her military interest than similar breaches would be for the Soviet Union. In short, complying with at least the qualitative provisions of SALT II is comparatively easier and, at present, more advantageous for the US than for the USSR. There was also a question about how much the Reagan Administration would be able to increase the defence budget. Much of the projected expansion will in any case go to manpower and conventional forces. The lead times for strategic programmes are long, and many of the 'quick fixes' discussed during the campaign are likely to yield only marginal gains at enormous cost. Yet the broad array of production and research and development programmes proposed by the new Administration in the strategic area, many of them not contrary to the letter of SALT II, might send a cautionary signal to the Soviet Union. How this signal would be received and interpreted in Moscow was one of the major question marks for the future of SALT in 1981.

The new Administration was therefore facing an exquisite dilemma: how to reconcile its earlier criticism of SALT II as negotiated by President Carter with budgetary and strategic realities that make mutual adherence to the SALT ceilings advantageous for the United States. For her part, the Soviet Union also faced a dilemma: whether to restrain her programmes so as to preserve the possibility of maintaining some American interest in the SALT II limits and in negotiating additional ones, or whether to dismiss the SALT process and take advantage of whatever time and productive capacity she has available so as to meet the likely expansion of US strategic forces after the mid-1980s.

In resolving these issues, both sides will have to give some thought to the one substantive SALT accomplishment: the 1972 Anti-Ballistic Missile (ABM) Treaty, which comes up for review in 1982. The decisions about offensive weapons and new defensive technologies which both sides take before then will bear on the ultimate future of this treaty. In the United States in particular, interest in strategic defence, including deployments that would require altering or abrogating the ABM Treaty, has been growing (for a detailed discussion, see pp. 43–4).

As both the SALT treaties and the SALT process hang in the balance, there will be a risk of misunderstandings and miscalculations during the period of internal reassessment and external signalling that began with the new Administration. However, unless there is a decision or miscalculation in Washington or Moscow that leads to a complete rupture, the likelihood is that the SALT I ceilings and major SALT II qualitative constraints will survive in some form, along with limits on defensive systems in the ABM Treaty. The process of Soviet–American dialogue on strategic arms control – through the SALT Standing Consultative Commission, and through *ad hoc* and diplomatic exchanges – would continue. But major substantive achievements in strategic arms control seemed unlikely.

Long-Range Theatre Nuclear Forces

Soviet–American discussions on long-range theatre nuclear forces (TNF) had been called for by both sides (albeit on different conditions), NATO having formed a Special Consultative Group beforehand, to ensure that European views were taken into account in US positions. Talks began in Geneva on 16 October and lasted for several weeks. Under the shadow of the American presidential election they took a rather tentative form. The fact that they began at all, however, suggested there had been some movement towards common concepts, since there did at least seem to be agreement that the talks should be bilateral and should initially focus on missiles. Yet in other respects the two sides remained far apart.

NATO's initial offer to negotiate (part of its December 1979 decision to deploy new long-range TNF in Europe) had reflected the widespread feeling in Europe that NATO could not deploy new weaponry without simultaneously offering to negotiate. (For the political aspects of the TNF talks, see pp. 81–3.) After at first insisting that talks could go forward only if NATO suspended its December decision, in July the Soviet Union agreed to preliminary talks but stipulated that any results could only be implemented after the SALT Treaty went into effect.

Though these talks did then begin in October, it was hard to see how negotiations could produce a 'balance', or even how the sides could agree on what was to be balanced. NATO insisted that any agreement should cover medium-range missiles, involve '*de jure* equality both in ceilings and in rights', and be adequately verifiable. However, the Soviet Union had consistently held that her long-range TNF were a response to the US forward-based systems – medium-range aircraft based in and around Europe and capable of hitting Soviet territory (even if only just) – and that it was the new cruise missiles and *Pershings* to be deployed as a result of NATO's December 1979 decision that threatened to disrupt the balance. And in agreeing to the preliminary talks the Soviet Union was adamant that they could only involve medium-range missiles if 'organically' combined with discussions on 'existing American forward-based nuclear delivery vehicles'. She did not concede that in this case Soviet medium-range aircraft should be included (though it was hinted that *Backfire* might be on the agenda) nor that those SS-20s based in the central part of the USSR, and thus capable of attacking either European or Asian targets, should be counted.

Even if the United States can persuade the Soviet Union to exclude shorter-range aircraft and those based on carriers assigned to the US Sixth Fleet, the negotiating problems are formidable. Since Soviet deployments of both the SS-20 missile and the *Backfire* bombers are well under way, and since the USSR has no pressing need to phase out her older systems, her bargaining position is strong. And it is difficult to see how the NATO principle of equal ceilings can be met without substantial Soviet concessions and only a slight cut in the planned NATO programmes. If aircraft were drawn in – most likely the US F-111s based in Britain, and probably the *Badgers*, *Blinders* and

Backfires on the Soviet side – that would only compound the problems caused by the growing Soviet numerical superiority in theatre systems.

In the end, it may prove possible to manage the TNF talks only by integrating them with those on central strategic systems in SALT III. An increased ceiling with some freedom to mix long-range TNF and central systems might allow for the appearance of parity while avoiding the awkward demands the principle of parity imposes on negotiations confined to the European theatre. It would also avoid the impression of 'decoupling' the European from the strategic context that might result from two distinct sets of negotiations. Yet there is no gainsaying that this would complicate, and thus prolong, SALT negotiations that will be protracted in the best of circumstances.

MUTUAL AND BALANCED FORCE REDUCTION TALKS

The MBFR talks in Vienna remained hostage to the deteriorating state of East–West relations and the demise of SALT II. The Presidential election and subsequent uncertainty over the policies the Reagan Administration would pursue, as well as the meeting in Madrid to review the Conference on Security and Co-operation in Europe (CSCE), cast their shadows over the Vienna negotiations. The Soviet Union appeared to be biding her time to see whether earlier Eastern proposals for a Conference on Military Detente and Disarmament in Europe would be accepted in Madrid. Similarly, the Western European MBFR participants were tempted by aspects of the French proposal, made at Madrid, for a European Security Conference limited to conventional weapons, focused on confidence-building measures (CBM) and taking in all Soviet territory west of the Urals (see p. 84). At the same time, neither side wished to bear responsibility for breaking up the Vienna talks, which both saw as a useful point of contact between East and West at a time when many other channels had dried up.

In December 1979 the Western side had proposed to facilitate agreement by beginning with a simplified first phase of reductions, comprising 30,000 Soviet and 13,000 US troops, before reaching agreement on the

second phase that would cover other participants as well. At the same time, the West tabled proposals for measures to accompany reductions. These so-called Associated Measures, to monitor withdrawals and verify remaining force levels, would apply not only in the Guidelines Area of the negotiations proper (the territory of East Germany, Poland and Czechoslovakia in the East, and West Germany and the Benelux countries in the West) but would also extend to the western USSR.

The East was critical of this package on four points: equipment reductions were excluded; the linkage between phases was too loose; the Associated Measures were more extensive and intrusive than was necessary to verify such simple reductions; and the measures went further geographically than originally agreed. Consequently, the Eastern side made an alternative proposal on 10 July, which envisaged the withdrawal of only 20,000 Soviet troops against 13,000 American, and took into account the *unilateral* withdrawal of 20,000 Soviet troops from East Germany resulting from Mr Brezhnev's announcement in East Berlin on 6 October 1979. The East also argued for collective equality, and proposed that no country be allowed to deploy more than half of the troops of either bloc – a proposal obviously directed at West Germany. As Chancellor

Schmidt had already expressed interest in committing the *Bundeswehr* not to exceed 50% of the Western collective ceiling, there was some convergence on this issue.

However, as the Western spokesman made clear at the end of the 243rd Plenary Session in December, data and assurance of verification continued to divide the sides: 'Until there is agreed data on Soviet ground forces, there is no way of identifying the net effect of the Soviet unilateral withdrawals ... It is only when Eastern participants enter into practical co-operation on the resolution of the data issue that Western participants will be able to take at full value the stated Eastern interest in concluding an early first agreement in these negotiations'. In November 1980, the Eastern side came forward with a proposal to freeze force levels between phases. Although in principle attractive, this turned out to be a rather empty political gesture because the data question would again intrude, and it would not be easy to verify satisfactorily that a freeze was being adhered to without implementing at least part of the West's Associated Measures.

It therefore remained to be seen whether a way round the data problem could be found which could satisfy the West's stated conditions and which did not force the Soviet Union to admit publicly that her earlier declarations were in error. There were scant grounds for optimism, not least since the Soviet refusal indicated a lack of political interest in overruling the military's insistence on secrecy. And it was likely that the new US Congress would demand high standards of verification before ratifying any MBFR agreement.

As 1981 began it was too soon to determine what impact (if any) the CSCE negotiations in Madrid would have on the Vienna talks. Given the stated Western interests in substantive negotiations, and in binding commitments rather than loose declarations of intent, the Western participants were unlikely to exchange the more technical Vienna talks for some wider and more political forum, even if they were attracted by aspects of the French CSCE proposal. Nor would they want to provide the Soviet Union with an excuse to lead the Eastern participants out of the MBFR negotiations. Even if movement remains sluggish, the transformation of Vienna into a kind of *de facto* multilateral standing consultative committee to exchange information and query suspicious deployments has some virtue, notwithstanding the lack of progress in the data discussion. MBFR might thereby become at least a forum for providing reassurance about the force deployments of East and West in Europe.

What the MBFR negotiations have served to demonstrate is that the kind of unilateral gestures represented by the reduction of 20,000 men in the East and of 1,000 nuclear warheads in the West are relatively meaningless unless associated with measures to assure the other side that what goes out does not come back. Soon after the much-publicized departure of the first of the 20,000 Soviet troops, suggestions were made in the press that the USSR was filtering men back to increase the strength of the formations remaining in Eastern Europe. Whether true or not, the fact remains that the absence of intrusive and continuous monitoring does raise such doubts. There can hardly be an enduring basis for mutual confidence if political gestures, which are obviously intended to convey important signals to the other side, are negated by mistrust.

NON-PROLIFERATION

In 1980 the prospects for nuclear proliferation worsened. Disagreements over the proper approach to the use and transfer of sensitive nuclear materials and technology revived with the ending of the grace period of the 1978 US Nuclear Non-Proliferation Act, which threatened the nuclear energy programmes in both the industrialized and developing world, and the conclusion of the International Fuel Cycle Evaluation (INFCE). Efforts to shore up the non-proliferation regime faltered at the second Review Conference of the Non-Proliferation Treaty (NPT), while developments in South Asia and the Middle East illustrated the new challenges to existing efforts to prevent the spread of nuclear weapons.

INFCE

In February, a Final Plenary meeting concluded the two-year International Nuclear Fuel Cycle Evaluation. INFCE had been proposed in 1977 by the Carter Administration as a way to discover and promote methods to further insulate civil nuclear programmes from military uses, with emphasis on minimizing the availability of weapons-grade plutonium and uranium. Despite suspicions that underlying American motives were essentially aimed at obstructing other countries' nuclear programmes, 66 governments and five international organizations agreed to participate – though they insisted that 'nuclear energy for peaceful purposes should be made widely available', that INFCE would be a technical study and not a negotiation, and that participants would not be bound by its results.

Eight working groups were created in October 1977 to study various aspects of the nuclear fuel cycle, including projected uranium and enrichment availability, fuel and technology supply assurances, plutonium reprocessing, fast breeder reactors, spent fuel management, waste management and disposal, and advanced fuel cycle and reactor concepts. The political aspect of INFCE's fundamental objective – reconciling energy needs with non-proliferation aims – was thus submerged in technical discussions about the expected growth rate of nuclear power, the merits of reprocessing plutonium for waste management and recycling through light water reactors, and the optimal timing of fast breeder reactor commercialization (see Steven J. Warnecke, 'Non-Proliferation and INFCE: An Interim Assessment', *Survival*, May/June 1979, pp. 116–24). This effort at depoliticizing the issue, however, could not remove conflicts rooted in divergent national resources and interests. For instance, the nuclear power programmes of Japan and Western European countries, unlike that of the United States, depend upon foreign uranium supplies. Their governments, understandably reluctant to add to their already painful oil dependence the further risks of long-term vulnerability to the vagaries of uranium suppliers, were eager to exploit their own nuclear fuel stocks (obtained from reprocessing plutonium) in the most efficient way by using the fast breeder reactor, which produces more plutonium than it consumes. On the other hand, American policy since 1976 had emphasized the danger of premature entry into the 'plutonium economy'. At the same time, the attitude of third-world countries tended to be guided by traditional demands for equal status, which in the nuclear field is often taken to mean having full access to the same nuclear technologies that the advanced industrial nations possess.

The final working group reports served as the basis for an overall report, drafted by a technical co-ordinating committee, and approved by consensus at the Final Plenary in February. The result could not satisfy earlier expectations. Inevitably the document reaffirmed energy views long held by nuclear proponents world-wide. The initial assumption that nuclear energy should be made widely available was reflected in palpably over-optimistic projections of nuclear power growth, which not only distorted all the related calculations of demand for different nuclear fuel cycles but also rendered the report's general conclusions open to question. Moreover, although INFCE could not have begun without it, the insistence that the study should remain technical yielded a final report which contributed few suggestions for coping with the fundamentally political problem of how to dissuade countries which do not have nuclear weapons from joining the ranks of those that do.

Despite its shortcomings, however, INFCE served a number of purposes. Its data and studies, though often biased, were still useful, especially for third-world nuclear scientists who lacked the resources to conduct independent analyses. INFCE also gave the US Administration an argument for deferring the seemingly intractable disagreements between the US and her European and Japanese customers for enriched uranium, who had been obliged by the 1978 Nuclear Non-Proliferation Act to renegotiate bilateral agreements for atomic co-operation in order to permit the US to apply stricter controls over the use of American-supplied nuclear fuel. The Act stipulated that the United States would terminate all nuclear co-operation with any nation which neither pledged to accept international safeguards on all nuclear facilities, nor acknowledged the right of the US to determine all subsequent uses of the nuclear fuel she had supplied.

By far the most significant achievement of INFCE, however, was to demonstrate a consensus. Even to discuss calmly for two years a subject on which proposals by certain governments had long seemed to elicit automatically hostile responses from others would have been notable. Yet INFCE went further, its participants jointly concluding without major dissent that civil nuclear technology and facilities 'could be drawn on for a subsequent nuclear weapons programme', and identifying a number of technical means to minimize this danger. This official acknowledgement was a signal accomplishment, in spite of INFCE's defects.

NPT Review Conference
The second quinquennial conference to review the NPT convened in a far less felicitous climate than its 1975 predecessor. In 1975, memories of India's disturbing detonation of a 'peaceful' nuclear device in May 1974 had still been fresh. Also, the nuclear-weapon states seemed to be making perceptible, if sluggish, progress towards their obligations under Article VI of the Treaty, 'to pursue negotiations in good faith on effective measures' of arms control and disarmament, through the 1972 SALT agreement and subsequent Vladivostok accords. Moreover, and reflecting the importance of the Conference, several important nations had acceded to the Treaty just before or during the meeting.

By 1980, in contrast, the issue of nuclear weapons proliferation had become encrusted with mutual hostility, not simply between states that had nuclear weapons and those that did not, but also between the buyers and sellers of civil nuclear technology, and even among the sellers themselves. Since, apart from the major nuclear-weapon states, no others had openly conducted any nuclear tests since the 1974 Indian explosion (not even India herself), earlier fears of a third-world stampede to obtain or test nuclear weapons had faded. On the other hand, the arsenals of the nuclear-weapon states had continued to increase, unrestrained by any significant arms-control, let alone disarmament, measures. By the time of the Review Conference in August 1980 the SALT II agreements seemed irretrievable, while a comprehensive test ban seemed no nearer than it had five years previously (see p.116).

From the outset, countries such as Argentina, Brazil and India had refused to sign the NPT on the grounds that it was a discriminatory document which countenanced immense nu-

clear arsenals in a few states while requiring the rest to forswear the nuclear option and submit their nuclear facilities to international safeguards and inspections. Those countries felt their criticism was given further credence by the London Suppliers Club, established in the wake of the Indian test by the seven nations most involved in exporting nuclear technology (originally the US, the USSR, Britain, France, West Germany, Japan and Canada). The Club aimed to establish common export guidelines which would extend the application of safeguards, assuring that competition for future nuclear sales would be based only on commercial considerations, not on who offered the most advanced technology or the least safeguards requirements. These guidelines were published in February 1978.

Just before the 1980 Review Conference, a number of countries ratified the Treaty, notably Turkey, Indonesia, Sri Lanka and Bangladesh. Nevertheless, this was a less impressive array than the list of countries which ratified at the time of the 1975 Review Conference, and it included none of the non-NPT members considered most able to develop nuclear weapons – Argentina, Brazil, India, Israel, Pakistan, South Africa and Spain. Still more disturbing were warnings that some NPT parties, such as Peru and Mexico, might withdraw from the Treaty on the grounds that the signatories possessing nuclear weapons had not honoured their NPT commitment to arms control.

The conference gave vent to the several disenchantments with the Treaty. At the outset, the Yugoslav, Romanian and Philippine representatives complained of obstacles to countries seeking to construct nuclear power plants. Two committees of the whole conference were established: the first to review NPT provisions relating to nuclear weapons, disarmament and security assurances; the second to review peaceful nuclear energy applications and safeguards. The Second Committee came close to agreement, but the First was deadlocked. The 'Group of 77' – a grouping of developing countries – insisted, with some sympathy from Sweden, that the Conference's final declaration should note that Article VI had not been fulfilled, should recommend steps towards the conclusion of SALT II and Comprehensive Test Ban (CTB) treaties, and call for an end to all nuclear co-operation with Israel and South Africa. Despite energetic last-minute efforts, the differences among the delegates could not be overcome, and the Conference adjourned without issuing any final declaration.

Diplomatically, then, the Second NPT Review Conference failed in a way that may damage the credibility of the Treaty and thereby undermine existing commitments to fulfil its obligations. The adjournment of the conference in discord set an unfortunate precedent against compromise, and could pave the way for wider rifts between the nuclear-weapon states and the other signatories. The lack of consensus on an Article VI declaration meant that both the Group of 77 and arms-control advocates within the nuclear-weapon states lacked a fresh indication of international pressure for more effective arms control.

Nevertheless, the Conference underlined the continuing relevance of the Treaty. This was shown by the high turnout (delegates or observers from 75 parties and 11 non-parties attended) as well as by the absence of any withdrawals. Despite the deadlock in the First Committee, the lack of acrimony in the Second Committee's review of safeguards and peaceful nuclear uses was encouraging – notwithstanding the earlier disputes about the unilateral and discriminatory nature of the London Suppliers' Club and the US Non-Proliferation Act. Nonetheless, it would be unwise for the nuclear-weapon states to ignore the warning represented by the Conference deadlock. In the end, the NPT is probably held together by the recognition of most countries that they are safer if both they and their neighbours forgo nuclear weapons. That is more important than any implicit link between horizontal and vertical non-proliferation, whereby non-nuclear states might remain so, provided existing nuclear powers reduced their nuclear arsenals. Still, the political symbolism of that link could play a role in decisions of third-world states, about whether to develop nuclear weapons.

Prospects for Proliferation

The most worrisome developments in nuclear weapons proliferation in 1980 took place in South Asia and the Middle East. Pakistan continued efforts to obtain facilities capable of producing weapon-grade materials, specifically through the clandestine construction of an unsafeguarded uranium enrichment plant at Kahota, near Rawalpindi (see *Strategic Survey 1979*, pp. 15–20). In 1980 US nonproliferation pressure eased in the wake of the Soviet invasion of Afghanistan, and the US embargo on military and financial aid to Pakistan (triggered in April 1979 by unsafeguarded nuclear activities) was replaced by an offer of $400 million in military assistance. Watching her neighbour with concern, India's Prime Minister Gandhi refused to rule out the possibility that the Indian nuclear explosives programme would be resumed (see p. 72).

In the Middle East concern centred around Iraq, an NPT signatory who had acquired a research reactor from the Soviet Union in 1968 and another (*Isis*) from France. More recently, she had purchased a 70-megawatt French research reactor (*Osirak*) designed to use uranium enriched to over 90% uranium-235, the concentration required for a nuclear weapon. The core of this reactor was mysteriously blown up by saboteurs in 1979, as it awaited shipment at the southern French port of Seyne-sur-Mer. The French Government, which had become more restrained in its nuclear export policy since Premier Chirac signed the original agreement in 1975, tried to convince Iraq to accept a new reactor using less-highly-enriched uranium instead. However, when Iraq refused, France resumed deliveries for *Osirak* and, in the summer of 1980, transferred 10–15 kg of weapons-grade highly-enriched uranium. The *Osirak* facility was bombed during the war with Iran, setting back its planned 1981/2 operational date. Suspicions about Iraq were intensified by her nuclear agreements with non-NPT party Brazil for the exchange of information and with Italy for the purchase of 'hot-cell' facilities (used to shield technicians from radioactivity during the separation of plutonium from spent fuel).

Although President Saddam Hussein denied any intention to manufacture atomic weapons, he alluded menacingly to improvements in Iraqi technology which would make his country a 'totally different' enemy in the near future. Further, after the bomber attacks during the opening days of the war with Iran, Iraq refused to permit International Atomic Energy Agency (IAEA) inspections of *Osirak* and *Isis* while war conditions persisted. This was the first time a refusal had been issued on such grounds for such dangerous material, and it cast doubt on prior French and IAEA assurances that the weapons-grade uranium supplied to Iraq would be adequately safeguarded against military use. These developments occasioned deep international concern, particularly in Israel, which moved in the United Nations to drop her long-standing objection to a nuclear-free zone in the Middle East. Meanwhile, fearful of an Israeli nuclear force, Syria reportedly obtained some Soviet assurance of protection from nuclear attack at the time the Soviet-Syrian Treaty of Friendship and Co-operation was signed in Moscow on 8 October.

Controversy also continued throughout 1980 over the possibility that a nuclear test had been conducted on 22 September 1979 in the South Atlantic. On that date, an American *Vela* satellite had detected two bright flashes within one second – the characteristic signature of an atomic explosion. US radio telescopes and sonar receptors registered some corroborating evidence that a nuclear test had taken place; on the other hand, no southern hemisphere monitoring station detected unusual amounts of radioactivity. A CIA report that South African naval forces were in the area at the time of the incident suggested South African involvement – which Pretoria, however, denied. The possibility of Israeli involvement was also alleged. Despite disputes within the American intelligence community and beyond it, a White House inquiry concluded that the evidence from the satellite was inconclusive and suggested that the 'explosion' was probably of non-nuclear origin, perhaps caused by the impact of a small meteoroid on the satellite's surface. Reports that the heat sensors of a *Vela* satellite had detected another nuclear explosion in the same area on 15 December 1980 reinforced scepticism over this conclusion.

The uncertainty as to whether or not nuclear tests had taken place underscored how hard it often is to determine the facts about clandestine nuclear programmes. When a government openly conducts a nuclear test, even if it insists that its intentions are 'peaceful', it unambiguously distinguishes itself from those states which have not yet done so. Should states, like South Africa and Israel, which have not exploded a nuclear device but are presumed to have one, be treated as having 'crossed the line'? To do so would weaken the NPT regime. Yet if they are still officially regarded as not having nuclear weapons, and so enjoy both the advantages of their presumed nuclear status and continued access to co-operation with existing nuclear powers under the Treaty, the NPT still suffers.

Implicit in the initial NPT bargain was a promise that, under Article IV, countries which forswore nuclear weapons would receive preferential treatment in the acquisition of nuclear technology for peaceful purposes. In practice, however, NPT parties have been taken for granted, while nuclear or near-nuclear non-signatories (like Argentina, Brazil and India) have often received sensitive technologies from suppliers who wish to discourage them from building their own unsafeguarded facilities. Unless some preferential treatment for NPT parties is introduced, not only may the Treaty gain no new adherents but some parties may one day exercise their right under Article X to withdraw, thus undermining the centrepiece of the world-wide consensus opposing nuclear proliferation.

Aware of this danger, governments may move to reform existing institutions through the newly-created Committee for the Assurance of Supply (CAS), a successor to INFCE which could establish norms designed to reward NPT adherents with guaranteed nuclear fuel supplies. It would be premature to pin many hopes on the CAS, which began slowly. Its first meeting in November was wholly devoted to negotiating the composition of the Executive Secretariat, and substantive discussion was deferred until March 1981, in part due to uncertainties surrounding future American policies. Because the United States will for many years remain the source and controller of most of the enriched uranium fuel now in use world-wide, the extent to which President Reagan chooses to modify his predecessor's vigorous attention to nuclear proliferation will fundamentally shape the nuclear debate for the next four years.

OTHER ARMS-CONTROL NEGOTIATIONS

With one exception, other arms-control negotiations met the same fate as their better-publicized counterparts during 1980. There was progress only in talks on controlling the use of certain dangerous conventional weapons against civilians. Otherwise, the deteriorating East–West climate eliminated what slim chance of progress there might have been. For instance, the Soviet–American talks on naval arms limitations in the Indian Ocean, moribund since the Spring of 1978, became a dead letter with the hostage crisis in Iran, the Soviet invasion of Afghanistan and the subsequent acceleration in military activity in the Indian Ocean; and the same developments also hung over the meeting in June to prepare for a proposed 1981 UN conference seeking to implement the General Assembly's declaration of the Indian Ocean as a zone of peace. Bilateral Soviet–American discussion of restraints on anti-satellite systems and on chemical weapons both also ran into the sands in the aftermath of Afghanistan. In April, the United States accused the Soviet Union of violating the two year moratorium on anti-satellite weapons by testing a 'killer satellite': *Cosmos* 1174. As she had announced in 1979, China took her seat at the 40-nation Committee on Disarmament for the first time in March. That forum, re-organized the previous year, continued to be a place for non-aligned and developing countries to vent their frustration at the lack of progress in super-power arms control, a sentiment also evident at the second review conference of the NPT in August and September. But some useful work was achieved in four new working groups on chemical weapons, radiological weapons, negative security assurances to non-nuclear weapon states, and the elaboration of a comprehensive programme for disarmament.

Comprehensive Test Ban Treaty

Tripartite talks between the Soviet Union, the United States and Britain resumed in February, picking up where they had left off in 1979. Verification remained the principal stumbling-block, even though the USSR had apparently agreed earlier to the principle of having 'black box' seismic recorders on her territory; moreover, it seemed clear that neither side was willing to move toward agreement in the existing political circumstances. Negotiators put the best face they could on the talks in July, when reporting on the tenth session. The report submitted to the Committee on Disarmament claimed 'significant advances', while cautioning that 'substantial work' remained to be done before the Treaty could be finalized. The report did state that, under certain circumstances, on-site observers might be permitted to inspect an area where a nuclear test carried out in violation of the Treaty was alleged to have occured. However, with the onset of the Review Conference of the NPT, the parties had reason to emphasize the progress that was being made. And it was far from clear that success in the three-year negotiations was any nearer, given the international climate, and in particular the growing American scepticism about the value of the Treaty.

Chemical and Biological Warfare

The Biological Weapons Convention, which came into force in March 1975, came up for review in March 1980 amidst allegations that the Soviet Union had violated it by continuing to conduct research and development on biological toxins designed for use in war. The 11th round of the bilateral Soviet–American talks on chemical weapons was due to have started in January but was postponed until February by the United States following the Soviet invasion of Afghanistan. The 12th round took place in May, and a statement on the progress of the talks was made to the Committee on Disarmament on 7 July. Verification remained the sticking point, and no date was set for the 13th round. There were also allegations that the Soviet Union had used chemical weapons in Afghanistan, and by the year-end the US was inclined less to negotiate over chemical weapons than to build up her own capabilities.

The incident which touched off Western concern about biological weapons allegedly occurred at a military compound in Sverdlovsk in the Soviet Union in April 1979. As a result of an explosion, quantities of a strain of bacteria identified as I-21 were released into the atmosphere. Estimates of resulting deaths ranged between 40 and 1,000, and large-scale evacuations apparently took place. The Soviet Union first denied the whole incident, saying it was a natural outbreak of anthrax. Soviet authorities vehemently denied that biological warfare experiments beyond the purely defensive ones permitted by the Treaty were being conducted in Sverdlovsk or anywhere else in the Soviet Union. American intelligence was unable publicly to confirm the details of the incident at Sverdlovsk but inclined to the conclusion that the USSR had in fact violated the 1972 convention.

There were similar allegations throughout the year that the Soviet Union and her allies had used chemical weapons in Afghanistan, Laos, Cambodia and Ethiopia. Such allegations were inherently difficult to prove, but the US State Department concluded in August, that chemical weapons probably had been used in the first three countries, with Ethiopia a more problematical case. These incidents increased the pressure on the United States to review her own chemical warfare posture. In late 1979 $195 million had been included in the American US defence budget to begin the construction of a chemical weapons facility at Pine Bluffs, Arkansas, but that money was withdrawn on objections from the State Department and the Arms Control and Disarmament Agency that the move would harm prospects for negotiations. Congress, however, insisted, and in September 1980 the House of Representatives voted overwhelmingly to include the original allocation in the fiscal 1981 defence budget. Momentum was clearly developing behind the argument that to deter Soviet chemical warfare capabilities the United States had to build up her own stock of offensive weapons, especially binary chemical munitions – pairs of chemicals that are harmless individually, and thus are easy to handle, but become lethal when mixed, for example by the explosion of a chemical shell.

'Inhumane' Conventional Weapons

The year's modest arms control success occurred in October, when 72 countries agreed in principle to curb the use of 'excessively injurious' conventional weapons and sent the Treaty to the United Nations General Assembly for approval. The Convention, which supplements the Geneva Conventions of 1949 and their protocols of 1977, required ratification by 20 countries before coming into force. It opened for signature at the UN on 10 April 1981. The last obstacle to completion of the two years of negotiations had been removed when the Soviet Union, embarrassed by pressure from Scandinavian and developing countries, agreed to a total ban on the use of incendiary weapons against civilians (she had earlier held out for limiting the ban to napalm). The Treaty prohibits the use of booby-traps and fragmentation bombs against civilians, and bans land-mines in civilian areas; mines may be used for military purposes only if their locations are carefully recorded so that they may be removed after the war. Fire bombs and defoliants may not be used in forest areas unless combatants are known to be hiding there. Importantly, the Treaty's protection is extended to national liberation movements engaged in an international armed conflict if they promise, in their turn, to enforce obedience to the agreements, but, in line with the 1977 protocols, the Treaty does not cover internal insurrection. None of the limitations apply to combatants, despite efforts during the negotiation to extend coverage to them.

CHRONOLOGIES

UNITED STATES AND CANADA

January

3　　State Department announces $280 m of defensive weapons to be sold to Taiwan, ending 1-year moratorium following full diplomatic recognition of China.

4–　　President Carter announces 17 m tonnes of US grain ordered by USSR will not be delivered, in protest at Soviet intervention in Afghanistan. Suspends sale of high-technology and strategic goods (9). At meeting of leading grain exporters in Washington, Argentina, Australia, Canada and EEC agree not to increase shipments to USSR to make up for US embargo (12). Argentina denies agreement (14).

13　　USSR vetoes US resolution in UN Security Council to embargo Iran.

14　　Carter promises US will take 'whatever action is required' to protect her interests in Asia.

15　　Three nuclear-powered US warships (*Nimitz*, *Texas*, and *California*) enter Indian Ocean; 21 US ships now in the area.

20–　　Carter gives the USSR until 20 Feb. to withdraw troops from Afghanistan, or US will boycott Moscow Olympics. In State of Union message to Congress declares that if US interests in Gulf are threatened 'such an assault will be repelled by use of any means necessary, including military force' (23).

24　　Italian Prime Minister Cossiga arrives in Washington on state visit.

28　　Carter's budget, sent to Congress, calls for defence budget of $142.7 billion – 3.3% real increase over 1980.

February

8–　　Carter announces plan to resume registration of men for draft and permit registration of women. Plan for women abandoned on Congressional objections (26). Rest of plan approved by Congress (25 June).

12　　Carter announces dispatch of amphibious assault force (1,800 Marines and 4 ships) to Indian Ocean. Force arrives (17 March).

18–　　Liberal party wins 48% of vote and 148 of 281 seats in Canadian general election. Pierre Trudeau sworn in as Prime Minister (3 March).

20　　Carter's deadline for Soviet troop withdrawal from Afghanistan passes unheeded; US will boycott Moscow Olympics.

26　　Ronald Reagan emerges as Republican presidential favourite after winning 50% of votes in New Hampshire primary.

27　　Pentagon asks Congress to fund development of 'binary chemical warhead' to counter apparent build-up in Soviet nerve-gas programme.

March

3　　Carter says US vote on 1 March for UN Security Council resolution condemning the Israeli settlement policy was an error (see Middle East).

April

1–　　Carter postpones sanctions against Iran as Iranian President Bani-Sadr undertakes that US hostages will soon be transferred to Iranian Government custody. US expels Iranian diplomats after Ayatollah Khomeini states that hostages should remain with their militant student captors (7). Carter announces new sanctions, including bans on Iranian imports to US and financial transactions with Iranians (17).

2　　Pentagon confirms American personnel to be stationed in Oman, Kenya and Somalia as part of build-up in Indian Ocean region.

14　　US offers asylum to up to 3,500 of the Cuban refugees sheltering in the Peruvian Embassy in Havana (see *Latin America*).

25–　　US reports failure of attempt by special military force to rescue hostages from Iran; 8 US soldiers die when transport aircraft and helicopter collide as rescuers withdraw. President Carter accepts full responsibility. Secretary of State Vance resigns in disagreement (28).

27　　US naval strength in the Indian Ocean reaches 34 ships as carrier *Constellation* and six escorts arrive.

29–　　Sen. Edmund Muskie named Secretary of State. Confirmed by Senate (7 May).

May

7–   US announces plans to sell India nearly 40 tonnes of enriched uranium despite her refusal to agree on safeguards against nuclear proliferation. Senate upholds decision 48–46 (24 September).

20   In referendum Quebec voters reject by 59.5% to 40.4% provincial government proposal to break Canada's federal structure by seeking 'sovereignty-association'.

25–   Chinese Vice-Premier Geng Biao in Washington for five-day visit. US tells China she is free to buy non-lethal military equipment, such as radar and helicopters (29).

26   George Bush withdraws from race for US Republican presidential nomination.

June

3   The number of Cuban refugees arriving in US since April passes 100,000.

3–   Computer error at NORAD falsely signals that US is under Soviet attack; mistake discovered after three minutes. Second false alarm occurs (6).

27   State Department announces US and Kenya have concluded agreement expanding US access to Kenyan military facilities in exchange for greater US military and economic aid.

July

16   Ronald Reagan nominated Republican presidential candidate; chooses George Bush as vice-presidential candidate.

31   Pentagon announces nearly a third of 1979 recruits to armed services were in lowest acceptable intelligence category.

August

6–   White House announces signature of Presidential Directive 59 on nuclear strategy, emphasizing limited nuclear options. Carter orders more effective protection for civilian and military leaders in event of major war with USSR (11).

11   Democratic Party convention opens in New York. Carter renominated as presidential candidate (14).

22   Defense Secretary Harold Brown formally announces 'stealth' technology which US believes will make aircraft virtually invisible to radar.

22   US and Somalia sign agreement giving US access to Somali port and airfield at Berbera. 'No formal security commitment' by US involved but provides for $40 m military sales credits in 1980–81. Congress demands assurances that no US-supplied arms will be used in conflict in the Ogaden.

25–   UN Special Session on world economy opens. Ends after bitter debates and no progress (15 September).

26   US Government sources say the US plans to spend up to $400 m to make Egypt's Ras Banas airfield into rapid-deployment site for US planes and a division of troops.

September

17   In Washington, President Carter and Chinese Vice-Premier, Bo Yibo, sign four agreements to complete the building of normal relations between the two countries.

18   US protests to Soviet Union that nuclear test on 14 September exceeded limit of 150 KT laid down in 1974 Threshold Test Ban agreement.

19   *Titan* II missile explodes in Arkansas silo, killing 1 and injuring 21; no evidence of radiation leakage.

November

4   Ronald Reagan elected President with 51% of vote. Republicans also win Senate majority for first time in 26 years.

17   Canada drops support for the US embargo on grain exports to USSR imposed in January.

18   Carter confirms approving export to USSR of equipment for building natural gas pipeline from Siberia to Western Europe.

December

16   President-elect Reagan nominates Gen. Alexander Haig, former Supreme Allied Commander Europe, to be his Secretary of State.

EUROPE

January

3 Portugal's new centre-right government sworn in under Prime Minister Francisco Sa Carneiro.

4 French aircraft makers Dassault confirm Iraqi order for 24 *Mirage* F-1 fighter bombers.

15 Central Committee of Yugoslav Communist Party holds emergency session to discuss the situation created by President Tito's illness and puts armed forces on 'low alert'.

24 Turkish Lira devalued by 33% against US dollar (second major devaluation in a year).

24 Defence Secretary Francis Pym, announces £1,000-m project (*Chevaline*) to improve British nuclear deterrent.

30 Proposed meeting of West German Chancellor Schmidt and East German President Honecker postponed in wake of Afghanistan invasion.

February

1 Spain breaks diplomatic relations with Guatemala over Guatemalan authorities' behaviour in siege of her embassy there (see *Latin America*).

5 France recalls her ambassador and diplomatic staff from Libya after burning of Tripoli embassy.

5 President Giscard and Chancellor Schmidt, meeting in Paris, condemn Soviet intervention in Afghanistan as threatening detente but do not call for economic sanctions; agree to produce new combat tank for 1990s and communications satellite.

5 Italy confirms a $1.5-bn deal with Iraq to sell four frigates, six corvettes and a support ship.

11– Greece discusses with NATO plans for her re-entry into the Alliance military structure (she pulled out in 1974). Rejects NATO's proposal (21).

11– Polish Communist Party Congress opens; Party leader Edward Gierek, forecasts five harsh economic years. Edward Babiuch replaces Piotr Jaroszewicz as Premier (15).

15 European Parliament calls for boycott of 1980 Olympics (to be held in Moscow), urges they be held on 'agreed international territory'.

19 EEC Foreign Ministers, meeting in Rome, support British proposal for Soviet withdrawal from Afghanistan against international guarantee of Afghan neutrality.

20– US Secretary of State Vance and Chancellor Schmidt meet in Bonn to try to resolve policy differences on the Soviet intervention in Afghanistan. Vance also meets French Foreign Minister François Poncet in Paris and British Foreign Secretary Carrington in London (21).

20– Turkish Government places two more provinces (Izmir and Hatay, near the Syrian border) under martial law in effort to stem terrorist violence. International Monetary Fund approves a new $93.8-m loan to Turkey (21). Turkey withdraws air traffic restrictions contained in NOTAM 714 (22); Greece responds by withdrawing NOTAM 1157, thus opening way for air services between them after six years (23).

28 West German Government announces it will increase defence spending by 3% in 1980, meeting NATO target.

28 Autonomy referendum in Andalusia shows defeat for Spanish Left and its campaign for regional autonomy.

March

9 In the first democratic election for home-rule legislature in Spain's Basque provinces, Basque National Party takes 25 out of 60 seats; extreme nationalist party takes 17 seats.

14 Six-day *Anorak Express* manoeuvres start in Norway involving 18,000 troops from 7 NATO countries.

21 In elections to Catalan Parliament, moderate nationalist *Convergencia y Unio* wins 43 out of 135 seats – the single largest party

30 US and Turkey sign Defence Co-operation Agreement which assures continued US use of military bases there in return for military and economic assistance.

April

7 USSR resumes her force withdrawals from E. Germany, removing over 1,000 troops and dozens of tanks from Oschatz, near Leipzig.

15 In Paris, the main OECD members pledge $1.16-bn aid package for 1980 to boost Turkish economy.

22–   EEC foreign ministers, meeting in Luxembourg, decide to apply full trade sanctions against Iran from 17 May unless US hostages there are released. First-stage sanctions imposed (22 May).

30   Queen Juliana of the Netherlands abdicates in favour of her daughter, Beatrix.

30   East and West Germany sign agreement to improve West Berlin's road, rail and canal links with W. Germany.

May

4   Yugoslav leader Tito dies. Succeeded by collective leadership.

4   France launches fifth nuclear missile submarine

5–   Greek Prime Minister Constantine Karamanlis elected President. Succeeded as Prime Minister by George Rallis, former Foreign Minister (10).

5   A 12-day 9-nation NATO exercise, *Dawn Patrol 80*, begins in central and eastern Mediterranean.

14   US begins withdrawing 1,000 outdated nuclear warheads from Europe according to December 1979 NATO decision.

14   Final communique of NATO defence and foreign ministers' meeting calls for 'total and immediate withdrawal of all Soviet forces' from Afghanistan and declares that holding of US hostages in Iran is 'exacerbating instability in the South-West Asia region'.

16   After ceremony for 25th anniversary of Austrian State Treaty US Secretary of State Muskie meets Soviet Foreign Minister Gromyko in Vienna – first high-level contact between US and USSR since invasion of Afghanistan.

18   Portugal readmitted to NATO's Nuclear Planning Group (excluded in 1975 because of Communist influence in the governments of 1974-75).

19   French President Giscard meets Soviet President Brezhnev in Warsaw – first Western head of state to do so since invasion of Afghanistan.

30–   EEC Foreign Ministers in Brussels apparently ending 3-year dispute over size of British contribution to EEC budget by agreeing a scheme for British payments. Britain agrees (2 June).

June

10   In Italian regional and municipal elections, ruling Christian Democrats gain 36.8% of vote (35.3% at the previous elections in 1975), Socialists 12.7% (12%), Communists 31.5% (33.4%).

13   EEC heads-of-government summit in Venice recognizes 'right to self-determination' of Palestinian people and declares PLO will have to be associated with any negotiations.

18   Turkish National Assembly extends martial law in 20 of country's 67 provinces for another two months.

22–23 In Venice, economic summit of Britain, Canada, France, Italy, Japan, W. Germany and US demands complete withdrawal of Soviet troops from Afghanistan. Energy crisis dominates talks but reduction of inflation is 'immediate top priority'.

24   Greek and Turkish Foreign Ministers meet in Ankara. First Greek ministerial visit in 20 years.

26   Final communiqué of NATO foreign ministers' meeting condemns Soviet intervention in Afghanistan and calls for 'immediate, unconditional and total withdrawal' of Soviet troops.

26   President Giscard confirms France has tested neutron bomb and decided in principle to acquire it.

July

1   After talks with Soviet President Brezhnev, Chancellor Schmidt says he has made progress towards negotiations with the USSR on medium-range missiles in Europe.

1–   Higher meat prices introduced in Poland. Labour unrest follows. Strikers blockade railway station in Lublin as unrest spreads (18).

3   France announces agreement for sale of 50 *Dauphin* 2 helicopters to China and eventual manufacture there.

15   Britain announces she will buy US *Trident* SLBM to replace *Polaris* as her strategic deterrent in mid-1990s. Cost, including British-built warheads and new nuclear powered submarines will be some $12 bn over next 15 years.

19–   Former Turkish Premier Nihat Erim assassinated; Marxist underground organization claims responsibility Interior Minister resigns as government is criticized for failing to deal with terrorism (21). Western Governments agree to rescheduling over 10 years of $3 bn of Turkey's debts due to be paid in next 3 years (23).

21   Western European Union votes to lift restrictions on West German military shipbuilding.

August

2   Bomb at Bologna railway station kills 76, injures nearly 200. Neo-fascist Armed Revolutionary Nuclei claims responsibility.

14–   Polish radio and television admits strikes are occurring, confirms stoppages in Gdansk, Lodz and Warsaw. Twenty-two factories in Gdansk, Gdynia and Sopot set up joint strike committee and issue 16-point demand to the Polish authorities (17).

18   Turkish National Assembly extends martial law in 20 provinces for another two months.

22   Chancellor Schmidt cancels proposed meeting with East German leader Honecker because of Polish situation.

24–   Emergency meeting of Polish Communist Party Central Committee drops 6 of 14-man Politburo, including Prime Minister Babiuch. Party leader Gierek promises trade-union elections by secret ballot (one of the strikers' demands). Strike movement leader Lech Walesa and Deputy Prime Minister Mieczyslaw Jagielski sign agreement at Gdansk allowing workers to set up their own trade unions and giving them the right to strike (31). Similar agreements reached in Silesia and southern Poland (2-3 September).

September

6   Polish Communist Party Central Committee replaces Gierek with Stanislaw Kania as party leader. Fresh wave of strikes reported in eastern Poland.

8   NATO and Warsaw Pact manoeuvres begin in both West and East Europe, involving 40,000 Warsaw Pact troops from 6 countries and 250-300,000 NATO troops.

9   Preparatory session for the second CSCE Review Conference opens in Madrid.

12   Gen. Kenan Evren, commander of Turkish armed forces, heads 6-man military junta which seizes power in bloodless coup. Prime Minister Suleyman Demirel's government dissolved and political activities banned.

16   Cyprus peace talks resume in Nicosia under UN auspices after 13-month break.

24   Polish independent labour organizers present charter of their movement, *Solidarity*, to the Warsaw District Court seeking legal recognition for first free trade unions in Soviet bloc.

October

5   Social Democrats win 42.5% of vote in W. German federal elections. Coalition with Free Democrats to continue with enhanced majority under Chancellor Schmidt.

9   E. Germany raises foreign exchange fees for W. German visitors. E. German leader Honecker demands formal recognition by W. Germany of 2 German states as precondition for easing of restrictions (14).

19–20 Warsaw Pact Foreign Ministers, meeting in Warsaw, renew their call for new disarmament initiatives.

20–   Greece and Turkey approve NATO proposals for Greek re-entry into NATO military structure after 6 years absence. Greek Parliament votes 182 to 20 in favour with the Socialist opposition PASOK abstaining (24).

24–   Warsaw District court grants registration to *Solidarity* but attaches a clause acknowledging supremacy of Communist Party. To allay union anger, Government agrees to change in the wording of clause and to let newly independent unions have some access to the media (31).

30–   E. Germany restricts travel with Poland. Czechoslovakia follows suit (19 November).

November

10   *Solidarity* wins appeal to Supreme Court against lower court's insertion in charter of phrase recognizing Communist Party's leading role. Polish Government announces meat and butter rationing from January 1981 (19). *Solidarity* demands major reform of Poland's secret police; government agrees to discussions to head off threatened general strike (26).

December

2   E. Germany closes areas along Polish border; a 24-mile strip is 'temporary restricted area'.

2–   Polish Communist Party Central Committee dismisses 4 from Politburo and names 2
      replacements – one of them the hard-line former Interior Minister, Gen. Moczar. Warsaw
      Pact leaders, after unexpected summit in Moscow, denounce use of force in Poland but vow
      Poland will remain a socialist state (5). Over 1,000 Polish private farmers gather in Warsaw
      and threaten to strike if government refuses their request for their own independent trade
      union (14). At memorial service in Gdansk for those killed in December 1970 anti-
      government riots, Roman Catholic Church, Communist Party and *Solidarity* all call for
      unity (16).
7   Portuguese President Gen. Eanes re-elected for a further five years with 56% of vote.
9–   NATO defence ministers, meeting in Brussels, ask US to send four AWACS surveillance air-
      craft to Europe in response to the Polish crisis. Planes arrive (10–11). NATO foreign minis-
      ters warn that Soviet intervention in Poland would alter entire international situation and
      threaten detente (11–12).
12   In Rome, Red Brigade kidnap magistrate Giovanni D'Urso and demand closure of high-
      security prison at Asinara.
17   W. German Government agrees to increase defence spending in 1981 but cannot guarantee
      it will meet NATO target of 3% in real terms.

THE SOVIET UNION

January
3–   USSR accuses President Carter of 'bellicose and wicked' statements on Soviet involvement
      in Afghanistan, and the West of a 'frenzied propaganda outcry'. Five complete Soviet div-
      isions (at least 60,000 troops) now in Afghanistan (7).
16–17 COMECON meets in Moscow to discuss the Olympics and its possible boycott by the West.
22   Leading dissident and Nobel peace prize winner Dr Andrei Sakharov stripped of his
      honours and sent into internal exile. Jacques Chaban-Delmas, President of French Nation-
      al Assembly, cuts short Moscow visit in protest.

February
4–   In first speech since intervention in Afghanistan Soviet President Brezhnev emphasizes
      detente must go on and 'reckless imperialist forces must not be allowed to destroy its fruits'.
      Says USSR is ready to withdraw troops from Afghanistan 'as soon as outside interference'
      ends (22).

March
5   USSR rejects plan by European Community to neutralize Afghanistan in return for Soviet
      troop withdrawal.

April
10   Second Soviet underground nuclear test in 6 days takes place in Semipalatinsk area.

May
1   Representatives of at least 15 nations boycott Moscow's May Day parade in protest at
      Soviet invasion of Afghanistan.
14   Political and military leaders of Warsaw Pact meet in Warsaw to celebrate 25th anniver-
      sary of the alliance.
19   Brezhnev and French President Giscard d'Estaing meet in Warsaw.

June
5   Two Soviet cosmonauts launched on 4-day orbital mission.
12   *Pravda* calls on W. Germany to abandon its central role in NATO decision to station US
      nuclear missiles in Europe.
18   Tass says Western press reports of recent large-scale strikes by car workers in Gorki and
      Togliatti are 'Washington propaganda'.
23   Plenary session of Party Central Committee resolves to increase military strength 'to the

maximum'. Brezhnev says situation in Afghanistan returning to normal and USSR can withdraw several units. Radio Moscow announces withdrawal of 7–11,000 men and 108 tanks.

30– W. German Chancellor Schmidt, first Western head of Government to visit Moscow since Afghanistan invasion, calls on Brezhnev to withdraw all Soviet troops from Afghanistan and begin talks without preconditions on limiting medium-range missiles in Europe. USSR say Schmidt's visit has not affected Soviet policy on Afghanistan (2 July).

July
3 Soviet Union and Vietnam sign agreement giving USSR oil drilling rights off Vietnam.
19 The Moscow Olympics open with 81 countries attending (smallest number since 1956), 62 boycotting the games.
23 Soviet and Vietnamese cosmonauts begin week-long mission.

August
8 Iranian Ambassador in Moscow warns USSR to stop arms shipments to Iraq.
19 Soviet media carries its first reports on the unrest in Poland, without comment.
20 For first time since 1973, the USSR resumes jamming of BBC and Voice of America broadcasts in Russian.
21 Fire on Soviet nuclear submarine 70 miles off Japan kills 9 and injures 3. No sign of radioactive leakage is found.
27 Tass says anti-socialist forces trying to subvert socialist system in Poland.

September
2 Soviet Defence Minister Ustinov urges Japan to sign a treaty of co-operation with Moscow, criticizes Japanese military co-operation with US and China.
11 USSR pledges to send Poland extra food and industrial goods.

October
1,3 Some 2,000 students demonstrate in Tallinn, capital of Estonia, against the presence of Russian settlers in Estonia.
4 Politburo candidate member Pyotr Masherov killed in car crash; believed to have been most likely successor to Prime Minister Kosygin.
8 President Assad of Syria in Moscow, signs treaty of friendship with USSR, providing for closer military, political and economic co-operation.
11 Soviet cosmonauts set record of 185 days in space flight.
16– Afghan President Karmal and President Brezhnev sign joint statement in which USSR pledges support for Karmal's government until opposition is crushed. Karmal remains in USSR for rest and medical treatment until 4 November. Kremlin says troops will stay in Afghanistan and may shortly increase (18).
21 Brezhnev declares Party's top priority is to feed the Soviet people. Mikhail Gorbachev, aged 49, agricultural expert, elected to Politburo: its youngest member.
23 Prime Minister Kosygin (age 76) resigns because of ill health; replaced by Nikolai Tikhonov (75), his first deputy.

November
7 Annual Revolution Day parade in Moscow boycotted by at least a dozen Western ambassadors. Defence Minister Ustinov says peace threatened by 'the actions of American imperialism and the aggressive NATO block'.
11 At the end of 2-week visit by Ethiopian leader, Col. Mengistu, USSR and Ethiopia describe planned US bases in Horn of Africa as threat to peace.
24 *Izvestia* issues strongest Soviet statement yet on situation in Poland, criticizing *Solidarity* by name for the first time.

December
2 Central Committee unveils draft economic plan for next five years, to be adopted in February 1981. Overall economic growth is projected at around 5% p.a; call for petroleum and gas production to reach 12.9 m barrels a day by 1985.
18 Former Premier Kosygin dies of heart attack.

ASIA AND AUSTRALIA

January

4–   President Carter imposes grain embargo on USSR in protest at invasion of Afghanistan (see *United States*). USSR vetoes UN Security Council resolution calling for immediate withdrawal of 'foreign forces' from Afghanistan (7). UN General Assembly approves similar resolution by 104 votes to 18 (14).

5   US Defense Secretary Brown in Peking for talks with Chinese military leaders; calls both countries 'very closely parallel about the need to strengthen other nations in the region'.

10–   Mrs Indira Gandhi unanimously elected leader of her Congress parliamentary party which takes a clear majority in elections to Indian lower house. Sworn in (14), keeping Defence portfolio herself.

12–   N. Korea proposes reunification talks between Prime Ministers. S. Korea accepts (24).

13–   US offers Pakistan $400-m aid package over 2 years. Offer rejected as too small (5 March).

16   Chinese Senior Vice-Premier Deng Xiaoping calls for curtailment of China's four principal freedoms, which include right of free speech and writing wall posters.

18–22   Chinese Foreign Minister Huang Hua visits Pakistan but does not offer increased military aid.

20   China indefinitely postpones the second round of negotiations with USSR on bilateral issues, including borders, due to start in February, because of invasion of Afghanistan.

24   The US and China sign a memorandum of understanding to build ground station for satellite data collection.

27   In Rawalpindi six major Afghan guerrilla groups form a common front – Islamic Alliance for the Liberation of Afghanistan.

27–   Foreign Ministers' Conference of Islamic Conference Organization begins in Islamabad. The 35 member states condemn the Soviet invasion of Afghanistan and the 'presence of the military forces of the Soviet Union and some of its allies in the Horn of Africa' (29).

30–31   First Filipino local elections in over 7 years of martial rule produce major victory for President Marcos's party.

February

1   US Deputy Secretary of State Christopher and National Security Adviser Brzezinski in Pakistan for talks on Afghanistan. President Zia ul-Haq says US has pledged to send forces if his country is attacked (3).

5–   China rejects Vietnamese proposal for a lunar new year truce along border. Vietnam announces collapse of peace talks with China (7). China suspends talks (6 March), then formally freezes them (23 June).

7   N. and S. Korea reopen telephone lines between Seoul and Pyongyang, closed since 1976.

13   After 2-day talks in India, Soviet Foreign Minister Gromyko fails to win full Indian backing for Soviet intervention in Afghanistan; joint statement omits mention of Afghanistan.

14   In Geneva, UN Human Rights Commission adopts Pakistani resolution condemning Soviet intervention in Afghanistan, voting 27–8.

21–   Nearly all shops in Kabul close in protest at Soviet intervention. Afghan Government imposes martial law in Kabul after rioting and mass demonstrations (22).

26   Japan joins naval forces of four Western countries in *Rimpac 80*, first Japanese participation in multilateral naval manoeuvres.

28   In Washington Australian and New Zealand Foreign Ministers agree to provide greater military presence in Indian Ocean.

29   S. Korean caretaker President Choi Kyu Hah restores civil rights to 677 political dissidents persecuted by former President Park Chung Hee.

29   Leadership and structure changes announced after plenary session of the Chinese Communist Party central committee strengthen the power of Vice Chairman Deng Xiaoping; four hardliners ousted from Politburo.

29–   Thai Prime Minister, Gen. Kriangsak Chomanan announces surprise resignation. Gen. Prem Tinsulanonda, Defence Minister and Army C-in-C, voted by Parliament to replace him (3 March).

March

13 Mrs Gandhi says India will explode a nuclear device if it is in her national interests to do so.

17 Pakistani President Zia admits his government crushed coup attempt on 11 March; retired Maj.-Gen. Tajmal Husain Malik arrested for leading it.

19 In Bangkok, Chinese Foreign Minister Huang Hua promises deposed Khmer Rouge government of Kampuchea 'full armed support' in guerrilla struggle against Vietnam.

24– North-east Indian state of Assam stages economic blockade in protest at settlers from outside the state. Blockade suspended (31).

April

9 China releases her 1980 economic plan and forecasts 5.5% increase in gross value of industrial and agricultural output (down from 8% in 1979).

17 Tass dispatch from Kabul announces Afghanistan has proposed regional security conference of south-west Asian governments and reduction of armed forces in the region.

19– Fresh protests in Assam. Indian troops remove pickets from oil installations (21).

May

7 Soviet Ambassador in Tokyo confirms USSR has sent estimated 10,000 troops to the four Japanese-claimed Kurile Islands because of closer Sino-US relationship.

14 Afghan Government calls for talks with neighbouring countries and end to hostile acts while the negotiations take place, saying this could lead to withdrawal of Soviet troops from Afghanistan.

14– Some 30,000 Korean students march through Seoul in the largest anti-government demonstrations in years. In provincial capital of Kwangju, a local demonstration becomes provincial rebellion against the military government, as 100,000 citizens battle with riot police and troops (21). Troops withdraw from the city (22), then recapture it (27).

17– Islamic Conference of 39 Muslim countries plus PLO opens in Islamabad; 8 Afghan guerrillas join Iranian delegation. Conference calls for a special committee to open contacts with Kabul to solve Afghan crisis (21).

18 China successfully tests first intercontinental missile, CSS-X-4.

27 Chairman Hua begins first official visit to Japan by a Chinese head of state for 2,000 years; assures Japan N. Korea will not invade S. Korea.

June

12 Japan's Prime Minister and Liberal Democrat leader Masayoshi Ohira dies aged 70.

12 President Choi Kyu Hah promises new S. Korean government by the end of June 1981, after general elections in first half of year.

15– Thai patrol boats on Mekong river attacked by Laotian forces; 1 Thai killed, 2 wounded. Thailand seals border with Laos (6 July), reopens it (29 Aug).

17– Over Vietnamese protests, Cambodian refugees begin to return from Thailand under voluntary repatriation programme supervised by UN High Commissioner for Refugees. Vietnamese forces attack across the Cambodian frontier into Thailand then withdraw (23). US orders $1-m emergency airlift of military supplies to Thailand (1 July).

21 S. Korea sinks N. Korean boat; North denies it was sunk in the South's territorial waters.

23 Sanjay Gandhi, son and close political confidant of Indian Prime Minister killed in air crash.

23 Ruling Democratic Party is returned to power with 284 of 511 seats in Japanese elections for Lower House of the Diet, its best performance since 1969.

25–26 ASEAN Foreign Ministers' meeting in Kuala Lumpur reaffirms opposition to Heng Samrin regime in Kampuchea and again calls for withdrawal of foreign forces from that country.

July

4 Leading S. Korean dissident Kim Dae-Jung and 36 others arrested and charged with conspiracy to overthrow government.

7 India announces recognition of Vietnam-supported Kampuchean Government of Heng Samrin.

10 President Carter and Chairman Hua meet for the first time after funeral of former Japanese premier Ohira in Tokyo. Agree USSR and Vietnam threaten peace and stability in Asia.

17 Zenko Suzuki (69) elected as Japanese Prime Minister.

August

17–   S. Korean President Choi resigns. After election by 2,540-member National Council for Unification, Gen. Chun Doo Hwan takes over as civilian president (27).

30–   Annual session of 5th National People's Congress opens in Peking. Discusses leadership changes and the economy; 1980 defence budget to be cut by $2 bn from 1979 (1 Sept.). Zhao Ziyang elected Prime Minister, replacing Hua Guofeng, who resigns (10 Sept.) but keeps post as Party Chairman.

September

1–   S. Korean President Chun Doo Hwan's promises national elections in 1981. Military court sentences Kim Dae-Jung to death (17).

8   Rebels reported to hold Herat, Afghanistan's third largest city. Travellers report heavy casualties on both sides in Panjshir valley.

12–   Vietnam asks China to resume negotiations suspended in December 1979. China refuses (23).

23   Vietnam informs UN she is ready to withdraw some forces from Cambodia if Vietnamese-sponsored demilitarized zone is established.

26   Helicopter gunships with Afghan army markings attack a Pakistani frontier post 60 miles north of Khyber Pass.

October

5–   China claims a 4-man Soviet patrol crossed into Chinese Mongolia (first border incident since July 1979). USSR denies the incident (8).

14–   Australia withdraws recognition from Pol Pot regime as government of Kampuchea. UN General Assembly rejects Soviet-Vietnamese move to replace Kampuchean delegation of Pol Pot regime by Vietnamese-backed Heng Samrin government delegation.

17   S. Korean government closes Korea University after 200 rioting students call for President's resignation and withdrawal of US and Japanese support for government.

19   Malcolm Fraser's Liberal Country Party return to power in Australian elections with reduced majority.

22   UN General Assembly adopts by 97 to 23 resolution calling for withdrawal of Vietnamese troops from Kampuchea.

22   China and US sign multi-billion-dollar agreement for Chinese grain purchases over next 4 years.

27   S. Korean President Chun Doo Hwan promulgates new constitution limiting future presidents to one term of office.

November

12   S. Korean Government bans 811 politicians and dissidents (including 210 out of 231 National Assembly members) from involvement in politics until 1988.

20   By 111–22 (12 abstaining), UN General Assembly calls again for the withdrawal of 'foreign troops' from Afghanistan.

20–   Trial of 'Gang of Four' (including Mao's widow Jiang Qing) and others begins in Peking. Prosecution demands death penalty for Jiang Qing (29 December).

December

8–   Soviet President Brezhnev, visiting India, differs with Mrs Gandhi, the Indian Prime Minister over Soviet occupation of Afghanistan. In speech to Indian Parliament, he proposes a 5-point 'doctrine of peace and security' for the Arabian Gulf (10). Mrs Gandhi announces major strengthening of Indo-Soviet political and economic relations (15).

11   US and Vietnam reach agreement allowing Vietnamese to leave for US.

MIDDLE EAST AND NORTH AFRICA

January
- 1– UN Secretary General Kurt Waldheim visits Iran to discuss US–Iran crisis. Ayatollah Khomeini refuses to meet him (3).
- 5 Libya suspends aid to Al-Fatah.
- 5 Brazil signs agreement with Iraq for peaceful use of atomic energy.
- 5 Ba'ath Party Congress in Damascus elects 21-man national party command; President Assad remains Party general secretary.
- 7–10 Israeli Prime Minister Menachem Begin and Egyptian President Anwar Sadat meet in Aswan but make no progress towards solving the Palestinian question.
- 9 Saudi Arabia executes 63 men for November 1979 attack on Grand Mosque in Mecca.
- 10 Delegation of militants holding US Embassy hostages meets Khomeini for first time since their seizure on 4 November 1979.
- 10 Iranian troops seal off Tabriz after clashes between supporters of Ayatollah Shariat-Madari and those of Khomeini.
- 25– Presidential elections in Iran. Abolhassan Bani-Sadr wins 76% of vote. Sworn in (4 Feb.); named head of Revolutionary Council (8 Feb.).
- 25– Israel ends first phase of Sinai withdrawal, pulling back to El-Arish /Ras Mohammed line. Egypt and Israel begin normal relations with the opening of Sinai border (26).
- 28– Saudi Arabia raises her oil price from $24 to $26 a barrel in effort to unify OPEC prices. Kuwait, Iraq, the United Arab Emirates and Qatar follow suit with $2 per barrel rise (29).
- 29 US State Department discloses 6 US Embassy employees escaped from Iran on 26/27 January, after hiding in Canadian Embassy since US Embassy was seized.
- 29 Israel rejects Egyptian plan for Palestinian autonomy in West Bank and Gaza Strip.

February
- 1 Iran raises oil price by $2.50 per barrel.
- 2– The Iranian Revolutionary Council agrees to the establishment of an international commission to consider the Shah's crimes. UN Secretary General Waldheim completes formation of commision with representatives from France, Syria, Sri Lanka, Algeria and Venezuela (17). UN Secretary General Waldheim announces 5-man commission to visit Tehran to 'hear Iran's grievances and allow early solution to crisis between US and Iran' (20); Commission arrives (23).
- 4 Ayatollah Khomeini pledges 'unconditional support' for the Afghan resistance.
- 4 Egypt and Israel agree to establish 8 joint sub-committees to speed up normalization of relations.
- 4 US National Security Adviser Brzezinski holds talks in Riyadh with Prince Fahd and Foreign Minister Prince Saud on Soviet invasion of Afghanistan.
- 11 S. Yemen and USSR sign 20-year Friendship and Co-operation Treaty.
- 11– In southern Lebanon, 4 dead and several wounded after clashes between Israeli-backed Christian militias and Palestinian guerrillas. Cease-fire negotiated by UN in August 1979 collapses (12).
- 19 Khomeini appoints President Bani-Sadr C-in-C of armed forces.
- 20 Kuwait to cut oil production by 25% from 1 April.
- 21–22 OPEC long term strategy committee (Saudi Arabia, Iraq, Kuwait, Venezuela, Iran, Algeria) meets in London to try to devise strategy on oil prices and production.
- 23 Khomeini states question of US hostages will be decided by Islamic Assembly to be elected in April.

March
- 1– The United States votes with other UN Security Council members to rebuke Israel for increasing number of settlements in Arab territories. President Carter declares vote an error (3). Israeli Cabinet denounces US (4); Begin says resolution invalid as far as Israel is concerned (6). His government seizes further 1,000 acres of Arab land east of Jerusalem (11).
- 10– Khomeini rules it inappropriate for Revolutionary Council to take custody of US hostages, after earlier announcements that they would be transferred. UN Commission suspends its

work and leaves Tehran after failure to see hostages (11). Secretary of Revolutionary Council Ayatollah Beheshti states return of the Shah remains condition for release of hostages (12).

12   Austria recognizes PLO.

14–   First-round Iranian elections for 270 parliamentary seats. In second round, clergy-dominated Islamic Republican Party emerges as the largest party (9 May).

17   Libya and Malta sign defence pact; Libya to strengthen Maltese defences against attack.

17   Talks between Iran and USSR on price of Iranian gas exports to Soviet Union break down.

18–   International Court of Justice hears US case against Iran. Orders the immediate release of hostages (24 May).

23   The deposed Shah of Iran leaves Panama for Egypt.

April

7–   Israeli commandos storm a children's dormitory in kibbutz near Lebanese border to free hostages seized by 5 Arab terrorists; all terrorists and 2 Israelis killed. Israeli troops take up positions in southern Lebanon (9), then withdraw (13).

8–   Khomeini broadcast urges Iraqi armed forces to overthrow President Saddam Hussein. Iran–Iraq clashes reported at Qasr-e-Shirin (9).

7–10 Sadat and Carter meet in Washington; main issue is new Jewish settlements in occupied territories.

14   Red Cross team visits US hostages held at Tehran Embassy; pronounces their general condition good.

14–   Begin and Carter meet. Carter says Israel and Egypt have agreed to immediate high-level negotiations on Palestinian autonomy (16). US vetoes Security Council Resolution calling for establishment of Palestinian state (30).

17   Israeli attack on Palestinian guerrilla base 30 miles inside Lebanon.

18   Morocco cuts diplomatic relations with Libya after Libya recognizes independence of Western Sahara under POLISARIO.

25   US military raid into Iran to free hostages fails; eight US soldiers die in plane crash during withdrawal.

May

2–   Five Israelis are killed, 16 wounded by gunmen in West Bank town of Hebron. Israel deports 3 West Bank Arab leaders in retribution (3). Security Council unanimously (US abstaining) calls on Israel to rescind expulsion (8).

8–   Egypt requests indefinite postponement of deadlocked Palestinian autonomy negotiations. Camp David target date for agreement on Palestinian autonomy passes with no breakthrough (26). Carter states US will veto any attempt by European allies to introduce resolution on Palestinian self-determination in Security Council (31).

8   OPEC ministerial meeting ends in Saudi Arabia with partial agreement on long-term pricing.

14   Knesset passes law declaring that Jerusalem will remain united under Israeli sovereignty.

22   EEC trade embargo against Iran goes into effect.

25–26 Socialist International delegation under Austrian Chancellor Kreisky visits Iran.

June

1   *Al Fatah* re-elects Yassar Arafat as leader and C-in-C of its forces.

9–10 OPEC meeting in Algeria agrees compromise oil price of $32 a barrel, but individual members to decide when to raise to that level.

17   The UN Security Council extends mandate of UN force in Lebanon until 19 December.

20   Iraq elects her first parliament since overthrow of the monarchy in 1958. President Saddam Hussein's Arab Ba'ath Socialist Party wins control of Parliament, which will share power with the ruling Revolutionary Command Council.

27   Khomeini orders immediate Islamic purge of Iran's civil service; almost 500 employees of national oil company dismissed.

30   Security Council unanimously (US abstaining) denies Israel the right to change the status of Jerusalem and declare it her capital.

July

2   US, Israeli and Egyptian negotiators meet in Washington to try to get deadlocked Palestinian autonomy talks moving again.

7–9   Over 80 killed in fighting between Lebanon's two largest Christian parties; former President Chamoun's militia surrenders to Phalange Party.

9   Bassam Shaka, Mayor of Nablus, returns from Jordan, five weeks after losing both legs in bomb attack.

10   Khomeini orders release of one of US hostages for health reasons.

24   Twenty Iranian servicemen executed for involvement in attempted coup two weeks earlier; over 300 alleged conspirators have been arrested.

27   Former Shah of Iran dies of cancer in Cairo hospital.

30   Knesset decides to perpetuate all of Jerusalem as the capital of the Jewish state by 69–15 votes.

August

2   Sadat delays a new round of Palestinian autonomy talks with Israel scheduled to begin in Alexandria, demanding that discussions cover sovereignty over Jerusalem despite new Israeli law.

5–   President Hussein of Iraq makes surprise visit to Saudi Arabia, first by Iraqi Head of State since 1958. Joint statement says the two countries will break diplomatic and economic relations with any country recognizing Jerusalem as Israel's capital (6).

11   Iranian parliament elects Mohammed Ali Rajai Prime Minister.

13   In a letter to Soviet Foreign Minister, Iranian Foreign Minister Ghotbzadeh denounces Soviet policies towards Iran, calls on USSR to withdraw troops from Afghanistan.

19   The biggest Israeli attack into southern Lebanon since invasion of 1978.

20   UN Security Council again votes 14–0 (US abstaining) to censure Israel for Jerusalem policy, calls on all states with embassies in Jerusalem to withdraw them.

September

1–   Libyan leader Col. Gaddafi calls on his country to merge with Syria. President Assad of Syria accepts the offer (2).

10   Clashes along disputed border between Iran and Iraq.

13   Khomeini sets terms for release of US hostages – US should return property of the late Shah, cancel all financial claims against Iran, promise not to intervene in Iran, and unblock Iranian assets frozen by President Carter.

17–   Iraq abrogates 1975 border agreement (17). President Bani-Sadr orders full mobilization of Iran's forces (20). Iraqi forces invade Iran at four points, capture border town of Qasr-e-Shirin and besiege refinery city of Abadan (23). Iraq declares she will fight until her main demands are conceded – recognition of Iraqi sovereignty over the Shatt-al-Arab waterway and areas allegedly taken from Iraq in violation of 1975 Algiers agreement (24). Iraqi planes attack Iran's main oil terminal on Kharq Island (24).

28–   UN Security Council unanimously calls on Iran and Iraq to stop fighting immediately and settle dispute by peaceful means. President Zia ul-Haq of Pakistan visits Tehran (28) and Baghdad (29) on Islamic goodwill mission.

30   US announces she is sending 4 Airborne Warning and Control System (AWACS) aircraft to Saudi Arabia at latter's request.

30   Ayatollah Khomeini rejects any compromise with Iraq.

October

1–   Iran promises not to block Straits of Hormuz. Iran and Iraq struggle for control of Abadan/Khorramshahr area (2); launch air attacks on each other's oil centres, Abadan and Kirkuk (7). Iranian jets strike Baghdad (14).

1   Saudi Arabia increases oil production by 900,000 barrels a day to 10.4 million barrels to off-set effects of war. Says she will help any Arab country attacked by Iran in any expansion of war (5).

17   President Zia of Pakistan, Chairman of Islamic Conference, appeals to Iran and Iraq for cease-fire.

20–   The Israeli military Governor orders the re-expulsion of Arab Mayors Fahd Kawasme and Muhammed Milhem, originally deported from the West Bank in May 1980 but allowed back the week before to appeal before military tribunal. For the first time since becoming Israeli Prime Minister, Begin meets 2 Palestinian leaders, Mayors of Bethlehem and Gaza (21).

26–   The Iranian Parliament meets in closed session to hear report on US hostages. Breaks up in confusion (29).

27   Jordan and Iraq set up a Joint Military Command to handle their co-operation in the Iran–Iraq war.

November
2   Iranian Parliament votes to release the 52 hostages when the US has met Khomeini's 4 conditions. US transmits response via Algeria, the mediator (10). Secretary of State says US has accepted the conditions in principle (20).

2   Israel establishes 2 new Jewish settlements in West Bank.

10   President Sadat discloses Egypt has given military aid to Afghan resistance fighters.

11   Iraq's Vice-Premier Tariq Aziz, goes to Moscow for second time since Gulf War started, presumably to ask for arms.

25   Arab League summit opens in Amman, with Syria, S. Yemen, Libya, Algeria, Lebanon and PLO not attending.

26   Syria mounts a major military build-up on border with Jordan.

December
2   US Deputy Secretary of State Warren Christopher gives Algerian intermediaries new US reply to Iran's terms for release of US hostages.

2–   Syria and Jordan agree on terms to alleviate tension between them. Syria withdraws 50,000 troops from border (14).

15–   OPEC meets in Bali; agrees on official oil price of $32 per barrel with producers able to add quality differentials up to ceiling of $41 a barrel.

18   Shimon Peres elected leader of Labour opposition in Israel.

19   Three Syrian soldiers killed, 2 wounded in Israeli commando raid into Lebanon (first clash of Syrian and Israeli troops there since Syria moved in, in 1976).

21–   The Iranian Government issues full text of conditions on hostages; includes demand that US deposit $24,000 m in Algeria before release. Secretary of State Muskie declares proposals are unreasonable and require actions beyond president's power. President-elect Reagan states he would not pay ransom for people 'kidnapped by barbarians' (28). Speaker of Iranian Parliament calls American leaders 'savages and thugs' (29). US rejects demand for $24,000-m deposit to release the hostages (29).

SUB-SAHARAN AFRICA

January
2   Leaders of Tanzania, Kenya and Uganda, the members of the former East African Community, meet for the first time in three years.

4–   The cease-fire deadline in Rhodesia comes into force at midnight. An estimated 18,500 guerrillas have gathered at 16 designated assembly points (6). In Rhodesia black parties register for the February election – Joshua Nkomo and Robert Mugabe register separately as the Patriotic Front and ZANU Patriotic Front (14).

30   South African force of about 250 men withdrawn from defensive position at Beitbridge on border with Rhodesia.

February
3   In the worst violation of Rhodesia cease-fire, 16 killed in rocket attack on bus 100 miles east of Salisbury.

13   President Arap Moi confirms he has agreed to US forces and aircraft operating from Kenya in an emergency.

25   The first stage in planned integration of guerrilla armies with Rhodesian military begins; 610 of Mr Nkomo's men report to Rhodesian Army training camp near Bulawayo.

26   Leaders of 'front-line' African states hold emergency summit in Dar-es-Salaam; condemn Britain's violations of the Lancaster House agreement and urge the guerrilla leaders to consolidate their alliance.

29   Independence elections in Zimbabwe-Rhodesia end with 93.6% of estimated electorate having voted.

March
2– The 11-nation Commonwealth observer group concludes Rhodesian election was 'free and fair'. Robert Mugabe, leader of ZANU-PF party emerges as Prime Minister designate after gaining 57 of the 80 black seats in the 100-member House of Assembly; Joshua Nkomo's Patriotic Front wins 20 seats, Bishop Muzorewa's United African National Council three (4). Mugabe and Nkomo agree to form a coalition government (5). Last British troops withdrawn from guerrilla assembly points (10).
22– In Chad, the most serious breach yet of August 1979 peace agreement signed by the 11 main political factions occurs. President Goukoni Oueddei and Defence Minister Hissène Habré agree to cease-fire after 36 hours of fighting between their private armies in Ndjamena (23). Cease-fire breaks down (24). Fighting in Ndjamena appears to escalate to full civil war (27).

April
12– President Tolbert assassinated in Liberia's first military coup; Sgt Samuel Doe, leader of the People's Redemption Council, takes power. New revolutionary government declares martial law and suspends country's constitution (25).
14 Second East African summit between presidents of Kenya, Tanzania, Uganda and Sudan to try and improve East African ties.
28– France begins withdrawing her 1,100 troops in Chad (last troops leave 17 May). President Oueddei agrees to sending of inter-African peace-keeping force to end civil war there;OAU charges presidents of Nigeria, Togo and Guinea to implement cease-fire (30).

May
12– Ugandan Military Commission announces it has taken over the powers of President Binaisa. Executive power will be wielded by a 3- or 4-man presidential commission (13).
13 In South Africa, the most concerted unrest in the black community since 1976–7 riots takes place. Worst centre of violence is Bloemfontein.

June
1 Three of South Africa's oil installations blown up by saboteurs; outlawed African National Congress claims responsibility.
7– Angola states 3,000-strong South African force is invading the south of the country. South Africa claims SWAPO'S operational command headquarters destroyed in largest raid into Angola since 1978; over 200 Namibian guerrillas and 16 South African soldiers killed (13). South Africa acknowledges her troops are in Angola; Security Council censures her and demands immediate withdrawal of troops (27).
18 Fighting continues between South African police and rioters, provoked by anniversary of 1976 Soweto riots; 42 killed, 200 wounded in two days of violence on Cape Peninsula.

July
1–4 OAU summit meets; postpones decision on membership for POLISARIO for three months, endorses Mauritius' demand for return of the British-owned American naval base on Diego Garcia.

August
20– OAU committee recognizes Ogaden region as integral part of Ethiopia. Somalia claims Ethiopian forces have invaded near Borama (27). Ethiopia denies attack (28).

September
5 POLISARIO guerrillas claim major raid into southern Morocco, killing 9 , wounding 27.

October
21 South African attack against SWAPO base in south-west Angola kills 28 guerrillas.
20–24 UN–South Africa talks held on Namibia; end with little progress made.

November
9 Worst fighting between guerrilla factions since Zimbabwean independence occurs in Bulawayo after ZANU party rally; 50 dead.
14 Bloodless coup in Guinea-Bissau deposes President Luis Cabral; new leader is Premier Joao Bernardo Vieira.

27   Chad denies Libyan troops are fighting in her civil war; claims Libya is merely providing government forces with equipment and ammunition.

December
10–   Uganda holds first general election in 18 years. Milton Obote's Uganda People's Congress party wins over half the 126 Assembly seats. Opposition Democratic Party claims election was not fair but Commonwealth observers disagree (13).
15–   Chad government forces capture Ndjamena; rebel Defence Minister Habré's forces flee to Cameroun. Habré agrees to cease-fire but stresses he considers the Chad government 'illegal' (16). Emergency summit meeting of OAU *ad hoc* committee on Chad condemns foreign interference in her internal affairs – veiled reference to Libya (23–24).
29   POLISARIO guerrillas claim nearly 300 Moroccan troops killed, 300 wounded in 3-day battle on Western Sahara border at Rous Lekhyalat.

LATIN AMERICA AND THE CARIBBEAN

January
3–   Salvadorian civil and military coalition government, formed 15 October 1979, collapses as the 3 civilians in 5-man junta and nearly all cabinet resign. New coalition of military and Christian Democrats formed (9). Leftists storm Panamanian embassy in San Salvador, take 7 hostages, demand release of 7 comrades arrested in December (11). Hostages released after prisoners are freed (14). Dozens killed and scores injured in shoot-out between demonstrators and security forces (22).
7   UN General Assembly votes Security Council seat reserved for a Latin American country to Mexico, ending Cuba's attempt to secure it.
31   In Guatemala, 39 killed after peasants occupy Spanish Embassy and police storm it.

February
5–   Guerrillas seize Spanish Embassy in San Salvador, take 13 hostages and demand release of 13 detainees. Leftists release 7 hostages; government frees 7 detainees; Spanish Ambassador and 5 others still held hostage (6). Spanish Ambassador released (12). Leftists again seize Panamanian Embassy, take 3 hostages, demand release of 23. Hostages freed (14).
27–   Guerrillas seize Dominican Embassy in Bogota, take 56 diplomats hostage. Demand $50 million, release of 311 political prisoners and safe passage out of country (28).

March
12   Colombian President appoints panel of lawyers to find way to speed trials of over 200 Leftists – first concession to guerrillas holding Dominican Embassy.
24–   Archbishop Romero, outspoken critic of military repression assassinated in San Salvador. After his funeral Mass, 27 killed outside cathedral in shooting sparked by clashes between Leftist guerrillas and soldiers (30).
25   Jamaican Prime Minister Manley announces breaking off negotiations with IMF on $504-m aid package.

April
4–   Police withdraw from around Peruvian Embassy in Havana; 10,000 Cubans seek refuge there. Government announces they may leave for Peru (5); announces those at Embassy, plus those with Cuban-American relatives may leave for US in private boats (21–22).
19–   One more hostage released in continuing series of releases from the Dominican Embassy in Bogota; 17 still held. Siege ends quietly after 61 days; guerrillas given safe passage to Havana, free all hostages (27)

May
11–   Cuban jets sink Bahamian patrol boat 75 miles off Cuba, killing 4; vessel was towing 2 Cuban fishing boats arrested for illegal fishing. Bahamas denounces attack and demands compensation (12). Cuba apologizes (28).

18   Brazilian President Figueiredo ends visit to Argentina aimed at improving relations.
18-19 In first Peruvian general election in 17 years, Fernando Belaunde wins Presidency, from which he was deposed in 1968, with 45% of the vote. Takes office (28 July).
22   In El Salvador, 7 rightist groups announce formation of secret army aimed at 'eliminating Communists' in the country

June
24-25 Two-day general strike in El Salvador, called by opponents of ruling junta; about 60,000 involved
30   Pope starts 12-day tour of Brazil

July
1–   Leftist candidate Hernan Siles Zuazo claims victory in Bolivia's election, with 40% of vote. Troops seize control of La Paz in nationwide military rebellion backed by rightists; President Gueiler overthrown and power seized by 3-man military junta headed by General Luis Garcia Meza (17). US cuts off $6 million military assistance to Bolivia (18). Bolivian Workers Confederation challenges new military government with 6-day general strike (21). US cuts economic aid and withdraws most diplomatic personnel (25).
21   Eugenia Charles becomes Prime Minister of island of Dominica after landslide victory by right-wing Freedom Party.

August
12   Foreign ministers of 11 Latin American countries, meeting in Montevideo, abandon continent-wide economic integration objective embodied in Latin American Free Trade Area for modest institutional framework: Latin American Integration Association.
25   After 24 hours' political violence, Salvadorean Government mobilizes hundreds of troops to stem spate of left-wing bombings.

September
2–   Attempted palace coup by rightists against moderate officers puts El Salvador in virtual state of alert. Crisis ends with rightists having firmer grip and moderate officers from key positions in forces ousted (4).
11–   Chilean plebiscite on constitution containing clauses that extend Gen. Pinochet's presidency for 8 years. Pinochet proclaims victory (12).
26   Sea-lift of over 125,000 Cuban refugees to US ends after 5 months.

October
30–   Jamaican elections held after campaign marked by extreme violence. Edward Seaga's right-of-centre Jamaica Labour Party beats Michael Manley's People's National Party, winning 52 of 60 seats and ending PNP's 8 years in office (31). Seaga sworn in and demands departure of Cuban Ambassador (1 November).
31   Cuba and USSR sign a 5-year, $35-bn economic exchange agreement.

November
3–   UN Decolonization Committee votes 130–1 for motion calling for independence for Britain's colony of Belize, with Britain ensuring its security against Guatemala. UN General Assembly calls for Belizean independence before December 1981 (11). Guatemala says she will never permit unilateral independence for Belize, which she claims will always be Guatemalan Territory (13).

December
1   In Uruguayan plebiscite, 53.37% of voters reject constitution intended to formalize rule of military regime which took power in 1974.
5–   US suspends economic and military aid to El Salvador after reports link security forces with murder of 4 Americans on 2 December. Announces she will resume aid (17).
13   Christian Democrat leader Duarte becomes President in reorganization of Salvador military-civilian coalition which increases power of conservatives.
15–   Guyana holds first general elections for 7 years. Despite international observation team's conclusion that they were neither free nor fair (16), Forbes Burnham declared winner with 76% of votes (17).

28   Army says it has halted attempted advance into northern El Salvador from Honduran border of column of 1,500 left-wing guerrillas.

EAST–WEST ARMS CONTROL

January
3   In response to Soviet intervention in Afghanistan, President Carter asks US Senate to delay debating SALT II treaty as its consideration is 'inappropriate at this time'.
9   US calls off talks with USSR on banning chemical weapons due to be resumed in Geneva on 10 Jan.
25   After the first meeting of special consultative group on arms control NATO renews offer to continue arms-control negotiations with Moscow.
31   MBFR talks resume in Vienna; NATO governments warn 'events elsewhere' may jeopardize progress, but both sides agree to continue.

February
4   The US, Britain and USSR resume comprehensive nuclear test ban (CTB) talks in Geneva.
5–   Geneva Disarmament Conference spring session opens (China participating for the first time). Session ends (30 April).
18   Soviet Foreign Minister Gromyko says USSR will agree to talks on reducing nuclear arms in Europe if NATO repeals its decision to deploy new US cruise missiles in Europe.

March
19   SALT Standing Consultative Commission resumes talks in Geneva. Soviet representatives not prepared to discuss plans for carrying out SALT II treaty, only 1972 SALT I agreements.
25   At Geneva Disarmament Conference USSR states she has 'never and nowhere' used chemical weapons.

April
17   Afghanistan claims at Disarmament Conference that 'American-made poison gas grenades' were captured from 'subversives' on 25 March.
18   US claims USSR has tested 'killer satellite' – Cosmos 1174 – in outer space, breaking her two-year moratorium on launching anti-satellite weapons.

May
15   Warsaw Pact summit meeting in Warsaw calls for European conference on disarmament and detente.

June
26   American, Soviet and British negotiators open 10th round of CTB talks in Geneva.

July
3–   Chancellor Schmidt tells Bundestag USSR has agreed to drop conditions for negotiating with US on limiting medium-range nuclear weapons in Europe. USSR confirms it (4).
10   At MBFR talks Soviet offer – to withdraw further 20,000 troops from Central Europe if US will withdraw 13,000 – is not well received by Western delegations.

August
1   Tass announces the completion of withdrawal of 20,000 Soviet troops, 1,000 tanks and other military equipment from E. Germany, as promised by Brezhnev in October 1979.
11–   Second review conference of the 1965 Nuclear Non-Proliferation Treaty opens in Geneva. Smaller nations warn defections from the treaty may begin, failing more progress by the large nations in curbing nuclear arms race (12). Conference ends in impasse over this issue (7 September).

September
7– Carter agrees to talk with USSR on medium-range nuclear weapons in Europe. Secretary of State Muskie meets Soviet Foreign Minister Gromyko in New York to discuss (25).
9 Preparatory meeting of CSCE Review Conference opens in Madrid. Deadlock over agenda.

October
6 US, USSR and Britain resume CTB talks in Geneva – 11th session since 1977.
11 In Geneva talks on banning inhumane weapons, 70 countries' representatives agree the principle of curbing use of 'excessively injurious' conventional weapons against civilians. Talks began in 1974.
16– US and Soviet delegations begin preliminary talks on limiting medium-range nuclear weapons in Europe. USSR specifies US 'forward-based systems' must be included. Talks end (17 Nov.) with no resumption date given.

November
12 After 11th hour compromise resolves agenda deadlock, main meeting of CSCE Review Conference opens in Madrid. Western delegates attack USSR over Afghanistan.
13 At MBFR talks USSR suggests both alliances collectively freeze troop levels in Central Europe for 3 years.

December
8– Polish delegation to CSCE presents a proposal, backed by Warsaw Pact nations, for 'conference on military detente and disarmament in Europe' in Warsaw on 20 October 1981. France proposes disarmament conference tied to CSCE and limited to conventional forces (9). Yugoslavia proposes European disarmament in two phases and closely related to CSCE (12).